DYLAN

DISC BY DISC

JON BREAM

INTRODUCTIONS TO THE ALBUMS AND LINER NOTES
BY RICHIE UNTERBERGER

Voyageur
Press

First published in 2015 by Voyageur Press, an imprint of Quarto Publishing Group USA Inc.,
400 First Avenue North, Suite 400, Minneapolis, MN 55401 USA

Voyageur Press titles are also available at discounts in bulk quantity for industrial or sales-promotional
use. For details write to Special Sales Manager at Quarto Publishing Group USA Inc.,
400 First Avenue North, Suite 400, Minneapolis, MN 55401 USA.

To find out more about our books, visit us online at www.voyageurpress.com.

ISBN: 978-0-7603-4659-4

Library of Congress Cataloging-in-Publication Data
Bream, Jon.
  Dylan : disc by disc / Jon Bream ; introductions to the albums and liner notes by Richie Unterberger.
     pages cm
  Includes index.
  ISBN 978-0-7603-4659-4 (hc)
  1. Dylan, Bob, 1941---Discography. 2. Dylan, Bob, 1941---Criticism and interpretation. I.
Unterberger, Richie, 1962- II. Title.
  ML156.7.D97B74 2015
  782.42164092--dc23
                              2015002775

Acquiring Editors: Dennis Pernu and Todd R. Berger
Project Manager: Caitlin Fultz
Art Director: James Kegley
Cover Designer: Amelia LeBarron
Page Designer: Brad Norr
Layout Designer: Erin Fahringer

On the front cover: *Bob Dylan* by Amelia LeBarron
On the frontis: Posin' at the Savoy in London, 1966. *Fiona Adams/Redferns/Getty Images*
On the title page: Taking musician John Sebastian for a ride in Woodstock, 1964.
Douglas R. Gilbert/Redferns/Getty Images

Printed in China

10 9 8 7 6 5 4 3 2 1

WITH COMMENTARY BY

Eric Andersen

Nicole Atkins

Kevin Barents

Jim Beviglia

Lin Brehmer

Jonatha Brooke

David Browne

Marshall Chapman

Robert Christgau

Charles R. Cross

Rodney Crowell

Anthony DeCurtis

Kevin J. H. Dettmar

Daniel Durchholz

Stephen Thomas Erlewine

Jim Fusilli

Holly George-Warren

Janet Gezari

Tony Glover

Gary Graff

Geoffrey Green

Joe Henry

Geoffrey Himes

David Hinckley

Frances Downing Hunter

Jason Isbell

Garland Jeffreys

Peter Jesperson

Joe Levy

Alan Light

Ron Loftus

Alex Lubet

Evelyn McDonnell

William McKeen

Don McLeese

Dennis McNally

Paul Metsa

Tom Moon

Ric Ocasek

Kevin Odegard

Ike Reilly

Kim Ruehl

Robert Santelli

John Schaefer

Joel Selvin

Bill Shapiro

Colleen Sheehy

Wesley Stace

Ahmir "Questlove" Thompson

Richie Unterberger

George Varga

Suzanne Vega

Dan Wilson

David Yaffe

Paul Zollo

CONTENTS

ACKNOWLEDGMENTS

Thanks to . . .

First and foremost, all the commentators for their time, preparation, and insights; Dennis Pernu for helping to conceive this project; Todd R. Berger and Richie Unterberger for helping to see this project through with the publisher's new vision; James Kegley for the design, and the rest of the staff at Voyageur/Quarto for their efforts; Lisa Dahlseid and Jeff Day for their efficient, accurate, and tireless transcribing and fact-checking; Randy Alexander, Marshall Chapman, Kevin Daley, Anthony DeCurtis, Holly Gleason, Lorna Graham, Jim Grant, Ilona Hmelnicka, Claire Jeffreys, Peter Jesperson, David Kinney, Alan Light, Dennis McNally, Steve Morse, Amber Newton, Carol Rothman, Bob Santelli, Colleen Sheehy, Traci Thomas, Alan Wolmark, David Yaffe, and Zarah Zohlman for helping to connect with the commentators; Don Sullivan for concerts; Dick Cohn and Marc Percansky for the stories; my *Star Tribune* colleagues Kate Parry, Tim Campbell, and Chris Riemenschneider for their support; Nancy Barnes for the Minnesota Profile; Ken Abdo for his counsel; Jan for her tolerance, advice, love, and muffins; Andrew for web mastery, tech support, tolerance, advice, love, and making me proud of him; Shookie for listening to every Dylan album and quietly sitting on my lap for parts of most of the discussions; and last and certainly most important, to Bob Dylan for the words and music that we can't stop listening to and talking about.

Opposite: Performing on BBC-TV, 1965. *Val Wilmer/Redferns*

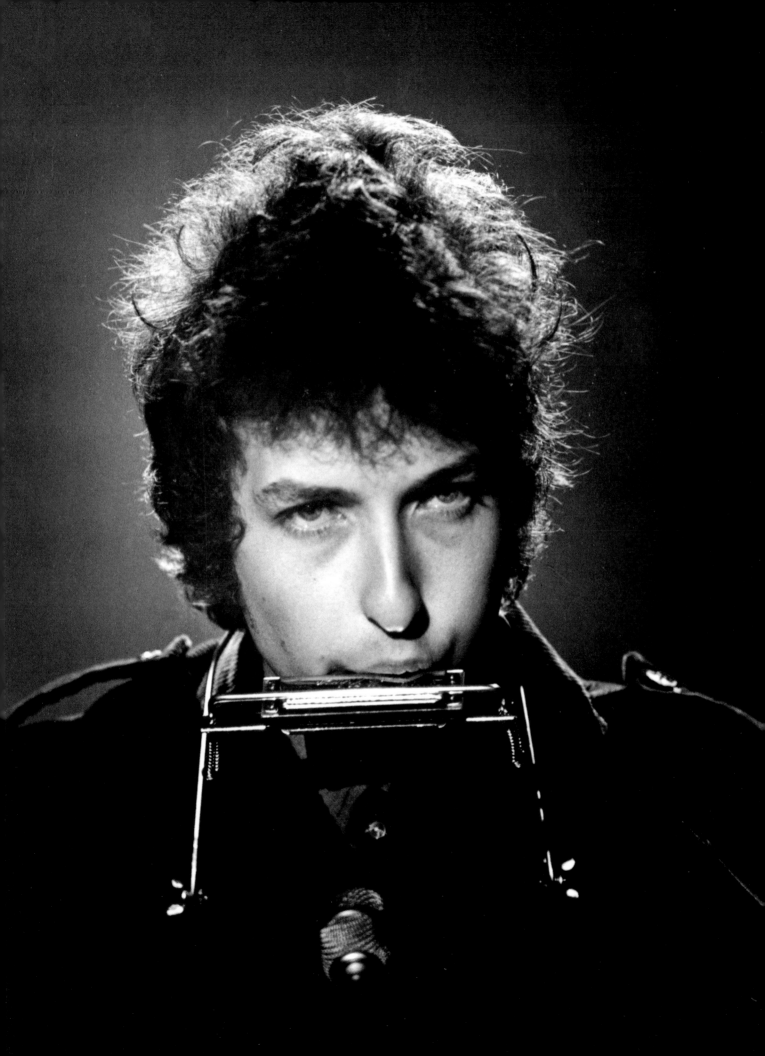

INTRODUCTION

Thirty-six studio albums. 406 songs. Fifty-five opinionated experts. And me.

People have been debating Bob Dylan for decades. Is he the voice of a generation or an unlistenable voice? There's no question that he is the most revered and influential American songwriter to emerge since 1960. "There is not a bigger giant in the history of American music," President Barack Obama said when presenting Dylan the Presidential Medal of Freedom in 2012. But Dylan's singing voice is another story—at times raspy, nasally, unpolished, and, more recently, ragged, gravelly, and croaky. For better or worse, the sound of his voice has been as distinctive as his songs. Admirers embrace his voice as wise and knowing, with phrasing that can be either studied or freewheeling depending on his mood. Detractors complain that, especially in concert, he's undisciplined in his enunciation, unconcerned about melodies, and unwilling to warm up to clear his phlegmatic throat before he takes the stage.

The Dylan debate can go as long as his storied career—which he launched professionally in 1961 after leaving his native Minnesota for New York City. In 2015, the unpredictable Rock and Roll Hall of Famer threw another curve ball by releasing *Shadows in the Night*, his first-ever collection devoted to the songs associated with another artist, Frank Sinatra. Is this tribute to Ol' Blue Eyes as surprising as when Dylan went electric in 1965 or when he became a Jesus freak in the late 1970s?

With this book, we will answer such questions by taking an in-depth look at each of Dylan's thirty-six official studio recordings—and those 406 songs. The goal was to bring many voices to the discussions, so we've enlisted fifty-five knowledgeable commentators to tackle *Dylan: Disc by Disc*. The concept was to assign two experts to each disc, so I reached out to critics, journalists, and radio DJs, some of whom had interviewed Dylan; professors who teach courses on Dylan; and musicians, producers, and industry executives who had a passion for Dylan and some of whom had worked with him.

Each of the commentators indicated the albums they'd prefer to discuss and then the matchmaking began. Some of it was intentional such as pairing veteran singer-songwriter Garland Jeffreys, a graduate of Syracuse University (where he palled around with Lou Reed), with Syracuse University professor David Yaffe, who is young enough to be Jeffreys' son. Some things were serendipitous. Who knew when connecting Kevin Dettmar, a Ponoma College professor who had edited *The Cambridge Companion to Bob Dylan*, and Paul Zollo, a songwriter/journalist who had interviewed Dylan for the magazine *American Songwriter*, that we'd end up with a born-again Christian and a proud Jew to discuss *Slow Train Coming*, the first Christian album by a Jewish-reared singer? Who knew that singer-songwriter Wesley Stace, who borrowed a Dylan LP title for his stage name (John Wesley Harding), records in the same Philadelphia studio as his co-commentator Ahmir "Questlove" Thompson, drummer for the Roots and *The Tonight Show Starring Jimmy Fallon*? And who knew that for both of them, Dylan's *Saved* had a big impact on their childhoods?

The process involved hour-long conversations with me as moderator. These were discussions, not debates, though there were some contentious moments. Robert Christgau, the self-dubbed "dean of American rock critics," was his predictable cranky and curmudgeonly self at times when assessing *New Morning* with Colleen Sheehy, a Midwest museum director who has curated a Dylan exhibit. Things got quite heated when critic Tom Moon, a regular on National Public Radio, analyzed *Oh Mercy* with

Opposite: London cool, 1966.
Blank Archives/Getty Images

Eric Andersen, a veteran singer-songwriter who has been buddies with Dylan since their Greenwich Village days in the 1960s. In the end, I pulled out my referee's whistle and told them that it was okay to disagree.

The assignment for *Blood on the Tracks* went to Kevin Odegard, a singer-songwriter in Minneapolis, Minnesota, because he played on the album and wrote a book about it. Tony Glover, who literally wrote the book on blues harmonica and has known Dylan since their Twin Cities coffeehouse days, was tasked with talking about *Highway 61 Revisited* because he attended some of the album's recording sessions. That discussion turned very journalistic with both the other commentator, producer/singer-songwriter Joe Henry, and me peppering Glover with questions about what happened.

Some conversations turned intellectual. Listening to San Francisco State professor Geoffrey Green, who once loaned his Woody Guthrie songbook to Dylan, and Yale-educated critic Joe Levy dissect *John Wesley Harding* felt like a grad-school seminar. Rodney Crowell, the distinguished country star turned Americana ace, started making references to Samuel Taylor Coleridge and Vladimir Nabokov, and Eric Andersen, the aforementioned singer-songwriter, brought up Albert Camus, Tennessee Williams, and Ezra Pound. He also had prepared a position paper on Dylan that he insisted on reading as a five-minute soliloquy during our discussion.

Inevitably, someone had to review the less praiseworthy albums in Dylan's catalog. After I asked the first question about *Knocked Out Loaded* to longtime critics Joel Selvin of the *San Francisco Chronicle* and Detroit's Gary Graff, the ever-sardonic Selvin announced, "Gary, I think what we need to ask ourselves here is, 'What did we do to piss off Bream to get this assignment?'" At the end of the discussion I explained to Selvin and Graff, both of whom I've known since the 1980s, that I'd had an even more challenging situation with *Knocked Out Loaded*: In 1986, I spent two days hanging out with Dylan in Berkeley, California, where he gave me a cassette of the album, which was to be released a few weeks later. *I* had to give my review of this decidedly inferior album to the artist himself. Somehow I found something positive to say about one—or maybe two—of the songs.

The commentators range in age from thirty-five to seventy-eight. One performs in an annual Dylan tribute, a few had interviewed Dylan, and a couple would call him a friend. The analysts came from as far as England (where Stace grew up) and the Netherlands (where Andersen now lives) and from all over the United States—from Connecticut to California, from Asbury Park, New Jersey, to Woodstock, New York. The one thing they had in common—besides their respect for Dylan—was they did their homework. Not only had they relistened to their album in question but they did research. Christgau was quoting from Dylan scholar Sir Christopher Ricks' definitive literary analysis *Dylan's Visions of Sin*, which Christgau had just read at the library. Several pundits referenced Zollo's exceptional 1992 interview with Dylan in *American Songwriter*. And countless commentators quoted from various album reviews in newspapers, magazines, and books.

The commentators got so invested in the project that many of the discussions stretched beyond our one-hour time frame—and a couple of the conversations lasted as long as two hours. The discussions were transcribed. Then Voyageur Press turned to Richie Unterberger to provide introductions for each album and to edit the discussions to a publishable length. So, in the commentators' words, we give you *Dylan: Disc by Disc*.

Chillin' in Woodstock, 1968. *Elliott Landy/Redferns/Getty Images*

with Dennis McNally and Robert Santelli

Released March 19, 1962

Producer: John Hammond

Recorded in Columbia Studio A, New York

Opposite: Heavyweight talent scout
John Hammond discovered Dylan in
September 1961. *Michael Ochs Archives/Getty Images*

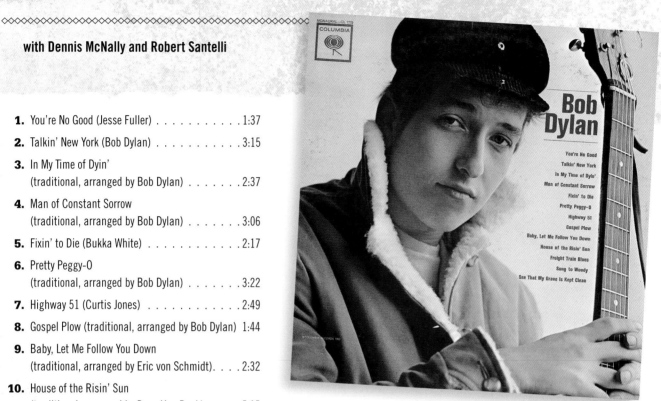

When Bob Dylan arrived in New York in January 1961, he was an unknown teenager with few career prospects and no particular agenda besides a mission to meet his idol, Woody Guthrie. Little more than a year later, he issued his debut album on one of the biggest record labels in the world, the sessions produced by one of the music industry's legendary figures. It was a remarkably rapid rise for a youngster who'd only been playing professionally for a year or two and was still known as Bob Zimmerman when he changed his focus from rock 'n' roll to folk at the end of the 1950s.

Dylan would soon be hailed as the greatest songwriter of the folk movement, but at this point he was still primarily an interpreter rather than a composer. Over the previous couple years, he'd learned a remarkably wide variety of folk songs in an equally impressive range of styles, from blues and traditional ballads to material drawing from gospel, country, and ragtime. The *Bob Dylan* LP was a showcase of what he'd mastered, all but two of the tracks being interpretations of folk tunes rather than original songs.

Although Dylan had been making inroads into New York's competitive folk circuit since his arrival in the city, it took a few fortunate breaks to get him into Columbia Records' Studio A by late November 1961. On September 29, *New York Times* music critic Robert Shelton gave the still-unsigned singer a rave concert review.

That same day, Dylan played harmonica at a Columbia session for fellow folk singer Carolyn Hester. Producing the session was John Hammond, a heavyweight known for his work with jazz greats such as Billie Holiday, Count Basie, and Benny Goodman. An impressed Hammond signed Dylan to Columbia as a solo artist, producing Dylan's first LP in sessions on November 20 and November 22.

Thirteen tracks couldn't hope to represent the depth of Dylan's repertoire, as he was known to have performed more than one hundred traditional folk songs in the early 1960s. Still, the selections gave him the opportunity to display his keening, grainy voice; searing harmonica; and versatile acoustic guitar, combining to stamp such well-traveled standards as "Man of Constant Sorrow" and "House of the Rising Sun" with his own distinct personality. He also fit in two of his own compositions, though these—like much of the album—betrayed his enormous debt to his chief influence, Woody Guthrie.

Despite a *Billboard* review praising "one of the most interesting and most disciplined youngsters to appear on the pop-folk scene in a long time," *Bob Dylan* was a commercial failure, selling just 5,000 copies in its first year of release. Hammond, according to Anthony Scaduto's *Bob Dylan: A Biography*, was even told his protégé would have to be dropped from the label. The producer's reply: "Over my dead body." Dylan stayed on Columbia, his next LP marking both his commercial breakthrough and his arrival as a major songwriter.

Dennis McNally, longtime publicist for the Grateful Dead and author of books about the Grateful Dead and *On Highway 61: Music, Race, and the Evolution of Cultural Freedom* (2014), debates the merits of *Bob Dylan* with **Robert Santelli**, CEO of the Grammy Museum and the author of *The Bob Dylan Scrapbook 1956–1966* (2005). Author **Jon Bream** moderates the discussion.

Bream: Not many people heard this album when it was released in 1962. When did you first hear it?
McNally: I was aware of Dylan as early as the March on Washington [in 1963]. I was aware of "Blowin' in the Wind" and the civil rights stuff. Otherwise, I didn't know his work seriously until I got to college in the fall of '67—I was a DJ on the college radio station and we had a rather nice library—and then I became a fan and worked back [through Dylan's earlier releases].
Santelli: In January of '64, when I was in seventh grade, a girl who had a crush on me got me that record. I didn't get into that record [at the time] because two weeks later the Beatles were arriving. After the Beatles, I wanted to play guitar seriously. So that summer of '64, I went back and listened to this record because of "Song to Woody." We had learned in fifth grade the [Woody Guthrie] song "This Land Is Your Land."

Bream: How has your impression of the album changed from the first time you heard it until now?
McNally: Dramatically over the years. In college, you see the first one as kind of a starter album. As I have studied it more recently, the

more I listened to it, the more impressed I am. Part of it, you're listening to a twenty-year-old man. He doesn't sound at all like a twenty-year-old. The depth of it, the texture of it.

Santelli: It remains one of my favorite Bob Dylan albums. If this record was made by anyone other than Bob Dylan, we'd be calling it a classic now because it is a great interpretation of American roots music done by someone whose voice is fresh and clean and eager. Someone with a brand-new take on some very old songs. However, because it was done by Dylan, who went on to show great brilliance at songwriting, the album has a tendency to be kind of discarded a little bit. The most important thing is we get to see where he was coming from before he comes to New York, what was he listening to, the fact that he knew who Blind Lemon Jefferson was and Jesse Fuller—that tells a lot about it. The authenticity that he captures in the first album—and you can follow his love of the music—it's done so well. Intimate, intuitive. It's unfortunate that so many great records will follow it—absolutely monumental masterpieces. I'm not calling this a masterpiece. I'm just calling it a great record.

Bream: How much of this is imitation, and how much is interpretation?

Santelli: He was accused of literally ripping off people. That's always been part of American folk music. There's always been "borrowing" going on, whether it is: interpretations, lyrics, phrases, full-on melodies. It's not negative or stealing. He was strictly following a tradition that was quickly coming to an end in the '60s but was alive and well in the folk and blues world.

McNally: "House of the Risin' Sun" was Dave Van Ronk's arrangement. In general, other people's arrangements are only starting points for Dylan. One of the interesting things about this album, very little of it was what he was doing on a regular basis [live]. Quite a lot of it, he only did for the record and stopped doing shortly thereafter.

The take-away from the material he chose is (A) a good deal of it is black music, and he resolves the division of American folk music into black and white spectrums by ignoring the divide, and (B) a lot of it is about death, which is not what you expect the average twenty-year-old to be singing about.

The new kid in town became a regular at the Bitter End folk club in Greenwich Village. *Sigmund Goode/Michael Ochs Archive/Getty Images*

Bream: Not only songs about death, but some are full of anger. I read a quote from Dylan saying about the first album: "Violent, angry emotions were running through me."

Santelli: I've interviewed Bob a couple of times, and I take what he says with a grain of salt. I don't know for sure that he was "angry" back then. He had a lot of reason to be happy. I think he was fascinated that these songs could carry such emotional intensity, especially when talking about something so profound as death.

He's a songster, someone who can carry himself across the American music treasury—play a gospel song, play a blues song, a hillbilly song, a folk song, a traditional song. He does all of that. For being twenty and being up in Minneapolis for a year and a half [where he was introduced to folk and blues], he has a great memory. Before this, he was into Little Richard, Hank Williams, and pop stuff. This album is an indication how good a student he was. His knowledge of the American folk tradition and the ability to interpret in such a way—that is profound, that is the real beauty of this record.

Bream: What sets his singing style apart from other folk singers?

McNally: He sang folk music with a rock 'n' roll attitude.... In *Chronicles* [Dylan's 2004 memoir], he eloquently describes hearing Robert Johnson for the first time. He had the biggest set of ears for all kinds of music. In *Chronicles*, he talks about when he first got to New York and went to gospel shows at Madison Square Garden, and he's listening to Cecil Taylor and all of it. He heard it all, he remembered it all, and he integrated it all. That's why he's Dylan.

Santelli: No one at the time in Greenwich Village would have known about Woody Guthrie like Bob did, and no one had the balls to become a Woody Guthrie jukebox—to talk like him, to act like him, to sing like him, to have some of Woody's idiosyncrasies. He doesn't learn it from listening to Woody Guthrie records. According to what he told me, he becomes extremely fascinated with Woody Guthrie because of his lifestyle and his life because of reading *Bound for Glory* [1943]. I've seen Bob's copy of *Bound for Glory* with notes in it. He read it like it was a textbook.

Bream: What do you think the two originals say about Dylan the songwriter?

Santelli: That he loved Woody Guthrie. Woody was a master of the talking blues. And the irony, the wordplay, the whole vibe of "Talkin' New York" is Woody Guthrie.

McNally: Two things come out from the two originals, neither of which are qualities that you generally associate with Dylan. The first is how incredibly funny he was. "Talkin' New York" is just hilarious. "Blowing my lungs out for a dollar a day" and "I love your sound, yeah a dollar a day's worth" are just hysterical. "Song to Woody," what comes across to me is humility, on many levels, and genuine gratitude. It's hard to remember he started out as a student. The way he writes that song is very honorable. It's very carefully crafted—his first great song—as an act of love for Woody.

Santelli: One song is cute and clever and the other heartfelt and deeply appreciative. Both of these things give an indication of what he is perhaps capable of.

Bream: The liner notes, which were reportedly ghostwritten by Robert Shelton of the *New York Times*, called Dylan "the most unusual new talent in American folk music" and "one of the most compelling white blues singers ever recorded." Hyperbolic or prophetic?

Santelli: I was at Experience Music Project [in Seattle, where Santelli developed a Bob Dylan exhibit], and we secured the Shelton papers. I always felt that Shelton understood Dylan and what he wrote, he absolutely meant. He was absolutely blown away.

McNally: Frankly, I don't think it was all that much hyperbole to claim that Bob was a great white blues singer. What he does with the blues on this album holds up.

Dylan proved to be a serious student of folk and blues music during his first recording session in November 1961.
Michael Ochs Archives/Getty Images

THE FREEWHEELIN' BOB DYLAN

with Anthony DeCurtis and Suzanne Vega

Released May 27, 1963

Producers: John Hammond and Tom Wilson

Recorded in Columbia Studio A, New York

All songs written by Bob Dylan, except where indicated.

Session musicians (on "Corrina, Corrina" only): Howie Collins (guitar), Leonard Gaskin (bass), Bruce Langhorne (guitar), Herb Lovelle (drums), Richard Wellstood (piano).

Dylan had started to write songs by the time he recorded his first album in late 1961. The following year, he emerged not only as a composer of distinction but also as the leading topical songwriter on the folk scene. Influenced by the civil rights movement, the threat of nuclear war, and his personal romantic tribulations, his songs tapped into the zeitgeist of a generation getting ready to embrace huge cultural and social change. Comprised almost entirely of original songs, *The Freewheelin' Bob Dylan* featured some of his most famous "protest songs." "A Hard Rain's a-Gonna Fall" was widely interpreted as an allegory for nuclear holocaust, "Masters of War" savaged the military machine, and "Talking World War III Blues" somehow found gallows humor in the Cold War. More universal in its wistful musings upon humankind's troubled journey was "Blowin' in the Wind," which became Dylan's first widely heard classic when Peter, Paul and Mary took their smoothly harmonized version to #2 on the singles charts in summer 1963.

Dylan also drew on his own experiences for more personal songs reflecting his transition from adolescence to adulthood. A serious romance with Suze Rotolo spurred "Don't Think Twice, It's All Right" (also taken by Peter, Paul and Mary into the Top Ten), while a ghost from his Minnesota past inspired "Girl from the North Country." Hit singles under his own name were still a few years in

the future, but *The Freewheelin' Bob Dylan* was a big success for a folk LP, nearly reaching the Top Twenty and establishing the singer as a star in his own right.

Despite the album's popularity and immense influence upon aspiring young folk singer-songwriters, the production of *Freewheelin'* was a protracted and at times fraught affair. More than a half dozen sessions were cut between April and December 1962, a period that saw Dylan's repertoire evolve so rapidly from traditional folk covers to idiosyncratic originals that he was almost an entirely different kind of artist by the end of the year. For the final session in April 1963, producer John Hammond was replaced by Tom Wilson, who would continue to work with Dylan in the studio for the next couple of years.

Without that last session, which included such acclaimed songs as "Girl from the North Country" and "Masters of War," *Freewheelin'* could have been a much different record, and one somewhat less in tune with a nation undergoing explosive transformation. As Suzanne Vega says of the LP, "It must have been an amazing time for him to have taken in all those influences and then put them out in songs. You really feel the flow of what's going on, through him, in that album. Maybe this is the most important Dylan album. It's the tip of the knife, and the rest of his work followed after that."

Suzanne Vega, a New York–based singer-songwriter and playwright who has released eight studio albums, and **Anthony DeCurtis**, a contributing editor at *Rolling Stone* and author of several music books, discuss *The Freewheelin' Bob Dylan*.

Bream: Is this the most important Bob Dylan album?
Vega: It's the most important album in terms of it being his beginning. It's the one that really announces who he is.

DeCurtis: When people who don't really even know that much about Bob Dylan think about Bob Dylan, an album like this is what they're thinking about—the protest songs, the voice of a generation, "Blowin' in the Wind," this kind of thing. It's certainly important in that regard, but Dylan has made so many important records. It's very difficult to say this is the most important.

Vega: Because of "Masters of War" and the five really classic songs that he has on this album, I was kind of surprised he had written those at the age of twenty-one and this was only his second album.

DeCurtis: It's pretty stunning in that regard. Also, some of these songs really hint at some of the things to come. "A Hard Rain's a-Gonna Fall" is a protest song, but there's a sense in which, in that kind of cascade of images, you're looking beyond the protest period in his work. And as protest songs go, often those type of songs, certainly back then, were "this happened and that happened," and they were almost kind of folk journalism, whereas this is really folk poetry.

Vega: Then he has "Oxford Town," which is like that folk journalism, in a way, but he twists it and makes it almost humorous. I would listen to it thinking I would be afraid to make a joke out of this, if I were to write a song about something that had just happened. But because he's got "Masters of War," which is so pointed and so deep and so angry, he feels his certainty in the material there. He's confident about twisting it around—"Somebody better investigate soon"—and having the right jokey term without folk journalism.

DeCurtis: The thing about "Oxford Town" that I really like, it doesn't really say, "James Meredith did this," in terms of integrating the University of Mississippi, but it takes some of the imagery, and obviously the place, and grounds it.

Vega: That's the great thing about "Masters of War." You can still apply it now, for any war, at any time. It's really personal, very angry, but at the same time he's not aiming it toward a specific leader or a specific time and place.

DeCurtis: What's interesting, too, is that it's aimed at a system. The focus is on arms manufacturers, people who profit from war. It isn't just "war is bad." It says certain people are benefiting from this and profiting from it, and it's not even necessarily about ideology. It's about just making money. That's a pretty interesting critique; it's not one you often hear.

Vega: Some of the most conflicted songs on the album are about Suze Rotolo, which I hadn't realized. I thought that didn't really happen until "Boots of Spanish Leather." I thought that's when they split, and I thought they were together happily during this album. But the songs imply otherwise.

DeCurtis: Yes. There are some specific references to travel and Italy.

Vega: I always thought "Girl from the North Country" was really nostalgic. I really thought that was more about Echo Helstrom [whom Dylan had known as a teenager]. That's more like talking about Hibbing [Minnesota, where Dylan grew up], talking about Minnesota. The main thing about this song that is so different than a lot of the other Dylan songs is in the chords. There's this beautiful sort of descending thing he does with the bass line. It's got beautiful, mysterious chords that I never associate with Dylan. Dylan's more straightforward, blues-based. But it's got this lovely quality to the guitar playing.

DeCurtis: I think the song we should say something about is "Blowin' in the Wind." Which, in a way, is so much a part of the culture that you can't hear it anymore, except that every time I actually hear it and listen to it, I still find myself just so profoundly moved by it. That kind of existential protest that this song represents—it's clearly grounded in the Civil Rights movement. But then you get to "The answer, my friend, is blowin' in the wind," that sense of "I don't know what will ever change this." That

feeling of "When will this ever end" is so powerful. At the same time, for that, it doesn't lose any of its righteousness. But not *self*-righteousness. The sense that it's talking about things that appeal to such an essential humanity, and how could that be resisted, and how could these changes not come? But, they didn't—or, they weren't, and people were still dying.

Vega: There's something beautifully simple about it, and yet at the same time it has a complexity.

DeCurtis: I think it's precisely that simplicity, actually; that's exactly the word. And it is why it has remained so profound.

And the interrogative tone of the song, in "Blowin' in the Wind," it's like that ballad form, where you're asking questions. But in this case, the questions, they sort of

A man for all seasons, he performed at the Singers Club Christmas party on his first trip to England in December 1962.
Brian Shuel/Redferns/Getty Images

implicate the listener. Like we all have to answer this. It implies a kind of communal answer, and that's kind of bracing, really.

One of the other songs that's on there that's obviously incredibly significant and kind of resonant in terms of his personal life is "Don't Think Twice, It's All Right." Suze told me there were people who sort of raised chickens, where you could go buy fresh eggs. So that line about the rooster crowing at the break of dawn, which sounds like it comes from some blues song in the 1920s, was in fact, I mean they would hear roosters in their apartment on West Fourth Street [in New York]. It's this incredible blending of something that's very, very immediate and something that's very deep in the musical culture.

Vega: It never occurred to me before that this is about Suze Rotolo. She's smiling on the [album] cover, but the songs inside, there's strife in there that you don't see unless you really think about it. I thought the split between the two of them had come earlier, but actually it's kind of present all through their relationship. This is not a romantic idolization. With the split coming later, these really tart songs are for her.

DeCurtis: On "Don't Think Twice, It's All Right," you get "You just sort of wasted my precious time." A friend of mine once described his ballads . . . there're a lot of ballads of taunting regret. I always thought that was a great sort of description. There's all this feeling, but then he just kinda recoils from it and can't resist.

Vega: Stabbing the knife.

DeCurtis: Yeah, exactly.

Vega: He even says it in the liner notes: songs you sing to make yourself feel better.

DeCurtis: And that is a kind of vulnerability, to admit that.

Bream: This album is also the first time we see his sense of humor. There was a thing that struck me in "Talkin' World War III Blues." There's a line, he says, "That's Abe Lincoln's line," and then there's a line that comes later, "And that's my line."

DeCurtis: He says, "Half of the people can be part right all of the time, Some of the people can be all right part of the time, But all of the people can't be all right all of the time. I think Abraham Lincoln said that." He took that talking-blues form from Woody Guthrie, and yeah, it really lent itself. People forget how funny he was and could be. There are so many things in this song that are really humorous, and pitted against the kind of incredible seriousness of "Masters of War" and "A Hard Rain's a-Gonna Fall," it's a really amazing contrast.

Vega: I think the album, without those moments of levity, would have been very heavy and ponderous.

DeCurtis: Suzanne, as a songwriter, what do you feel were his gifts to you?

Vega: What I try and soak in is the sense of expansion that you get from his songs. You really hear it in "A Hard Rain's a-Gonna Fall." Just the sense of limitless possibilities. My songs tend to be a lot tighter; they're very condensed. So sometimes it's a great release even just to sing one of his songs. It's so interesting to actually sing his songs and feel the thought process that he must have gone through when he wrote the song. It's so much wider and so much broader than what I can think of on my own. That's what I go to Bob Dylan for—the mystery and the beauty of the images, and the sense of unlimited possibility.

DeCurtis: Some of these songs—like "Blowin' in the Wind," certainly "A Hard Rain's a-Gonna Fall," certainly "Masters of War," and in a very different way "Don't Think Twice, It's All Right"—seem very contemporary. They only gain significance over time. For someone who's responding in a certain way, so immediately to things around him, to escape chronology that way, into timelessness, that's extraordinary.

Vega: And that's what makes it modern. He takes these images from the past, and he also responds to things that are absolutely of the moment, but we still feel them as modern because it's timelessness; it's out of time.

DeCurtis: The thing about "Bob Dylan's Dream," this idea that—that combination of youth and age, and sort of old and modern, and the kind of incredible quality of looking back in that song. I'm always moved when he gets to that last verse and he goes, "I wish, I wish, I wish in vain, That I could sit simply in that room again," describing himself in a group of friends. His sense of, I guess, that maybe his world was speeding up so much, and that heat was beginning to gather around him, and the future was kind of becoming clear. But also this sense of loss of something . . . just comes through very forcefully in that song. It's a hard emotion to imagine somebody who is twenty-one feeling, but maybe you feel it really most powerfully when you're that young.

Vega: He's feeling it on "Girl from the North Country," that sort of deep nostalgia for something that he feels is gone. There's a great line in "Bob Dylan's Dream": "And our choices they were few and the thought never hit, That the one road we traveled would ever shatter and split." The idea that everyone's paths and destinies are just gonna scatter off in all different directions. It's such a great line, 'cause it's like a rock hitting a windshield or something.

Bream: What do you think the significance of the title *The Freewheelin' Bob Dylan* is?

Vega: It really shows him in motion. He's traveling. He's going to Italy; he's on a train, going west. He's out and about. He's in Greenwich Village but he's also—he's freewheeling. He's not tied down. But you know, he sort of wants to be tied down. You get the feeling that he's angry at Suze Rotolo for not staying home and being with him. But you get the sense of a guy just out in the world, and free. Free.

But it's also ironic. Because something so heavy and deep and dark as "Masters of War," there's nothing freewheeling about the sentiments there. Imagine if the album had been called *Masters of War*. But it's better to have it called *The Freewheelin' Bob Dylan* because it sort of belies the depth of what's coming.

CHAPTER 3

THE TIMES THEY ARE A-CHANGIN'

with Lin Brehmer and Jonatha Brooke

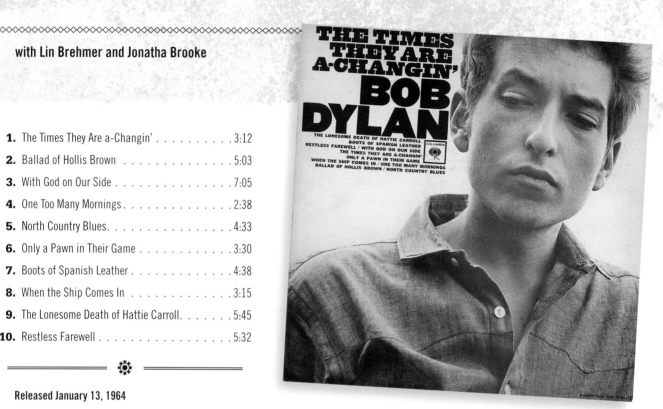

Released January 13, 1964

Producer: Tom Wilson

Recorded in Columbia Studio A, New York

All songs written by Bob Dylan.

Although Dylan has often been labeled a protest singer, the period in which protest songs were a big part of his repertoire was fairly brief. Such songs were a major factor, however, in establishing his folk stardom and cementing his image, whether he wanted it or not, as a spokesperson for his generation. No other album captures this phase of his career as strongly as *The Times They Are a-Changin'*; the title song is one of the most famous protest songs of all time.

When the album was recorded between August and October 1963, things were changing fast not just in the world at large but also for Dylan himself. The release of his second album, *The Freewheelin' Bob Dylan*, in spring 1963 had vaulted him into national stardom. Folk star Joan Baez, by featuring Dylan's songs in her concerts and albums, and also allowing him to share the stage at events like the 1963 Newport Folk Festival, exposed him to a wider audience than he could ever have hoped to reach on his own. The pair also appeared together that summer at the March on Washington, affirming his commitment to social justice in action as well as song.

The first of his albums to feature only original compositions, *The Times They Are a-Changin'* was awash in tunes commenting upon, and at times railing against, social inequity, racism, and the madness of war. "With God on Our Side" attacked the hypocrisy of warmongers the world over, "Only a Pawn in Their Game" was inspired by the murder of civil rights activist Medgar Evers, and "The Lonesome Death of Hattie Carroll" was based on the death of an African-American barmaid. The song "The Times They Are a-Changin'" was itself a declaration that a new generation of baby boomers had emerged to usher in a new way of looking at society.

Yet, like *The Freewheelin' Bob Dylan*, the album balanced the diatribes with gentler, more personal ruminations. "Boots of Spanish Leather" reflected the ups and downs of his relationship with Suze Rotolo; "One Too Many Mornings" had a world-weary poetry that couldn't be tied to any cause in particular. "Restless Farewell" hinted at a restlessness to move on—as he would, indeed, on his next album, leaving protest itself behind.

When *The Times They Are a-Changin'* was released in January 1964, however, Dylan was still very much viewed as folk's foremost topical songwriter. In accordance with his rising status, it became his first album to reach the Top Twenty. But much had changed after "Restless Farewell" concluded the LP's sessions on Halloween 1963. President John F. Kennedy had been assassinated, puncturing the idealism of youthful activists across the globe. The singer's romance with muse Rotolo was coming to an end. And the Beatles' "I Want to Hold Your Hand" was rocketing to #1 in the United States, ushering in a new phase of both musical and cultural change that would impact Dylan and the rest of the music world.

Lin Brehmer, a longtime radio programmer and DJ at WXRT in Chicago, and **Jonatha Brooke**, a New York–based singer-songwriter who has released nine albums under her own name and wrote and starred in the one-woman musical play "My Mother Has Four Noses," discuss *The Times They Are a-Changin'* in the context of a world in transition.

Bream: Is this the most topical, most protesting-est album of all time?
Brehmer: I don't think there's an album he did that is more Ezekiel or Jeremiah, forecasting what's going to be happening fifty years from when he was writing these songs. "With God on Our Side," "Only a Pawn in Their Game," he could have released those this year, and people [would] go, "Well I'm not going to tweet about this, a little too controversial."

Even though this is part of the rash of albums that are among my favorites, this is not an album that I went back to and listened to a lot. I bet you that's true for a lot of Dylan fans because it is so dour and filled with prophecies of doom. This is really 1963, I'm on the road at the March on Washington, I'm at civil rights demonstrations. This was the backdrop to what he was writing.
Brooke: They are real folk songs, real protest songs where the words are really paramount. These are beautiful, powerful songs, and very crafted. I just love

He was only twenty-two years old when he wrote these songs. *Michael Ochs Archives/Getty Images*

the turnarounds where he'll change that hook in the last verse and just rip your heart out, "Now's the time for your tears"—that's just awesome, and beautiful. "God on Your Side," it's amazing—wow, this is prescient, this is all of history in one song.

Bream: Let's talk about the title track. Dylan said when the box set _Biograph_ [1985] came out about that song, "I knew exactly what I wanted to say and who to say it to. I wanted to write a big song, some kind of theme song, with short, concise verses that piled on each other in a hypnotic way."
Brehmer: Pound-for-pound, there are more great lines packed into one short song than anything I can think of. Each verse of "The Times They Are a-Changin'," it's like they were taken out of _Bartlett's Familiar Quotations_. All these lines you know from start to finish, all of those lines can stand alone, and also as part of the song.
Brooke: "Get out of the new one if you can't lend your hand . . . the battle outside is raging . . . it will soon shake your windows and rattle your walls." This could be a church song. The references to the flood, the waters rising, the first will be last.
Brehmer: It does sound biblical.

Bream: "The Times They Are a-Changin'" has the same opening line as the "North Country Blues" song on this album, "Come gather round people."
Brehmer: That's sort of a classic folk introduction, isn't it? That goes back to folk traditions—one hundred years or something, sort of a sit around the campfire or sit around the meeting house and come gather round people because I'm going to tell you a story in the finest troubadour tradition. I'm going to lay it out for you right here.
Brooke: The melody of "Times They Are a-Changin'" is also verbatim in "One Too Many Mornings." It's pretty much the same melody that he's employed in a more personal musing.

Bream: He owned up copying these melodies from Irish and Scottish folk songs. He's even named the songs he took them from.
Brehmer: The guy was originally this obsessed folkie.
Brooke: That's what Woody [Guthrie] did; he copped old, traditional work songs, folk songs, and just wrote new words to them.

Bream: "North Country Blues" is a very Minnesota song, talking about outsourcing jobs on the Iron Range in Minnesota where he grew up. That's also the first song that Dylan wrote from a woman's perspective.
Brehmer: Right, because she's singing about the rough times and how hard it is, and talking about family, these people that don't come home. Then her husband doesn't come home, and it just gets worse and worse. It's talking about outsourcing and cheaper labor, and who is talking about that in popular music in 1963 and 1964?
Brooke: And how many guys were trying to speak from a woman's perspective?
Brehmer: "North Country Blues" is one of my favorites on that album, and again it seems very traditional folk. You know it comes from a place that goes back a long time.
Brooke: The line that stuck out to me on that song is, "My friends they couldn't have been kinder." I just thought that was such an unusual thing to put in.
Brehmer: It is in this kind of dour, unremitting, horror story.
Brooke: Like crediting your community for bolstering you up.
Brehmer: Here Dylan is fifty years ago eviscerating values and institutions and coming at it from different directions. Writing from a women's point of view, writing what it was like with the dynamic whereby American society and upper-class society ghettoizes even poor whites, only a pawn in their game.

Folk singers Bob Dylan, Joan Baez, and Paul Stookey (of Peter, Paul and Mary) had a cause when they performed at the Lincoln Memorial during the March on Washington for Jobs and Freedom. But that day, another person on the podium had a dream—Dr. Martin Luther King delivered his historic "I Have a Dream" speech. *Fred W. McDarrah/Getty Images*

If I were Bob Dylan, I would not release that album in 2014. It would be a bad career move.

There's no "I Shall Be Free No. 10," no kind of jokey Bob Dylan winking at me, "I'll be in your dreams, you can be in mine," "Talking World War III Blues" kind of wry smile on his face stuff. It's really down to the marrow of some of the toughest issues of the time.

Bream: No humor on this at all.
Brooke: A good deal of sarcasm for sure, which I think is brilliant. In "The Lonesome Death of Hattie Carroll," doing his best to really pay attention to how justice goes down. He's going to give the guy the heaviest sentence he can, and he gets six months. I think it's really great.

Bream: I was struck by the really vivid details in that song.
Brooke: The rich, wealthy parents, and he reacts to his dead with a shrug of his shoulders, in a matter of minutes on bail was out walking, he keeps repeating "table" like a mantra. She never sat at the table, she cleared the table, she cleared the ashtrays from the table, it was never her table. Those lyrics are killer.
Brehmer: That's something my English professors used to talk about all the time, the importance of minute particulars in writing. You don't say, "It's raining hard outside." You give them something much more specific.
Brooke: And he's pointing his finger at all the philosophers and the critics and taking the rag away from *your* face, now is the time for your tears. He's twisting it all up and then he's just nailing you at the end with "now is the time for your tears." It's a brilliant

turnaround. It's quintessential great writing where the last hook just twists it and nails you with the message.

Brehmer: He's poking us all the time through the whole album. He sets us up and it's sort of like, "Well what are you going to do about it? Where are you coming from?" I think he's also on this album starting to feel the pressures of being a future icon. There's no way he can anticipate the kind of stature that he's enjoyed over the years, but I think he's starting to get bugged. Bob Dylan is, in a much bigger way, discovering that he can't take it for granted that he can just say what he wants or do what he wants. Everything is being shoved under this microscope, although a much smaller microscope than it would be today. If I were in his position it would definitely inspire me to barb my message a little bit more. Some of the turnarounds that you talk about, I'm telling a story and you're following along with me, but in the end how hypocritical are all of us?

Bream: Does that come along in the "Restless Farewell" song?
Brehmer: Yeah. Look at that, "It can pierce through dust no matter how thick, so I'll make my stand, and remain as I am, and bid farewell and not give a damn."
Brooke: From what I understand, he wrote this song kind of in a pique of anger after a *Newsweek* article sort of falsely accused him of plagiarizing on something.
Brehmer: Another thing strikes me about this album. Here it is, this monumental work, and it's his voice mixed pretty loud in terms of how you would mix a guitar and voice. It's just him strumming a guitar. Just guitar and voice.
Brooke: And with his own cadence, and his own sense of time and where the next verse will fall and how he's going to frame that next thing. The music itself is stream of consciousness because many of the songs have no set time signature or cadence. If you were trying to learn it, copy it exactly, I think it would take years because it is so loose and free-form.
Brehmer: That's why so many people enjoyed covering the songs because it almost gave them a license to construct it any way they want it. "I can't do it like Dylan does it, but I'll take these chords and these lyrics and I can do my own thing with it."

Bream: Let's talk about some of the more personal and romantic songs on the album.
Brehmer: "Boots of Spanish Leather" is one of the most beautiful romances put to music. It's just a beautiful song. I don't know where that comes from. Girlfriends or a girlfriend or Joan Baez?
Brooke: My heart really responded to the "One Too Many Mornings." I love that refrain and how personal it felt. It was really poignant to me.
Brehmer: Both of those songs are just beautiful. In terms of looking at the album as a whole, you know it's not a comedic interlude, but at least it's an emotional interlude. You go from "The Ballad of Hollis Brown" to "With God on Our Side," which is just eviscerating, pointed, sarcastic, and to the point. Then you slip into "One Too Many Mornings," which is beautiful. Then he's back to the Iron Range and people losing their jobs, then "Only a Pawn in Their Game" and then "Boots of Spanish Leather," almost as if you take a breath there. It's really one of his most dour albums, but at the same time lyrically one of the most powerful albums he put out.

Opposite: During rehearsals for the influential and top-rated TV variety program *The Ed Sullivan Show* on May 12, 1963, Dylan played "Talkin' John Birch Paranoid Blues." After an executive from the CBS Standards and Practices department heard the controversial lyrics, Dylan was asked to perform a different song during the live show. He refused, marched out of the studio, and never appeared on the Sullivan show.
CBS Photo Archive/Getty Images

CHAPTER 4

ANOTHER SIDE OF BOB DYLAN

with Ric Ocasek and Ike Reilly

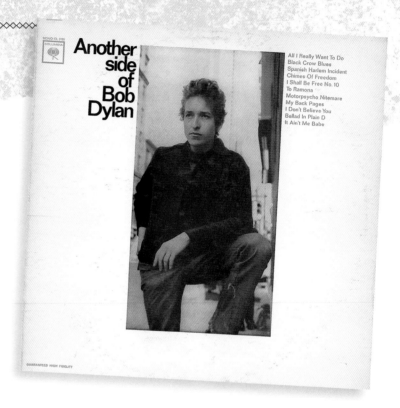

1. All I Really Want to Do 4:02
2. Black Crow Blues 3:12
3. Spanish Harlem Incident 2:22
4. Chimes of Freedom 7:09
5. I Shall Be Free No. 10 . . . . 4:45
6. To Ramona 3:50
7. Motorpsycho Nitemare 4:31
8. My Back Pages 4:20
9. I Don't Believe You 4:20
10. Ballad in Plain D 8:15
11. It Ain't Me Babe. 3:30

Released August 8, 1964

Producer: Tom Wilson

Recorded in Columbia Studio A, New York

All songs written by Bob Dylan.

Another Side of Bob Dylan did indeed deliver a quite different side of Dylan than his first three albums had. For the first time, and not the last, the shift in direction was not welcomed by everyone in his fan base. Having spent much of the previous two years building his reputation on protest songs, or at least compositions with acute social commentary, he now presented no such songs at all. In their place were observations about interpersonal relationships and floundering romance, as well as abstract poetry that replaced narrative storytelling with impressionistic states of mind.

Forces in both Dylan's private life and the entire popular music scene were reshaping his music in ways no one could have foreseen just six months before he cut the LP in one marathon session on June 9, 1964. His romance with Suze Rotolo, rarely a smooth one since the pair met shortly after Dylan moved to New York in 1961, finally came to an end—as documented, in painful detail, on the album's "Ballad in Plain D." Around the same time, the Beatles conquered America, wowing Dylan as thoroughly as the teenagers forming the bulk of the Fab Four's audience. "I knew they were pointing the direction of where music had to go," he enthused to biographer Anthony Scaduto. "I was not about to put up with other musicians, but in my head the Beatles were *it*."

His admiration of the band notwithstanding, on *Another Side of Bob Dylan*, he remained a solo acoustic folk musician, occasionally playing piano as well as guitar and harmonica. Traces of the Beatles and the other British Invasion acts springing up in their wake could be detected, perhaps, in the choruses for "It Ain't Me Babe," "All I Really Want to Do," and "My Back Pages," which verged on the catchy. Indeed, all of those songs would become hit records—but not for Dylan, their chart placings reserved for electric rock cover versions by the likes of Sonny and Cher and the Byrds that would soon follow.

For that matter, *Another Side of Bob Dylan* didn't do all that well on album charts, peaking at a considerably lower position (#43) than either of his previous two LPs had. In addition, some of his longtime supporters were dismayed by his apparent abandonment of the protest idiom. As Paul Wolfe wrote in *Broadside* after the 1964 Newport Folk Festival, "His new songs, as performed at Newport, surprised everyone, leaving the majority of the audience annoyed, some even disgusted, and, in general, scratching its collective head in disbelief. The art that had, in the past, produced towering works of power and importance, had, seemingly, degenerated into confusion and innocuousness."

The record did make the Top Ten in the United Kingdom, where other Dylan LPs were also invading the upper reaches of the charts. And half a year or so later, his next LP would cause shock waves that made the controversy surrounding *Another Side of Bob Dylan* seem mild in comparison.

Ric Ocasek, lead singer of the Cars and a producer who has worked with Weezer, No Doubt, Hole, and many others, and **Ike Reilly**, an indie-rock singer-songwriter from Chicago who has released six albums, place *Another Side of Bob Dylan* in the pantheon of the bard's work.

Bream: Ric, you were in high school when this album came out. What did you make of the album?

Ocasek: I was probably more inspired by *The Times They Are a-Changin'*, which came out the same year. I was learning how to finger-pick—"One Too Many Mornings" and all kinds of finger-picking styles. I thought that was a beautiful album, *The Times They Are a-Changin'*. I guess *Another Side* had one of the great lines that he ever wrote—"I was so much older then, I'm younger than that now." But it also had "All I Really Want to Do," which Sonny and Cher did, and "It Ain't Me Babe." So he had a couple people making pop singles out of his stuff.

Reilly: That was a strange record, 'cause "It Ain't Me Babe," "All I Really Want to Do," and "My Back Pages"—you could say those are canonized into the American songbook now. And this is just a real acoustic record. He recorded it in one session. It's a poetic record, too.

My dad was a master chief in the navy and a big Sinatra fan, and not closed-minded but not certainly seeking out any rock 'n' roll when we were kids—I was trying to prove to him that Dylan was far beyond anybody poetically—so I played him "Chimes of Freedom." Then I played "My Back Pages," and he's like, "Wow, that guy is an incredible writer." And I said, "Yeah, you think Sinatra would do that?" My dad said, "When you look like Sinatra, you don't have to write like that. Look at this guy; he needs to write like that." So I thought it was funny. But those words on record, it surpasses anything anybody has ever done, as far as the combination of poetry that is accessible.

Some of these songs have all these pop culture references like Cassius Clay, Barry Goldwater, and stuff that's really in that moment. Then it's apocalyptic time with songs like "Chimes of Freedom" and "My Back Pages." It's invigorating. Every time I listen to that, I still get the chills.

Bream: Ric, what was your reaction when this came out following _The Times They Are a-Changin'_, which was a heavy protest album, and all of a sudden, hey, he's not that protest dude anymore?
Ocasek: I wasn't analyzing the records back then like that. I got just as much poetry out of "Motorpsycho Nitemare" as I would have out of "Boots of Spanish Leather." I never really got upset about anything he did, as time went on, even when he changed to rock. I didn't think of it as a big departure or anything. I was just happy to have new songs.

Bream: At the time, Nat Hentoff was doing a profile of Dylan for the _New Yorker_, and Dylan invited him to the session. Before he started recording, he said—and I'm quoting from this interview—"There aren't any finger-pointing songs in here. Those records I've made, I'll stand behind them, but some of that was jumping into the scene to be heard, you know, pointing to all the things that are wrong. I don't want to write for people anymore or be a spokesman. From now on, I want to write from inside me."
Ocasek: He probably didn't want to be locked into what everybody wanted him to be. But that's kind of a natural kind of thing to feel after you've made some records.
Reilly: I think that quote was more of an indictment of what he did at first. We have him doing the finger-pointing songs to jumping into the scene to be heard. He's a song freak, so for him to move into those more personal songs, I couldn't get bummed at anything the guy did.

The one thing I notice about these songs is they're really funny. The departure from the heavy-handedness of some of the protest songs to the really sillier shtick—like he uses the farmer's daughter joke as a whole premise for a song—I think it's great. A little bit of the frivolous nature of this record is interesting, too. It's like, "These are the songs I'm writing right now; I'm not gonna analyze the protest, the apocalypse. I can cover all bases—love and sex and humor."

Bream: He recorded this entire album in one day—he actually recorded fourteen songs, but there are only eleven on here that they used.
Ocasek: That doesn't seem so unusual to me, for Bob to do that. He seems like he could play probably a thousand songs, and get all the lyrics right as well, any time he feels like it. He pretty much just records one take.
Reilly: What's cool, it's just a guitar. I'm not a guitar specialist, but it seems like there's some weird tunings. The arrangement—just the guitar and his voice. This is a guy whose guitar arrangements are so supportive of the melody and the lyrics and the performance.
Ocasek: He's a phenomenal guitar player. He always gets the stuff right. He's phenomenal on acoustic guitar—or on anything.

Bream: There are some pretty loose things. Like he's giggling during "All I Really Want to Do" in the last chorus. Some people have said he seemed a little loaded at certain times during the recording session. We weren't there, but he does seem to be having some fun.
Reilly: He sounds pretty succinct, though. He's doing all that yodeling. We laugh when people rip his voice. There's such melody, and complicated melodies.
Ocasek: He sings a lot in a pretty high key. He probably liked Little Richard and all those really high singers. I think he thought that he had to sing things high.

Opposite: Coffee, wine, and cigarettes fueled Dylan's imagination as he wrote in the work room above a coffee shop in Woodstock. Douglas R. Gilbert/Redferns/ Getty Images

Dylan and Ramblin' Jack Elliott were friends who both went to school on Woody Guthrie. *Douglas R. Gilbert/Redferns/ Getty Images*

Reilly: The "Spanish Harlem" song, it's a really weird little—like I think these are open G tuning, but then I couldn't really figure out what he was doing. He'd go to like this little run that doubles his voice almost. That's the part that blows me away in a lot of ways. Some of the melodies are obviously derived from Irish songs, but that song just kinda, it seems so just him.

Bream: You both mentioned "My Back Pages." What was your interpretation of that song? Was it a reflection on his looking back at his career?
Ocasek: I just thought it was extremely poetic. That's why I kind of like it, but I didn't try to analyze where it came from. I usually don't.
Reilly: It would never even dawn on me to think he was writing about his career. I, again, was just soaked up by the imagery and how it made me feel. I would listen to that, and when I'd sing along, I'd be, "I was so much older then, I'm younger than that now"—what does that mean to me, you know?

Bream: So what did that line mean to you?
Reilly: I can only say it means to me that maybe you're more liberated from trying to follow somebody else's rules when you get older. Like I was confined by what people thought you should do with your life or what you should believe in. The minute you shed

all that—whether it's oppressive religion and all that shit—once you can shed that, you can be maybe chronologically older but a lot more youthful and free.

Bream: What did it mean to you, Ric?
Ocasek: I pretty much interpreted it the same way. It is one of the lines in his songs that I always remember. It's one that you could use in life if you were talking to your kids, and kind of get into a story like that.

Bream: How much do you think the Byrds owe to this album and to Bob Dylan? They recorded almost half these songs.
Ocasek: They were obviously huge fans. And they had commercial appeal, so really they were the messengers for Bob. Because maybe regular people, the less esoteric song listeners, probably found that easy to swallow.
Reilly: They made it more palatable.
Ocasek: Yeah. And you still got to hear the words. And they were cool. They sounded good; the Byrds were good. There were a lot of people doing that for Bob at the time. There was Joan Baez and Judy Collins, and some other folk singers who would do his songs.

Bream: Peter, Paul and Mary had the first big hit of a Dylan composition. But this was the album where people took it into mainstream, Top Forty radio hits, whether it was the Byrds or the Turtles or Sonny and Cher.
Ocasek: They were really jumping on it, which was great. It was like changing the culture, getting those words out into the general public. That was making people think, and really part of the movement that we really haven't seen since. No matter what era has gone by, none has been as important as that era for change.

Bream: Do you think this album helped change the way the public perceived Dylan as an artist, because people were having big commercial success with his hits? Or was he still sort of seen as the outsider kind of guy?
Ocasek: He was still seen as the outsider. People who like the Byrds or people who covered his songs, they usually like Dylan, too. He had his own niche, and I don't know that anybody could take him out of it and put him into a normal kind of music scene. He was always the king of that whole thing. He just kept it. It would be hard to imagine another person coming up and able to say things in a different way that everybody's gonna pay attention to. His work is gonna be around for hundreds of years.
Reilly: Him just being the messenger that had the ability to poetically speak in a hip language and in a literary language, and combine it with rhythm and melody, reaches people. It's not gonna happen again. He had a combination of everything—work ethic, unbelievable thirst for song, and ambition.

Bream: What do you think the overall significance is of *Another Side*?
Ocasek: Up to *Blonde on Blonde*, all those albums were to me equally as amazing and equally as important. You could take 'em and do like when I choose random play. You can just play 'em randomly, whichever songs come up, and I think they'd all fit into the same—they'd all be like just a huge piece of work. So I can't say that I think that stands out more than *Times Are a-Changin'* or any of the records after that as well.

If you say "What's your favorite Dylan record?" it would probably be *Freewheelin'* or *Times They Are a-Changin'*. Or the first Dylan album—even though that didn't have any songs he wrote except for "Song to Woody" and "Talking New York." Those are the ones that inspire me the most. I still get excited when there's a new Dylan album, to hear what his words are gonna be.

CHAPTER 5
BRINGING IT ALL BACK HOME

with Rodney Crowell and Anthony DeCurtis

Released March 22, 1965

Producer: Tom Wilson

Recorded in Columbia Studio A, New York

All songs written by Bob Dylan.

Session musicians: Steve Boone (bass), Al Gorgoni (guitar), Bobby Gregg (drums), Paul Griffin (piano), John Hammond Jr. (guitar), Bruce Langhorne (guitar), Bill Lee (bass), Joseph Macho Jr. (bass), Frank Owens (piano), Kenny Rankin (guitar), John Sebastian (bass).

Before 1964, it seemed unimaginable that folk and rock would combine to take popular music to heights that neither style could have reached on its own. Folk was the authentic voice of the people, played on acoustic instruments, and grounded in age-old traditions; rock was loud, brash, electric, unabashedly commercial, and still aimed at a largely teenage audience. Yet in 1965, they fused into folk-rock, which would forever change the way music was made and heard. As much as any musician, Dylan was crucial to pioneering the folk-rock evolution, making his first strides into electric sounds in early 1965 with *Bringing It All Back Home*.

A rabid fan of early rock 'n' roll greats like Chuck Berry and Little Richard as a teenager, Dylan had never abandoned his love for the music, even after he abandoned it for folk as a performer. The Beatles' invasion of the United States in early 1964, however, turned his head back toward his roots. "They were doing things nobody was doing," he told biographer Anthony Scaduto. "Their chords were outrageous, and their harmonies made it all valid. You could only do that with other musicians."

Dylan had actually recorded an obscure rock single in 1962, "Mixed Up Confusion." But as far as virtually all of his fans knew, he was an acoustic folk performer who'd stay that way. In January 1965, however, he began recording an electric rock—or at least half-rock —LP with "other musicians." From a sonic standpoint, this was his riskiest and most radical shift of all.

Any doubt as to what Dylan was up to got removed the minute the needle hit "Subterranean Homesick Blues," an all-out blast of blues-rock. Side One of the record had its share of other pounding rockers, such as "Maggie's Farm," but their stream-of-consciousness wordplay—sometimes verging on the edge of surrealism—shared little with the other rock 'n' roll on the market in early 1965. But Dylan wasn't all assault, balancing the ravers with the tenderly romantic, lighter folk-rock ballads "She Belongs to Me" and "Love Minus Zero/No Limit."

Perhaps hedging his bets a bit, Dylan made Side Two entirely acoustic, though Bruce Langhorne added luminous guitar fills to Dylan's own sturdy axework. The compositions, however, were no less ambitious in their enigmatic, poetic juxtapositions, whether jubilant ("Mr. Tambourine Man") or apocalyptic ("Gates of Eden"). "Mr. Tambourine Man" became the first huge folk-rock smash when the Byrds gave it their Dylan-meets-the-Beatles jingle-jangle treatment, while "Subterranean Homesick Blues" became Dylan's first Top Forty single.

Dylan's raucous electric rock caused displeasure and occasional outrage among folk fans who didn't even want him abandoning protest songs, let alone embracing rock 'n' roll. But *Bringing It All Back Home* was a big hit, becoming his first Top Ten album and gaining more new converts than old fans it alienated. "Dylan as an individual has finally found his natural medium," declared *Boston Broadside* in its review of the LP. "And folk music as a whole has found another step forward that can be taken."

Rodney Crowell, a two-time Grammy-winning singer-songwriter who has released sixteen studio albums, talks about this Dylan-goes-electric album with **Anthony DeCurtis**, a *Rolling Stone* contributing editor who was introduced in Chapter 2.

Rodney Crowell: "I always thought: Is Dylan our Samuel Taylor Coleridge?"
Michael Ochs Archives/Getty Images

Bream: A lot of people think this album is a turning point for Dylan and for rock 'n' roll. What do you think?
Crowell: It was pivotal for me. A lad down the street from where I lived said, "You need to come hear this." Went down to his place, put it on, and I didn't get past "Subterranean Homesick Blues" on the first day. We must have played it twenty-five times before we moved to the second song.

To me that was Hank Snow and Chuck Berry and Bob Wills all rolled in. It was a brand-new paradigm in language, truly, jumping into a parallel universe. Then later on, when I got into the whole album, the bar gets set higher and higher as you go into it.
DeCurtis: Within a year or thirteen months we had *Another Side of Bob Dylan*, *Bringing It All Back Home*, and *Highway 61 Revisited*. That is a level of achievement that is just stunning. It's also an evolution that is just extraordinary. In my listening to this record, I always go back to those four essentially acoustic songs on the second side: "Mr. Tambourine Man," "Gates of Eden," "It's Alright Ma (I'm Only Bleeding)," and "It's All Over

Now, Baby Blue." The level of writing there, the level of performance, the level of the ideas—they are peerless. As a kind of run of twenty minutes of music or something, it would be hard to top that.

Bream: What did you think of the approach that one side of the album was electric and one side was acoustic?

Crowell: I think a lot about the first half of it is based on his understanding of rock 'n' roll and how he was going to approach it. It was in many ways based on the twelve-bar blues. "She Belongs to Me" is a brilliant fusion of the twelve-bar blues tradition, taking the main opening line and repeating it and then summing it up with the kick line at the end, but he adds a II chord in there and elevates twelve-bar blues to another level. Much in the same way that "Mr. Tambourine Man" and "It's Alright Ma" are kind of taking the folk tradition. If I have any criticism of this record, it's deep into the first side you get into "Outlaw Blues" and "On the Road Again," which I think is Dylan experimenting with rock 'n' roll and the twelve-bar blues form. But I don't think his sensibility for rhyme scheme [on those two songs] worked so well for me.

DeCurtis: "She Belongs to Me" and "Love Minus Zero/No Limit" are about as straightforward of love songs as you're going to get from Bob Dylan. The language is complicated, and they're certainly not moon/June love songs, but they seem very heartfelt and beautiful. Their complexity is not necessarily in the emotion being expressed but in the quality of the language being used.

That protest singer idea—the protest kind of shifts here. "Subterranean Homesick Blues" refers to the heat, the police, and a kind of paranoid sense of the culture. "Maggie's Farm" was a great metaphor for oppression in all its forms. But they lend themselves to so many other situations; they're not the kind of songs that come from a specific event, like "The Lonesome Death of Hattie Carroll," which was about something very specific that happened to a particular person. Or "Only a Pawn in Their Game," about Medgar Evers and his killer. This is a whole different order of things, and I think it's part of that transition out of the folk world and into the rock 'n' roll world. In a sense, Dylan moves in both of those worlds still. But at this point it was very important for him to put some distance between himself and the folk world and make some inroads into rock 'n' roll. That sense of transition is, I think, one of the exciting things about this work.

Crowell: I've sort of taken "She Belongs to Me" as a love song to like an archetypal goddess, rather than addressing who we might have thought of as Joan Baez at the time. He articulates something profound about the perfect woman, which is only archetypal. That puts him in a place where he's far enough from a one-on-one relationship that he can stretch it out there as far as it can go.

DeCurtis: "It's Alright Ma (I'm Only Bleeding)" reminds me of parts of Shakespeare, how when you're reading *Hamlet* or any of the well-known plays, so much of the language has entered our language. "Even the president of the United States sometimes must have to stand naked." "Money doesn't talk, it swears." These expressions have a sort of aphoristic quality. At the same time, it's so wild and swirling that you know you're hanging on by your nails trying to just keep up with him.

Bream: You know he recorded that acoustic side with a full band but then scrapped it. Some of it has come out on the bootleg series.

Crowell: Which brings me to something that I think we should address, which is the actual sonic recording. It's a living, breathing entity, in terms of what was technically available at the time and the way the studio is used and the way music is produced. I listen to "She Belongs to Me," and if you listen very closely, it's obviously a live performance. He sings, [and] when he moves away from the mic, the compression that he has on the vocal brings the strum of his rhythm guitar up about two or three DB, which gives the recording kind of a living, breathing quality to it. Even when it shifts from the band to the acoustic Side Two, it's still just really, really great recording. Engineered and compressed and with all the pre-amps working. To this day when we're working with Pro Tools, I say, "Why can't you make them sound like 'Subterranean Homesick Blues,' that raw, that electric?"

DeCurtis: That sense of immediacy, I have felt that as a listener. That kind of false beginning to "Bob Dylan's 115th Dream" where he starts laughing and goes back into the song—it's such a kind of nice moment. There's a lot of humor on this album, too, for all the kind of seriousness of all of its aspects, and certainly the seriousness of its achievements. But there's a kind of fun, shaggy dog quality to "Bob Dylan's 115th Dream" with Captain Ahab and all this other business, where he's just stringing along this episodic tale of the discovery of America. "He said his name was Columbus, I just said good luck." It sounds like he's making it up as he's singing, and he just sounds so loose and free.

All was good for Dylan at the Newport Folk Festival in 1964, but it would be a different story for him at that fest the next summer. *Douglas R. Gilbert/ Redferns/Getty Images*

Crowell: Framing himself as a smart-ass in just the perfect way. It takes a lot of belief in oneself to have that much swagger to deliver "Subterranean Homesick Blues" or "Maggie's Farm" the way he does. It's fully realized. Few get there. Maybe Hank Williams got there a few times. Chuck Berry got there. Howlin' Wolf got there. Ray Charles got there. But I don't know if a poet got there. A poet who fused music and performance and recording studio and the whole ball of wax the way this particular record does. This is my favorite Bob Dylan record—I would say one of the best records ever made.

DeCurtis: It is one of those records that whenever I reapproach it, I never feel that thing that you can sometimes feel about even very great records which is, "I got this." There still seems to me something that is just so open-ended about it. What he's doing with such limited instrumentation on those four tracks [on Side Two], talk about psychedelia. When we say that term, we think of certain types of effects and guitar sounds, whereas here it's all with words and very simple kind of guitar parts. In terms of expanding your mind and language right to the brink, those songs are just amazing.

Crowell: Indeed they are. When psychedelia hit Houston, I had enough of an understanding to realize these weren't poets. These were guys who had some amps and could get a light show going, a wah-wah pedal, some fuzz. You could bend the shape of reality using electricity and the instrument to try to affect psychedelia. But Dylan had already done it with poetry and language.

At the end of it, it's the language that Bob Dylan was able to seemingly effortlessly combine with the natural melodic sense that he had. It was profound. To me, the two greatest rhyming songwriters of all time were Chuck Berry and Bob Dylan. But Dylan pushed it out there into no man's land at about this time of *Bringing It All Back Home*.

DeCurtis: Dylan's phrasing on this album is just perfect. And not in some studied way but in a natural way. The record opens with that kind of jangle of "Subterranean

Homesick Blues," and you're right in the middle of the thing. "Mama's in the basement, mixing up the medicine, I'm on the pavement, thinking about the government," you're already racing to keep up with him. Then finally you get to the end and he's singing at the top of his register that "You must leave now, take what you need, you think we'll last." "Whatever you wish to keep, you better grab it fast." It so much captured what just happened to you listening to this album, but also what was happening at that moment in time where things seemed to be moving so quickly. These are songs you can live by, as complicated as they are. There are messages in here for you that are as deep as anything you're going to encounter in any aspect of the arts.

Crowell: "Subterranean," "She Belongs to Me," and "Maggie's Farm" hit, and I'm going, "There he goes man." He's rhyming, rhyming, the rhyming genius, and then he hits, "Love Minus Zero/No Limit," and he doesn't rhyme. There is no rhyme in it at all. It's like I've got you on the carpet, and now I'm going to yank it out from under you. It's a beautiful pivotal point in that record for me any time I listen to it. "He did that on purpose!" I have to think you put that song there for that reason, to shift.

DeCurtis: That song starts out, "My love she speaks like silence/without ideals or violence." Silence and violence is a masterful rhyme, and then it turns into like a prose poem. Your point about the abstractness of the women in these songs is well taken. There's such a calmness to Dylan in those songs, too. It's a different kind of song for him. It's almost as if he's just kind of reciting them or something. There's a great kind of relaxed beauty in them.

Bream: Do you interpret "Maggie's Farm" as a workman's protest, or is it his protest about not being boxed into a certain role?

Crowell: As a younger man, I read it as a metaphor for the old ball and chain: I'm not going to be held down by you anymore, woman. But as I have gotten older, I think you might have your finger on, "I'm just not going to live up to your expectations. Whoever you are out there. I'm not. I'm an artist. If I start thinking about living up to your expectations, then I can't even get close to the next work I'm going to do."

DeCurtis: It could be about "Maggie's Farm" specifically, could be about a relationship, could be about a society, could be about the folk movement, or all of that. It's about the struggle to be who you are and discover who you are with some sense of freedom.

"It's Alright Ma," the whole song is like an explanation of, "It's life and life only." I can only do what I can do. Even if by virtue of being so amazing, creating an overwhelming sense of expectations, he's also saying, "You can't hold somebody to expectations. You have to let somebody just be who they are." That is maybe one of the final messages of the album. What is being brought back home is that sense of who you are. Just discover that, be that, and realize that.

Bream: How did you interpret "Mr. Tambourine Man"?

Crowell: I interpret it as possibility, possibility beyond the mundane. I can't say that having heard "Mr. Tambourine Man" and feeling what it was reaching out there wasn't the reason that I took that first puff on a joint. Maybe this is a way to get there. It didn't turn out to be that puff on that joint was going to be the thing that allowed me to write like that, but I certainly had to go see.

DeCurtis: When all of those questions were being discussed back in the day—this was right around the time I smoked pot for the first time—that was part of it. You don't want to overemphasize it, but certainly at that time that idea of mind expansion and psychedelia weren't just musical styles. The song seemed to be about that, about visions, or about that open-endedness, what Rodney is calling possibilities. It seemed to be about seeing new things, seeing other things, seeing in a poetic way.

CHAPTER 6

HIGHWAY 61 REVISITED

with Tony Glover and Joe Henry

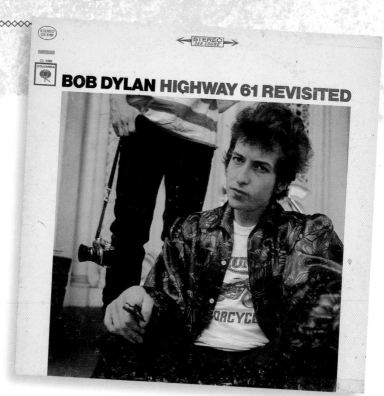

Released August 30, 1965

Producers: Bob Johnston, Tom Wilson
(for "Like a Rolling Stone" only)

Recorded in Columbia Studio A, New York

All songs written by Bob Dylan.

Session musicians: Mike Bloomfield (guitar), Harvey
Brooks (bass), Bobby Gregg (drums), Paul Griffin (organ,
piano), Al Kooper (organ), Charlie McCoy (guitar),
Sam Lay (drums), Frank Owens (piano/maracas),
Russ Savakus (bass).

Even after *Bringing It All Back Home* hit the Top Ten and "Subterranean Homesick Blues" made the Top Forty, some of Dylan's more purist folk fans were hoping his detour into rock was a temporary aberration. He was, after all, continuing to play as a solo acoustic artist in his live shows, as seen in the documentary of his spring 1965 British tour, *Dont* [sic] *Look Back*. Any thought of his venture into rock as just a passing phase, however, vanished in the summer by his chaotic, brief electric set at the Newport Folk Festival, the audience's hailstorm of boos and cheers fighting it out for supremacy. At the same time, his all-out rock single "Like a Rolling Stone"—all six minutes of it—was climbing the charts, rising all the way to #2. And later that summer, it was featured on his first all-out rock album, *Highway 61 Revisited*, which completed his transformation from folk-music hero to rock 'n' roll star.

With his studio backup crew now including seasoned electric blues-rock musicians Mike Bloomfield (guitar) and Al Kooper (organ), Dylan dove into fully arranged, powerful recordings with greater volume and dizzyingly surreal lyrics. While blues remained at the core on romps such as "Tombstone Blues," he also unveiled a deft, almost pop-flavored melodic touch on "Queen Jane Approximately," as well as putting the kind of descending tunes favored by Ray Charles through a doom-laden lens on "Ballad of a Thin Man." The longer songs were epic in their narrative, none more so than the eleven-minute closer "Desolation Row," the LP's sole acoustic track.

While some folk purists continued to rail against Dylan's new direction as a commercial sellout—and a betrayal of the protest folk movement he'd spearheaded—it was a losing battle. Retaining many of his fans from his folk days and adding legions of new ones, *Highway 61 Revisited* leapt to #3 in the charts, doing about as well in the UK (where "Like a Rolling Stone" was a big hit). And now Dylan was blasting out rock in concert as well, to mixed but often enthusiastic response, though onstage he wasn't quite as uncompromising as he was on record, splitting his concerts into electric and acoustic sets. With Simon and Garfunkel, the Lovin' Spoonful, the Mamas & the Papas, and other young folkies also moving from acoustic to electric sounds, folk-rock became a major trend in popular music, introducing a new level of lyrical sophistication into the hit parade.

Highway 61 Revisited is often regarded not just as Dylan's best record but as one of the greatest ever, *Rolling Stone* listing it as the fourth best album of all time. In Anthony Scaduto's biography of the singer, even Dylan himself conceded, "I'm not gonna be able to make a record better than that one. *Highway 61* is just too good. There's a lot of stuff on there that *I* would listen to."

The landmark moment when Dylan went electric at the Newport Folk Festival on July 25, 1965. *Alice Ochs/Michael Ochs Archives/Getty Images*

Tony Glover, who literally wrote the book on blues harmonica playing, has known Bob Dylan since their days on the Minneapolis folk scene in 1959. He discusses *Highway 61 Revisited* with **Joe Henry**, a Los Angeles–based singer-songwriter who has released twelve studio albums and served as producer for records by Bonnie Raitt, Rodney Crowell, Solomon Burke, Elvis Costello/Allen Toussaint, Ramblin' Jack Elliott, and many others.

Bream: Tony [Glover], how many of the recording sessions for *Highway 61* were you at?
Glover: It looks like three of them. The first session: "Tombstone Blues," "Takes a Lot to Laugh," "Positively 4th Street." Second session: "From Buick 6," "Ballad of a Thin Man," a version of "Desolation Row" with a band that was scrapped. The last one I was at was "Highway 61 Revisited," "Just Like Tom Thumb's Blues," and "Queen Jane." He played Newport, which was Sunday, and the first session was Thursday. The blood was still hot.
Henry: Only "Like a Rolling Stone" had been recorded before Newport, right?
Glover: That's correct. It was done mid-June. I remember hearing it on the [Newport] grounds. People had transistor radios, and I think I heard it a couple of times.
Henry: Since it was the first time Bob Dylan worked with [producer] Bob Johnston [after Tom Wilson produced "Like a Rolling Stone"], was it noticeable to Dylan that

Dylan recording "Like a Rolling Stone."
Joe Henry: "I think the challenge of
the song is 'what does it mean to feel
completely unmoored?'" *Michael Ochs
Archives/Getty Images*

there was a new man at the helm? Or was it the feeling, "The label's here, I'm going to carry on anyway."

Glover: That was the feeling that it looked like to me. Albert Grossman [Dylan's manager] was the one saying, "Let's try another take on that." Or "that's got it."

Bream: How much instruction was Dylan giving to the other musicians?

Glover: He'd maybe run down [the song] once. He'd stand maybe over off-mic near where the bass and drum guys were set up and kind of play through the changes and idea. He didn't have a "you play this and then you go with a double shuffle, da da da." He would run it down and then the people would show it. We'd gone up to Woodstock and [Al] Kooper had come along. And him and Kooper spent a lot of the day Saturday going over and charting the tunes. He would play them and Kooper could notate the changes so at the Monday session he was able to give the guys a chord chart like they do in Nashville.

Bream: What was the vibe like in the studio?

Glover: I got to feel that there was some really heavy stuff happening. "It Takes a Lot to Laugh, It Takes a Train to Cry" was really nice, the first version with the band doing an up-tempo, kind of heavy riff thing. Then it stopped, and Bob sat at the piano and the band was on break and Bob reworked lyrics. They came back, and another take was a slowed down, really pretty version that's on the album. An improvement over the first one, which is kind of so-so.

"Ballad of a Thin Man," the guy playing the organ was doing like a maniacal sound, doing some of those octave swoops. It made me think of Vincent Price movies.

Bream: In that first verse, Dylan chuckles, and they didn't take it out or recut it.
Henry: It reminds me of [critic] Greil Marcus writing about the earliest performances of those songs, and he said, "With time, you forget how funny that stuff was when people first heard it." Audiences when they first heard "Desolation Row," they'd laugh out loud. It hadn't become an iconic set piece, they were hearing it like a new song.
Glover: Context does make a difference. In these songs, there's a lot of funny stuff and humorous puns going on and references that nowadays are written on the wall.
Henry: I first heard "Like a Rolling Stone" in 1970. I was nine or ten. Even though it's become so ubiquitous in our culture, I can hear it randomly and be jolted back to that first memory and what it was like to hear it as a new song and not as a classic.
Glover: It was a definite turn from the way things had been going. One of the things that kind of set it off for me is he did a tour following that [album] with The Band, and he came to Minneapolis in the fall. He did the first half acoustic and the second half with The Band. He's out there acoustically, and there's this guy sitting next to me, and he leans over and says: "Do you know who that is?" I said: "Didn't you get tickets for Bob Dylan?" He said: "Yeah, but that's not what he sounds like." I realized this guy had never heard of Bob before "Like a Rolling Stone." I thought things are going to be different now.

Bream: Does it feel in retrospect that this record changed everything for the music, culture, and the music business?
Henry: I think you liken it to something like *Citizen Kane* or Louis Armstrong doing "West End Blues" or Charlie Parker doing "Now's the Time." It changed everything that followed.
Glover: It also affected radio. Here was a single ["Like a Rolling Stone"] that some of the jocks were just playing one side of. Half the song. Columbia [Records] got nervous about a six-minute song so they put it out in two parts. DJs were putting it together at the station and making it into one song. Columbia got word of this and started putting it out as a one-sided six-minute song. That really changed things. Before that if it was over two twenty-five, DJs didn't have the time of day for it. Now they were forced to pay attention to something.
Henry: There's a sonic aggression on that record that is as much a departure as anything. I go back and listen to *Bringing It All Back Home,* and even though it was the first quote-unquote "electric" record, it still sounds like it was produced and recorded sort of like a Johnny Mathis record. It was very well balanced. Instruments are cleanly played and a little bit distant to me as a listener; there's a bit of a flat screen in front of me, whereas "Highway 61" sounds fucked up. For instance, the compression distortion on Bob's vocal on something like "Desolation Row," it's not about hi-fi. It sounds like a definite statement that's being pushed so aggressively forward. I hear that as a choice. It's a real shift to think that a Columbia record would be made deliberately to sound in a way that's appropriate to the song and not appropriate to recording standards. It sounds like a mess in the best sort of way.
Glover: Things like the guitar's out of tune with the harp on "Queen Jane." There's a certain kinetic energy there that's being captured that's more important than anything with Johnny Mathis.

Henry: There's an immediacy to it that has obviously trumped everybody. That was an exciting take no matter how messed up it is—whether the bass player was making the change a half bar later than the rest of the band.

Glover: It seemed to me at the time there were two ranks of musicians. Sort of like us and them, us being Bob and Al and Mike Bloomfield on guitar and them, regular studio musicians. This was their three- to six-o'clock booking. There was a bass player who went kind of nuts on one tune, he was goofing around at the end of the tune, and he was replaced by Harvey Brooks, who is a little more one-of-us kind of bass players. There was a plan maybe to make Bob feel more comfortable. For that matter, uncredited Sam Lay, the drummer with Butterfield [Blues Band] that Bloomfield brought along, was playing drums on "Highway 61 Revisited." You can tell by the double shuffle thing he's got going on. There was definitely a feeling of experimentation to some extent amongst some people, and others were just punching their time card.

Bream: How well did Dylan know Bloomfield, and why did he pick him for this project?

Glover: Legend has it that they had met in Chicago some years before and spent an evening hanging out and playing tunes at each other, which could be true. He was certainly aware of the [Paul] Butterfield Band. At some point, there was a question whether Bloomfield was going to go with the Butterfield Band or with Dylan. He ended up picking the band.

Henry: I remember reading that when Bloomfield got to the session for "Highway 61," Bob said to him, "Just don't play me any of that BB King shit." He wants the energy of blues but nothing as identifiable as a particular genre approach to blues playing.

Glover: As to why he picked Bloomfield, he was a really good player, and he had a hell of a grounding in blues. He worked with Big Joe Williams, who Bob had also played with. Bloomfield was not a shy player. He knew how to integrate as well as do flash runs.

Bream: Some people have suggested that *Highway 61 Revisited* might be the first punk-rock record—an aggressive shout of disillusionment.

Henry: I can't disagree with it. Especially if you go back to the reissued mono recordings, it's a much more guitar-forward record and less piano/organ–driven.

Bream: Let's talk about your interpretations of some of the key songs. "Ballad of a Thin Man," one which is still in his live repertoire, almost nightly.

Glover: It's a story. It's a bunch of different people in situations. A lot of it is "You don't know what it is, do you Mr. Jones." There's all these stories that go back to *Dont* [sic] *Look Back* where there's this reporter who's trying to get him to say things, and he basically chews him up and spits him out. There's stories about that's who Mr. Jones is. There are other ways you can take it.

Henry: I've always been inclined to think that Mr. Jones is not a particular person, but the point of the song is nothing in this moment is as we perceived it necessarily. Everybody is going to have to reimagine their own reality for lack of a better term.

Bream: My interpretation is, like Tony said earlier, it's us versus them, the new world—the hip, the counter culture—versus the old world, the straight world that doesn't really understand.

Glover: I agree with that.

Bream: Let's tackle "Desolation Row."

Glover: There was another version done at the end of the session on Friday night. He got a half of verse into it, and it was pretty obvious his guitar was way out of tune.

Opposite: Tony Glover on Newport: "By the time he got up, they were running late and running out of time, and they had a curfew. So he did three tunes. People were pissed about that. They were yelling. 'You've done three tunes and now you're gone. What's the deal?'" *Alice Ochs/ Michael Ochs Archives/Getty Images*

I looked at [friend and musician Bob] Neuwirth and he looked at me and we both looked at Albert [Grossman] and said, "Hey man, the guitar's way out of tune." He said, "Let him go." Bob played the whole thing through and came in the booth to hear a playback and went, "Hey, that guitar is way the fuck out, why did you make me go through eleven minutes of the damn thing?" Albert just shook his head.

Bream: Did he have the lyrics written out for that song?
Glover: Yeah. There was like a music stand, and he had notes on it. A lot of his stuff—there are a lot of arrows here and crossing out there, sticking in a word here, going back to there. So it's kind of a mess. It's not neatly typed out. It ain't like a cue card. I'm always amazed at the memory he has as far as being able to recall lyrics.

Bream: The final song, "Desolation Row," was the only acoustic song on the record. Did that heighten its impact?

Glover: The way it sits in the album, it's kind of like a benediction in a way. It's very cinematic, little scenarios happening. Like Marty Robbins' "El Paso." That whole thing is a movie, and this is a movie in the same way. It starts out selling postcards at a hanging. That's something that happened in Duluth in the 1920s. There were some black guys who were accused of rape and ended up getting lynched by a mob and hanging from a bridge, and there were photos taken and put on postcards and sold that way. One line is that whole story. So a lot of lines have little stories in them.

Henry: It is a movie. It's like a Bunuel movie compared to a Billy Wilder movie as far as being a nonlinear story. But you can see the whole thing.

Bream: How does the mood and the vibe of this album capture what was going on at the time?

Henry: If I go back and listen to the record as a complete statement, it sounds human and raw. I associate the sound of "Ballad of Thin Man" with what the Vietnam War looked like to me on the cover of *Life* magazine.

Bream: Let's talk more specifically about the content of "Like a Rolling Stone" and what it means.

Henry: Has there ever been a piece of popular music that is directly and personally aggressive toward somebody? Not without a sense of compassion, because that's there, too. He was definitely calling somebody out, maybe a lot of people. I don't think that had ever been done in a pop song before. He's saying, how does it feel to be completely disconnected and ungrounded? I think the challenge of the song is, what does it mean to feel completely unmoored?

Bream: Where does *Highway 61 Revisited* rank in the canon?

Henry: You'd have to put it in the top two or three. Not just in his catalog but also in the Rock Age.

Glover: It's definitely up there. It's one of the ones that makes him worth remembering and thinking and talking about.

Henry: As a record maker, I recognize the distinction between things that might have been recorded two weeks ago and already sound like an artifact to me versus certain music—Charlie Parker is in that category, Robert Johnson is in that category—where it just sounds like living persons jumping out of a speaker. It sounds completely electric and alive, not a sealed document. On many days, *Highway 61* strikes me as that. It sounds like it's still evolving because we as listeners are evolving as we hear it. It does not sound like a done deal to me.

Joe Henry: "There's no question [*Highway 61 Revisited*] changed the paradigm and it changed the dynamic and it changed everybody's estimation of not only what was possible but also what they were obliged to try to do."
Fred W. McDarrah/Getty Images

CHAPTER 7

BLONDE ON BLONDE

with Geoffrey Himes and Jason Isbell

Released May 16, 1966

Producer: Bob Johnston

Recorded in Columbia Music Row Studios, Nashville [except "One of Must Know (Sooner or Later)," recorded in Columbia Recording Studio A, New York]

All songs written by Bob Dylan.

Session musicians: Bill Aikins (keyboards), Wayne Butler (trombone), Kenneth Buttrey (drums), Jerry Kennedy (guitar), Al Kooper (organ, guitar), Wayne Moss (guitar), Robbie Robertson (guitar), Charlie McCoy (guitar/bass/harmonica/trumpet), Joe South (guitar/bass), Hargus "Pig" Robbins (keyboards), Henry Strzelecki (bass).

On "One of Us Must Know (Sooner or Later)" only: Rick Danko or Bill Lee (bass), Bobby Gregg (drums), Paul Harris (piano), Al Kooper (organ), Robbie Robertson (guitar).

O f the three mid-1960s electric rock albums regarded by many as Dylan's holy triumvirate, *Blonde on Blonde* is often considered the best. With more than a year of recording with other musicians under his belt, the singer-songwriter expanded his melodic range even as his lyrics grew more enigmatic in their blend of romantic yearning, cynical putdowns, and surrealistic wordplay. The upbeat "I Want You" and graceful-yet-probing "Just Like a Woman" were Top Forty hit singles, with the boisterously zany "Rainy Day Women #12 & 35" stopping just short of the #1 position. Several other songs on the double LP—rock's first, along with the Mothers of Invention's *Freak Out*, also released in 1966— are just as highly esteemed in Dylan's pantheon, especially "Visions of Johanna" and the epic "Sad Eyed Lady of the Lowlands," whose nearly twelve-minute-length was unprecedented in rock music.

Although the first few sessions for *Blonde on Blonde* were recorded in New York (some with the Hawks, soon to evolve into The Band), Dylan and producer Bob Johnston made the unusual decision to cut most of the album in Nashville in February and March 1966. Organist Al Kooper and Hawks guitarist Robbie

Geoff Himes: "In that one interview where he talks about the thin-wild-mercury sound he was looking for, *Live 1966* and *Blonde on Blonde* are the two albums that really capture it." *Jan Persson/Redferns/ Getty Images*

Robertson remained key collaborators, but most of the backing was supplied by Nashville sessions musicians such as multi-instrumentalist Charlie McCoy and soon-to-be-star Joe South (bass, guitar). Unaccustomed as many of them were to working with rock musicians, they picked up the complex songs with remarkably rapid efficiency, even when "Sad Eyed Lady" went on and on and on without any indication as to when it would end.

In the contrasts between the melodies of the bridges and verses of songs such as "I Want You," "Just Like a Woman," and "Absolutely Sweet Marie" (as well as the smooth transitions between those sections), Dylan might have been picking up a few tricks from his friends the Beatles. Not that he was too reverent; it's often speculated that "Fourth Time Around" is a parody of the Beatles' "Norwegian Wood." The influence of country music on *Blonde on Blonde* is light, but as Johnston has recalled, he and Dylan appreciated the lower-key atmosphere Nashville studios offered. As *Hit Parader* magazine noted in its review at the time, "The Nashville musicians give his typically ambiguous lyrics the most relaxed and solidly musical backing he's ever received on records."

"What makes this all work is there's this great mixture of very realistic description and very surreal description," observes critic Geoffrey Himes. "When people try to imitate Dylan, they forget the realistic part of it, and they just give you the surrealism. It doesn't work as well."

Among those most satisfied with the results was the artist himself. "The closest I ever got to the sound I hear in my mind was on individual bands in the *Blonde on Blonde* album," Dylan told *Playboy* in March 1978. "It's that thin, that wild mercury sound. It's metallic and bright gold, with whatever that conjures up."

An award-winning critic who writes for the *Washington Post*, *Oxford American*, *Paste*, *Downbeat*, and many other publications, **Geoffrey Himes** is well-suited to dissect *Blonde on Blonde*. As is **Jason Isbell**, the 2014 Americana Music Association's artist of the year and an acclaimed singer-songwriter who has released four solo studio albums and tattooed a lyric from Dylan's "Boots of Spanish Leather" on his arm.

Bream: This is often regarded as Dylan's best album. Is it?
Himes: There have been times when I've thought it was. It's definitely one of my favorite albums of all time by anybody.
Isbell: I love it, too. I think it's the most "Dylan" Dylan album. I think it's a culmination of a lot of work in a certain direction that he was trying to go. I think he probably did very close to what he meant to do with that record.

Himes: *Highway 61 Revisited*, which is a great record, too, is a more conventional type of electric blues. This is something very different; this has a carnival feel to it that mixes with the blues. The core elements are Dylan's harmonica and Al Kooper's organ, which are similar, almost reedy instruments that create a hum through the whole album, with the guitars and rhythm section poking at it. Throughout these long songs he often refuses to resolve the chord progression—the changes keep approaching a climax and never quite find it.

Isbell: Having those really great Nashville session players on *Blonde on Blonde*, I think made a huge difference. Because it's so good for keeping people standing on one foot. And he did that for it feels like the whole session.

Bream: Unlike the standard Nashville session, there were no charts or chords to play. Dylan may have taught part of the song to Kooper, who in turn showed it to the musicians, and they were almost winging it.

Himes: I think the real hero of the sessions was [drummer] Kenny Buttrey. When you talk about people not knowing where they are going, Kenny, with those little punch rolls and things he did, sort of kept the tension in the songs when they could have gone out of control.

Isbell: His performance on the record is probably as good as anybody else's, if not the best. The snare drum on "Most Likely You Go Your Way and I'll Go Mine," that's Olympic.

Himes: Dylan tried to cut this album with the Hawks [later known as The Band] in New York before these sessions. If you listen to those tracks, there's a lot of great stuff there, but it doesn't have that sort of understated suspense we've been talking about. They're more like live performances than studio performances, which is not surprising because the Hawks are more a live band, a bar band. They'd only played with Dylan for a few weeks.

Isbell: If you listen on The Band box [set], it's really hard to tell the difference between the outtakes and the ones that make the record. Those guys are studied. They spent a lot of time practicing those songs, and there wasn't a lot of room for improvisation. With the players Dylan wound up using in Nashville, they didn't do that; they didn't have to.

The 1966 tour of London became the subject of a little-seen documentary, "*Eat the Document*," directed by D. A. Pennebaker, who had helmed *Dont Look Back* chronicling Dylan's 1965 visit to London. *Jan Persson/Redferns/ Getty Images*

Himes: Let's talk about the songwriting. The thing that strikes me is that a lot of the songs are in the putdown mode, like "Positively 4th Street" and "Like a Rolling Stone." Dylan had found a way to take the structure of a romantic pop song and use it to talk about other issues. At the same time, "Visions of Johanna," he's talking about this Johanna who is not there, this woman he's really obsessed with. It's almost like she's a muse or a state of consciousness that he's grasping for, like she's the sister of "Mr. Tambourine Man," the sort of visionary conscience that allowed him to write these songs and see beyond the conventions of the world. And then there's all these distractions preventing him from getting to her. This pompous, draggy boyfriend, the night watchman, and the jelly-faced woman. So, on the one hand, it's about a love triangle or quadrangle, but I think the images are all about the quotidian distractions in life that we all have to put up with and the state of higher consciousness that we all sort of are hoping for or trying to find. Does that make sense?

Isbell: It does to me. I see the life that he's leading as Louise, in the things that she represents—the pop stardom and sex and the money and all that—and then I see Johanna as what he's moving toward. Going home and being his own person. The one woman in the song is part of what he desires, which is pop stardom and touring and being Bob Dylan; Johanna was this kind of ideal, wholesomeness and innocence that home life offers that he always seems to be getting pulled away from.

Himes: There's a lot of humor. The humor doesn't mean he couldn't be serious. It's more like you could be funny even while you were being serious.

Isbell: There is a contrast to all that seriousness and all those lines that make you take the record off and listen to it for a minute in your head to figure out the depth of what he's saying. Sometimes he just wants to make a joke.

Bream: Did you take "Leopard-Skin Pill-Box Hat" as serious or see that as a joke?

Isbell: There's a lot of both. I think that one pairs with "Just Like a Woman." They almost have to be about the same person. I think he's under that weakness and that pop culture kind of sensibility that the trust-fund kids have at that point in time. A lot of lines are hilarious double entendres that don't make any sense.

Himes: One of the effective ways to attack the rich and powerful is to make fun of them. A "Leopard-Skin Pill-Box Hat" was the kind of hat that Jackie Kennedy wore; it was the height of rich people fashion.

He turns twenty-five between the recording and the release of this record. He's still a kid. He's very much caught in this bohemian world—that beatnik, hippie, iconoclastic culture—and when he's talking to these women who are symbols of a certain class, it's not just rich and poor he's talking about, it's also hip and square. Both of those dialectics are really alive on this record.

Isbell: He makes fun of both of them, almost equally, too. "Rainy Day Women" sounds so much like he's making fun of bohemians. He can write songs what we'd call diss tracks now that don't sound bitter or desperate in any way. He's finally reached a point in his own life when he can see things a little bit more objectively, and he can point the finger at all sides at the same time.

Bream: About the third or fourth line, he chuckles as he's singing. What did you make of that?

Isbell: I think he's laughing at the trombone, myself.

Dylan waits for a press conference in London where he recorded *Live 1966: The "Royal Albert Hall" Concert*, which wasn't released until 1998. *Express Newspapers/ Getty Images*

Himes: It has a circus horn band feel. He's singing off-key a lot of times as if he's stoned. The whole song seems wobbly to me, in the best possible way.

Isbell: Like a wheel's about to come off the wagon. Every time you hear someone like that laugh, you think it's an inside joke. For him to leave it on the record, you think he must have thought something to himself that was hilarious.

A lot of people have spent a lot of time after that to try to recreate that kind of party track. It's a hard thing to recreate that line where it makes everybody feel comfortable listening to it no matter what the situation is. When you hear that song first thing in the morning, it's going to be hard to wake up grumpy.

Bream: Let's talk about "Sad Eyed Lady of the Lowlands," the first song to occupy an entire side of a vinyl LP in rock history.

Himes: It's just a gorgeous love song.

Isbell: He gets totally lost and off-track and winds up not making any sense to himself. It's a beautiful song written for one person, specifically. It's really hard to do that.

Himes: People say: Is this song about Joan Baez or Sara Lownds or Edie Sedgwick? It's more about what it says about us as a listener.

Bonjour, Bob! The American rock star meets the press in Paris.
RDA/Getty Images

Bream: Let's talk about "Stuck Inside of Mobile with the Memphis Blues Again."

Himes: "Stuck Inside of Mobile" is a more comic version of "Visions of Johanna." There's the same tension of where he wants to be and where he is.

Isbell: It's pretty obvious in hindsight that he was getting tired of the machine. I like the characters he's sort of mocking in this one.

Bream: Al Kooper said of these sessions something like you take this New York hipster and put him in Nashville, and we threw all these things that didn't make sense into the test tube, and all of a sudden it exploded into this great record.

Himes: There's definitely tension between Bob, Robbie, and Al from New York and all of the Nashville guys. In this song in particular, you get this tight country shuffle that [drummer] Buttrey is playing, this brooding organ that Kooper is playing, and somehow they got the right amount of tension and balance between them to create a sound like nobody had ever heard before.

Isbell: You come here expecting to not understand somebody, and then during the course of making music together, you realize that you have so much in common. Two days ago when we first started these sessions, we thought we weren't going to get along with each other, and now after playing with each other, we're smitten by each other. It gives everybody more motivation to work harder to impress the guy sitting next to you. Probably Robbie played his best because [guitarist] Joe South was sitting in the room.

Bream: It was the first double album by a major artist, and there are no words on the album cover—other than on the spine. What do you make of those two things?

Isbell: That obviously came out of having so much great material. As far as the album cover and the album title, I think they're more throwaway than anybody realizes. It's Dylan pointing at a picture [and saying] "that one's fine" even though it's blurry. "My hair looks cool."

As for the title, when you're in the studio and say, "I'm going to play the Tele[caster guitar] through the Vibralux," some people would call that blonde on blonde. It's a blonde amp and some people refer to that era Telecaster as blonde.

Himes: There were some other songs that could have found a place on this record, but I think he didn't get good takes on them. "Obviously 5 Believers" and "Pledging My Time" are straightforward lyrics, but the playing on them is so great and the vocals are so great. He kept them on the album for that, not because they're great songs.

Bream: Do you think the harmonica was inspired by the great Charlie McCoy being at the sessions and some competitiveness coming out of Dylan?

Himes: There's a lot of harmonica playing on this album. It's like his alternative voice; when he runs out of words, the harmonica is talking for him. It's like a sax part. It's a reedy horn instrument. If you look at the hooks, mostly they're first stated by the harmonica.

Isbell: I think he knew he wasn't a great harmonica player.

Himes: I think he is a great harmonica player in sort of a primitive, limited technical sense. It's like his singing. He's not a great technical singer. But he's a great singer.

Bream: *Blonde on Blonde* is such a remarkable record. Has there ever been another studio album quite like it?

Isbell: The juxtaposition of the life he was leading and life he wanted is so important to the content of the record. Once you make a decision, there is no going back.

CHAPTER 8

JOHN WESLEY HARDING

with Geoffrey Green and Joe Levy

Released December 27, 1967

Producer: Bob Johnston

Recorded in Columbia Music Row Studios, Nashville

All songs written by Bob Dylan.

Session musicians: Kenneth Buttrey (drums),
Pete Drake (steel guitar), Charlie McCoy (bass).

Throughout the last half of 1966 and virtually all of 1967, Dylan released no new records and performed no concerts, leaving the public wondering what he could possibly do to top his mid-1960s albums if and when he finally reemerged. When the release of *John Wesley Harding* ended the silence in the final week of 1967, as *New York Times* critic Mike Jahn wrote in his book *Rock: From Elvis Presley to the Rolling Stones* (1973), it "thoroughly stood folk and folk-rock on their heads." As Jahn elaborated, "It sounded more like folk music than any Dylan album since 1965. . . . For whatever reason, *John Wesley Harding* emerged bearing a large sign reading *Calm*. A polite strum on an acoustic guitar predominated."

At a time when rock's leading lights were rushing to outdo each other with albums ever more conceptual, loud, and psychedelic, *John Wesley Harding* faced a totally opposite direction. It wasn't quite a retreat to his pre-1965 folk—bass, drums, and (on just a couple songs) steel guitar backed Dylan's voice and guitar. But it was certainly softer and gentler, and more country-influenced, than anything he'd done since he'd plugged in back at the beginning of 1965. Like most of *Blonde on Blonde*, it was recorded in Nashville, though just three session musicians were used for the basic-to-the-point-of-bare-bones arrangements.

To the satisfaction of Dylan's followers, however, his lyrics remained about as challengingly enigmatic as they'd been for the last three or four years. Yet, a more narrative, almost biblical flavor than he'd deployed in the past ran through much of the material. Few of the hooky riffs that had made some of his early electric outings hits were heard, and *John Wesley Harding* didn't generate any chart singles, though "All Along the Watchtower" made the Top Twenty via Jimi Hendrix's forceful hard-rock interpretation. The album itself did very well in the marketplace, however, reaching #2 in the United States and topping the UK charts.

Dylan could have cut a much different album. In mid-to-late 1967, he'd recorded many new compositions with The Band on what would later be called *The Basement Tapes*, some of which would be hits for other artists (as "The Mighty Quinn" was for Manfred Mann, for instance). *The Basement Tapes* might have been too informal and lo-fi for general release, but certainly Dylan could have re-recorded the highlights with The Band or other musicians in a professional studio. Instead he opted to polish *John Wesley Harding* off in just three sessions, using none of the material heard on *The Basement Tapes*, and closing the record with a bona fide country love song, "I'll Be Your Baby Tonight."

In hindsight, *John Wesley Harding* is viewed as heralding a "back-to-basics" movement throughout rock. The Beatles, Rolling Stones, and Byrds released LPs in 1968 boasting a distinctively earthier, rootsier sound than the ambitiously conceptual, electronic styles they'd explored the previous two years. Dylan would get even more deeply into country music on his next album, though without the almost universally positive critical reaction that greeted *John Wesley Harding*.

Joe Levy, an editor at large at *Billboard* magazine and former executive editor of *Rolling Stone*, and **Geoffrey Green**, a singer-songwriter and professor of English at San Francisco State University who has taught classes about Bob Dylan, hold forth on *John Wesley Harding*.

Distinguished New York graphic designer Milton Glaser designed this Dylan poster in 1967, which was inserted inside *Bob Dylan's Greatest Hits*. The next year, Glaser co-founded *New York* magazine. *Michael Ochs Archives/Getty Images*

Bream: *John Wesley Harding* is considered a pivotal album. In what ways and why?

Levy: It's a pivotal album in a number of different ways. Dylan has briefly disappeared, after having a motorcycle accident. Though it seems brief historically speaking, it's at a time when there is no way of communicating with rock stars except seeing them perform or getting their records. And the public is used to getting a record every six months or so. The Dylan that returns with *John Wesley Harding* is a different Dylan. We've seen different Dylans surface before, but this is a radical difference. These songs are unfolding dreams. They unfold somewhere in the past where Tom Paine can come running up to you, free you from the grip of some mysterious woman who walks in chains. This is some weird stuff, and weird in a very different way than Dylan's been weird before. The way he's used language becomes minimal and focused.

Green: To people at the time, it seemed like an interminable absence from Dylan, and with this album, it was an amazing, almost rebirth. While dreams were always a part of Dylan's writing, there's a very meaningful indeterminacy and ability for the songs to open out in many different directions and be seen in many different interpretive perspectives. That was very new and quite striking to listeners, at the same time combined with a simplicity of arrangement and particular musical instruments.

Levy: The Dylan who supposedly caused riots by playing with electric guitars can now shock people by playing an acoustic guitar, bass, and drums. *Rebirth* is a very interesting word here, because this record so consciously goes back to the original source material. "I Dreamed I Saw Joe Hill Last Night," a union song decades old by the time Dylan got to it, is the source material for "I Dreamed I Saw St. Augustine." And the Woody Guthrie song is the model for the title song.

Green: "As I Went Out One Morning" is an old Child ballad. The motifs he uses— of wandering and hobos and drifters, and arriving from one place to another like immigrants, or coming to the country—go back to the folk tradition as well.

Levy: This is a deeply personal album in a way no other Dylan album has been personal before. He speaks now through all these different voices on this record. He's the wandering drifter, the judge, the jury, the nurse, the attendant—he is all of these figures. If we're gonna locate Dylan in this record, we have to inject that every face is his. So many songs are about being trapped and being set free, or judged and being righteous, or not righteous. This is Dylan beginning to come to terms with his own legacy and persona, and he's doing it in a very public and human way. This is an album consumed with vision for the past, vision for the future. It's a biblical record, very explicitly. Yet one of the fascinating things it does is actually take all of that stuff in the past and make it present. Because these songs present themselves as parables, they often include very explicit morals, little summations, and those things are reinforced repeatedly.

This is a period in which Dylan feels put upon by the public. In *Chronicles* he complains, "There were people climbing on my roof, and the sheriff told me if I shot them, I was the one that had to go to jail." And in the light of that kind of sentiment, the album's fixation on outlaws, particularly the retelling of the story of the real John Wesley Hardin as a fictional John Wesley Harding, who was always known to lend a helping hand, and who never killed an honest man, becomes particularly interesting. Because that's a fabulistic telling of that story. It's not the story of the real man who, by all accounts, was a bad dude, who bragged killing some forty-four people and shot a guy for snoring.

Green: The whole album is an act of fabulation, and there're a lot of unified themes that run through it. Dylan's going through a contemplative period where he's had the ability not to travel from one place to another but to stop and think and to consider issues like becoming a father, what life means, what it's all about, and what's important. In *Chronicles*, he describes how he wanted a sense of making music and being kind of famous, and be careful what you wish for. That seems to be what's being said in "I Am a Lonesome Hobo," though the sense of that wish is really very open to possibilities.

Levy: It's a very unusual record, I think. Unusual in that I'm not sure there's another one like it. Often, I think it's the best one in the canon, which is to say there's not a bad song on it. There's also not a wasted word on it. Even if you want to argue whether or not there are bad songs on other great Dylan records, you'd kind of have to agree there's a wasted word, or a thousand, on many of them.

Green: There's an artistry to the way each song is shaped. So that even what seem to be simple songs are open to possibility. If you look at "All Along the Watchtower," there seems to be a story, and yet what actually is being presented is an intense description of a mood of anticipation and waiting. It's almost like *Waiting for Godot*.

Levy: It's also one of the many songs that asks what's of value and says that people don't know what is of worth. People drink my wine, they dig my earth, they don't know what it's really worth. Anyone can fill up his life with things he can see but cannot touch. This is a taking-stock moment. That's what makes this a powerful and interesting record.

What he's doing here provides a kind of summation, and it's almost as though having summed it up, it's difficult to then know what to say next.

Bream: What do you think of his voice on this project?

Green: I think the performances are very effective for the kind of multiple characters and multiple roles that this really is. The album is like a stage, and Dylan is acting out a one-man play in which he plays all different characters. He's kind of a stoic comedian. His performance works very, very well on this stage, and the music is as economical as the vision of the songs we've been talking about.

Levy: The music is quite economical, and yet it's almost sort of that sleight of hand. If you listen closely, this rhythm section is really cooking. It's a very placid record that reminds me of the sort of punk minimalism of the Feelies. It sounds relaxed, but it's really rather frantic. And that's a pretty neat trick. So it soothes and energizes at the same time.

Green: And just because there's a selectiveness of the instruments doesn't mean that they're not making very nuanced and rich musical statements. It's a great rhythm section, and the interactions are very important. It's one reason we can see that Jimi Hendrix was so inspired by this album, and wanted to do a recording of the "Drifter's Escape," and did "All Along the Watchtower" and could identify with the strands that were in this.

Levy: One of the most significant things about the music on this record is it is not The Band. The decision to step outside of working with his crew consciously or subconsciously adds to the sense of speaking in the persona of the immigrant, the drifter, the hobo, the outlaw.

Bream: What do you make of the cover photo?

Green: The cover was perhaps enigmatic, yet it's showing a Dylan who is looking both comfortable and uncomfortable at the same time. There's even a bit of a grin on his face, which he had striven not to have in his tours in '65, '66.

The idea of the moral that's being preached in "I Am a Lonesome Hobo" connects kind of with the cover. "Once I was rather prosperous, There was nothing I did lack, I had fourteen-carat gold in my mouth, And silk upon my back. But I did not trust my brother, I carried him to blame, Which led me to my fatal doom, To wander off in shame." And on this cover—arrangement, coincidence, feel, or design—Dylan is standing inclusively with his brothers. At a time that the country is very polarized, this is a kind of arrangement of elements that bridges a kind of perceived gap. Here it's a painterly kind of posing that is inclusive.

Levy: You look at this type of photograph and you think, *Who are these guys? Where are these guys? When are these guys? Where and when is this taking place?* Up 'til now, Dylan iconography has been pretty rock-star driven. The black-and-white movie-star photo on the cover of *Another Side of Bob Dylan*; the devilish bohemian on the cover of *Bringing It All Back Home*; the tired rock star on the cover of *Highway 61 Revisited*; the wait-a-minute, out-of-focus, what's happening here, what drugs are we taking rock star on the cover of *Blonde on Blonde*. And here's a guy in the woods, surrounded by some other guys who we don't know who they are. Are these guys playing on this record? 'Cause it's an album cover. Is it a band? Doesn't really look like a band. The thing is, you don't know what this is, and you kinda don't know when it is. It always struck me as really weird, a little mysterious, a little normal at the same time. And that's apt to this record. But weird.

Opposite: Dylan wrote on both guitar and piano at his Woodstock home known as Byrdcliff. *Elliott Landy/Redferns/ Getty Images*

CHAPTER 9

NASHVILLE SKYLINE

with Marshall Chapman and Holly George-Warren

1. Girl from the North Country 3:41
2. Nashville Skyline Rag 3:12
3. To Be Alone with You 2:07
4. I Threw It All Away 2:23
5. Peggy Day 2:01
6. Lay Lady Lay 3:18
7. One More Night 2:23
8. Tell Me That It Isn't True 2:41
9. Country Pie 1:37
10. Tonight I'll Be Staying Here with You 3:23

Released April 9, 1969

Producer: Bob Johnston

Recorded in Columbia Music Row Studios, Nashville

All songs written by Bob Dylan.

Session musicians: Norman Blake (guitar), Kenneth Buttrey (drums), Charlie Daniels (guitar), Pete Drake (steel guitar), Charlie McCoy (bass), Bob Wilson (piano).

On "Girl from the North Country" only: Johnny Cash (guitar/vocals), Marshall Grant (bass), W. S. Holland (drums), Carl Perkins (guitar), Bob Wootton (guitar).

When Dylan concluded *John Wesley Harding* with a sentimental country love song, some listeners might have thought it was a temporary aberration, or a tongue-in-cheek satire. Instead, it was a signpost to where he'd head with his final album of the decade, 1969's *Nashville Skyline*. *John Wesley Harding* was country-flavored, but *Nashville Skyline* was actual straightforward country music, or as straightforward as Dylan ever got with the form.

Like its predecessor, the LP was recorded in Nashville, but the pronounced shift toward country wasn't the only change. Dylan's husky and at times grating voice, so often the target of insults by unsympathetic listeners, was at times almost unrecognizably deeper and smoother. To the dismay of some longtime fans, his lyrics were simpler and more romantic than anything he'd written previously. As Dave Marsh wrote in *The Rolling Stone Record Guide* (1979), "Dylan's diminished energy [on *John Wesley Harding*] cost him almost nothing in the way of adulation, but *Nashville Skyline*, which painted a picture of a blissfully romantic, decidedly uninteresting fool, nearly did."

More appreciative listeners and critics sometimes pointed out that in doing a country album, Dylan was revisiting a deep-seated love of country music he'd harbored for many years, much as he'd re-embraced his rock 'n' roll roots in the mid-1960s. Some also felt that in playing the favorite music of many rural Americans of modest means, Dylan was in his quixotic way acting as a voice of the common people. And he wasn't the only rock musician of the late '60s to make an about-face toward country, as the Byrds, Flying Burrito Brothers, and others issued pioneering country-rock records before *Nashville Skyline*'s release.

For all its mixed reception, *Nashville Skyline* was another big seller, hitting #3 on the US charts and #1 in the UK. And if few of the songs would be ranked among his more oft-covered or influential, one gave him another Top Ten hit—his last one, in fact, to this day. Paced by Pete Drake's steel guitar and Kenneth Buttrey's devised-on-the-spot combination of drums, cowbell, and bongos, "Lay Lady Lay" also featured the "new" Dylan croon at its most accessible.

Like several Dylan albums, *Nashville Skyline* could have taken a much different shape. Just a day after the principal sessions wrapped up, Dylan recorded more than a dozen duets—mostly covers, rather than originals—with longtime friend Johnny Cash, the band including rockabilly star Carl Perkins on guitar. However, just one track from the session, a remake of "Girl from the North Country," was used on the LP. Dylan would also make his first TV appearance in almost five years, on Cash's variety show a few months later, and give his first major concert since 1966 at the Isle of Wight Festival in England in August, though a return to touring was still five years in the future.

Holly George-Warren, an award-winning editor of rock encyclopedias and author of more than fifteen music-related books, assesses *Nashville Skyline* with **Marshall Chapman**, a Nashville renaissance woman who has recorded more than a dozen albums; written songs

This was one of the outtakes from the photo session for *Nashville Skyline*. From the album cover, who knew it was winter? *Elliott Landy/Redferns/Getty Images*

Even though he sought privacy in Woodstock, Dylan was comfortable with Elliott Landy photographing him. *Elliott Landy/Redferns/Getty Images*

for Emmylou Harris, Jimmy Buffett, and others; authored two books; co-composed an off-Broadway musical; and acted in two movies.

Chapman: Did you know that Dylan wrote "To Be Alone with You" for Jerry Lee Lewis? I'm a Jerry Lee Lewis freak. I just love *Nashville Skyline*. It's a happy record. I play it in the kitchen, and it makes the food taste good.

Bream: It's Dylan's happiest record and maybe Dylan's most loving record.

George-Warren: That's probably why all the rock critics hated it when it came out. I was looking at the old reviews, and they're all quite snarky about it. Like "it's wimpy country" and "it's all the bad part of country" and stuff like that. It's weird, because I love it. I loved "Lay Lady Lay." I lived in North Carolina in a small town and just remember hearing it on the radio and loving it.

Chapman: It's his most romantic record, for sure. And here's another word to associate with this record—sexy. "Lay Lady Lay," it just gets in you, man.

George-Warren: You think: How did this get to be on the radio? Because he's talking about getting laid, in a way.

Chapman: I read somewhere that Dylan didn't particularly like "Lay Lady Lay." He had written it for [the movie] *Midnight Cowboy* and didn't finish it in time. He didn't think it was one of his better-written songs. The couplet I love is so goofy and so Dylan-y: "Why wait any longer for the world to begin / You can have your cake and eat it too." When Clive Davis [head of Columbia Records] said, "We're going to release this as a single," Dylan said, "No, no, no." And this was Dylan's quote: "Clive had his way. I was the most shocked that it ended up being a hit."

George-Warren: In late 1968 or early '69 he went to see the Everly Brothers in New York City. He went backstage and offered them "Lay Lady Lay" to record, and they turned him down.

Chapman: I know critics thought Dylan was taking a step back with this album, but I think he was taking a step forward. People suddenly saw him for the genius musician he was instead of this Communist folk singer.

   I think the [Cash] TV show did something for Dylan. And *Nashville Skyline* really did something for how Nashville was perceived, because, next thing you know, Ringo Starr hears Pete Drake [playing pedal steel], so then *he* comes to town to record an album with Pete Drake. Then George Harrison does an album with Pete. Then Joan Baez comes to town. Suddenly country music is sliding into pop.

Bream: Let's talk about the "Girl from the North Country" version that Bob and Johnny do. They transpose verses two and three and leave out verse four completely. And then when they're singing together, they come up with different words a couple of times.

George-Warren: Since they cut them down and dirty, quick and didn't fuss over them, it could have been just a simple they screwed up and left out a verse by mistake.

Chapman: My take is there might have been pharmaceuticals involved. I'm sticking with that for the lost verse.

George-Warren: That cover shot is by Elliott Landy, who took those really famous pictures of The Band in that field. That picture of Bob tipping his hat, he took it up in Woodstock. I wrote a book about Woodstock [the festival] with [promoter] Michael Lang, who told me that his major priority was that he really wanted Bob Dylan to play at Woodstock, but he didn't want to put any pressure on him because Dylan was notorious for not wanting to be bothered by people.

Finally, Michael went to [manager] Albert Grossman and made his big play and said Bob could just come and hang out. Of course, it didn't happen, sadly. But Woodstock is a teeny little town and right after Woodstock, Michael was walking across the street and here comes Dylan in a convertible car and he's got that same hat that's on the cover of *Nashville Skyline*, and he tips his hat to him just like he's doing in the picture.

Bream: Is that the happiest, most smiling Bob Dylan picture you've ever seen?
George-Warren: I love the cover. The sunlight hits his face. He looks like the young hipster artist of today. He looks like he could be a member of Mumford & Sons in that picture.
Chapman: This is a happy album. I'm going through a divorce right now, and listening to this album has really cheered me up. You can understand every word. I think he was really making a point to let the lyrics shine.
George-Warren: I used to work at *Rolling Stone* and [editor/publisher] Jann Wenner was a huge Dylan fan. Dylan told Jann about *Nashville Skyline*: "The new songs are easy to sing, and there aren't too many words to remember."

Bream: This album also has his smoothest and maybe prettiest singing ever.
Chapman: I love his voice on this.
George-Warren: I think it's beautiful. Another tidbit I read is he quit smoking before he did the album.

Bream: Two other things struck me about *Nashville Skyline*. It's his shortest album, and it's the first time he had an instrumental on an album.
Chapman: What record company would let your first cut be a duet and your second one be an instrumental? C'mon. No artist could get away with that except Bob Dylan, I guess.
George-Warren: They cut "The Nashville Rag" [instrumental] first to just get warmed up, but they kept it. If you listen to the end, it just kind of fizzles out a little bit. It's got that live, loose, jammy vibe to it.
Chapman: I love the segue between "Nashville Skyline Rag" and "To Be Alone with You." Like they'd just taken a lunch break, and we hear, "Are we rolling, Bob?" I thought someone was saying that to Dylan. But it's Dylan talking to [producer] Bob Johnston. I imagine it was Dylan's decision to leave that in there. . . . Don't you think this is a sexy record?

Bream: What makes it a sexy record?
George-Warren: "Lay Lady Lay." "Tonight I'll Be Staying Here with You."
Chapman: "Peggy Day." Just take our word for it. [laughs] This might just be a female point of view.

Bream: There're no politics on it. Maybe that makes it sexier.
Chapman: There's a lot of longing, too, like in "Girl from the North Country." And Cash is in such great voice. It's almost like they were egging each other on.
   Nashville is known for songwriters writing songs for other artists to record. All these songs, in the best sense of the word, sound like songs anybody could record.
George-Warren: The simplicity of the music is what makes it so powerful. It seems like at that time of his life, Dylan was really trying to simplify his life and live this low-key life in a tiny village, just a few hundred people, back to hanging out on the land, chopping the wood, back to the basics.

Bream: This album came out at a turbulent time. The Robert Kennedy and Martin Luther King [Jr.] assassinations, the Vietnam War, the riots

at the Democratic National Convention, and all of a sudden Dylan does a straightforward love album, completely devoid of politics. Why? Was he trying to send a message that he's not the spokesman for his generation?

Chapman: I think it's *so* Dylan. There's nothing worse for an artist than being pigeonholed by even your audience and the press and your record company. They think they know what you're going to do. It's such an artist thing to do the opposite. When everyone wanted him to stay a folkie playing acoustic guitar, he goes electric. It just seemed the most natural thing in the world for Bob Dylan to do.

George-Warren: Part of it, too, could have been a reaction to what had happened in music with psychedelia, which was getting pretty heavy-handed and over the top and kind of contrived. Musical simplicity would be the opposite of that. Just acoustic instruments. Then also, some early, early influences that Dylan had. He loved Jimmie Rodgers, and he loved country music as a kid growing up in Hibbing. When you're having kids yourself, you start thinking back to your own childhood. You think about that song "Country Pie." Mom and apple pie. He was looking for that kind of bucolic, simple life. It's reflected in these songs. And he was in love with his wife.

Think about the huge divide at that time with rock music and the counterculture and what was considered very conservative, right-wing politics—this is the stereotype—[of] the older folks in Nashville. Dylan, who had been the spokesman for his generation and done all these anti-war songs and worked on behalf of civil rights earlier in his career, did seem to be aligning himself with a kind of music—and even a city—that was considered to be more aligned with the pro-war, segregationist stuff. It was brave of him to declare *Nashville Skyline*. It wasn't subtle. It was all the way country-sounding. Ironically, I don't think the album at all was embraced by the country audience. It did not even chart on country charts. It's got the pedal steel, it's got acoustic instruments, and it's got players who played on big country hits.

Jon, you said it was Dylan's shortest album. I'm guessing this: that was pretty standard length for a country record back in those days.

Chapman: They always had ten songs on them.

George-Warren: Maybe that was another little message from Bob: he's gone country.

Bream: In retrospect, this was when country-rock was starting to rise with the Byrds, Flying Burrito Brothers, and others. Where does this fit in with that whole country-rock thing? Or does it?

George-Warren: Famously, Bob Dylan gave the Flying Burritos Brothers his seal of approval when *Gilded Palace of Sin* [1969] came out. When a *Rolling Stone* reporter asked Dylan, "What are you listening to now?" he pointed to that Burritos album. As far as being a morale booster to Gram Parsons and those long-haired guys who were trying to play country music and were not finding much success among the counterculture and traditional rock audience, it gave them a little boost. I don't think it helped to spread country music so much except maybe among other musicians. I don't think country-rock got that much of a fan base until the Eagles and Linda Ronstadt came along with the much more slick country-rock sound.

Chapman: What do you think of calling this the first Americana album?

George-Warren: It should definitely be considered one of the first.

Bream: You might have to give that to The Band, whose *Music from Big Pink* was out for maybe ten months before *Nashville Skyline*.

George-Warren: That's probably another huge influence on this record. He was already starting to explore that kind of stuff with The Band. *Nashville Skyline* should be considered one of the pioneering Americana albums for sure.

Opposite: Having retreated to Woodstock since 1966, Dylan elevated his public profile once again with his June 7,1969 appearance on his pal's popular TV program, *The Johnny Cash Show. Michael Ochs Archives/ Getty Images*

CHAPTER 10
SELF PORTRAIT

with Geoffrey Green and Kim Ruehl

Released June 8, 1970

Producer: Bob Johnston

Recorded in Columbia Music Row Studios, Nashville, and Columbia Studio A, New York. Dylan recorded live "Like a Rolling Stone," "The Mighty Quinn (Quinn the Eskimo)," "Minstrel Boy," and "She Belongs to Me" on August 31, 1969, at the Isle of Wight Festival at Wootton, United Kingdom.

All songs written by Bob Dylan, except where indicated.

Session musicians: Byron T. Bach (cello), Brenton Banks (synthesizer/violin), George Binkley (violin), Norman Blake (guitar), David Bromberg (guitar/dobro), Albert W. Butler (saxophone), Kenneth Buttrey (drums), Fred Carter Jr. (guitar), Marvin Chantry (viola), Ron Cornelius (guitar/dobro), Charlie Daniels (guitar/dobro), Rick Danko (bass/vocals), Dottie Dillard (backing vocals), Pete Drake (steel guitar), Dolores Edgin (backing vocals), Fred Foster (guitar), Solie I. Fott (violin), Bubba Fowler (trombone), Dennis Good (trombone), Hilda Harris (backing vocals), Levon Helm (mandolin, drums, backing vocals), Freddie Hill (trumpet), Karl T. Himmel (drums), Garth Hudson (keyboards), Lillian Hunt (viola), Martin Katahn (violin), Doug Kershaw (fiddle), Millie Kirkham (backing vocals), Al Kooper (guitar/keyboards/horn), Sheldon Kurland (violin), Richard Manuel (piano/vocals), Charlie McCoy (bass/marimbas), Martha McCrory (cello), Barry McDonald (violin), Ollie Mitchell (trumpet), Carol Montgomery (backing vocals), Bob Moore (bass), Gene Mullins (trombone), Joe Osborn (guitar/bass), June Page (backing vocals), Rex Eugene Peer (trombone), Bill Pursell (piano), Robbie Robertson (guitar/backing vocals), Albertine Robinson (backing vocals), Alvin Rogers (drums), Frank C. Smith (trombone), Maeretha Stewart (backing vocals), Gary Van Osdale (viola), Bob Wilson (organ/piano), Stu Woods (bass).

For live recordings at the Isle of Wight Festival only: Rick Danko (bass/vocals), Levon Helm (drums/vocals), Garth Hudson (keyboards), Richard Manuel (piano/vocals), Robbie Robertson (guitar/vocals).

For much of the 1960s, Dylan surprised and at times alienated fans with unexpected shifts in direction. The 1970 double album *Self Portrait*, however, marked the first time such a move was greeted with almost universal derision. Even more charitable listeners were confounded by Dylan's decision to issue a double LP dominated by a mish-mash of folk, pop, and rock covers. The haphazard insertion of some original compositions and live recordings, as well as the casual execution of the studio tracks, made some feel almost as if he was deliberately trying to destroy his reputation by compiling a quasi-bootleg.

In some ways, the manner in which *Self Portrait* was assembled didn't differ all that much from the way he'd recorded in the 1960s. The sessions were done in the two studios where he'd cut virtually all of his previous discs. Still working with producer Bob Johnston, he also used a number of musicians who'd been key players on his '60s Nashville recordings. As for his decision to concentrate on covers, he'd always played some non-originals in concert, and his very first album was almost exclusively devoted to such material.

The album's gestation was quite protracted, however. The tracks were drawn from Nashville sessions in April and May of 1969 and additional recordings made in March and April of 1970, Dylan concentrating on family life in the interim. To the dismay of some listeners, female backup vocals and orchestral instrumentation were overdubbed on some songs. At a time when many rock fans were hoping Dylan would return to the cutting-edge lyrics and musical experimentation that had characterized all of his '60s work, *Self Portrait* was often viewed, as Dave Marsh wrote in the *Rolling Stone Record Guide*, as "a disaster that crossed all generic boundaries." For good measure, Marsh called it "almost certainly the worst double set ever done by a major artist."

The same level of vitriol was found in some reviews upon the record's 1970 release, most famously in *Rolling Stone*, where Greil Marcus began his critique, "What is this shit?" That didn't stop the record from reaching #4 in the US charts (and #1 in the UK), but Marcus was hardly alone in his outrage. "I don't know anyone, even vociferous supporters of this album, who plays more than one side at a time," exclaimed Robert Christgau in his *Village Voice* review.

Dylan passionately defended the record in Anthony Scaduto's biography of the singer. "It's a great album," Dylan contended. "There's a lot of damn good music there. People just didn't listen at first." Decades later, *Self Portrait* finally underwent a critical rehabilitation of sorts, some outtakes from the sessions even getting issued on the 2013 archive release *Another Self Portrait*. Enough so, in fact, that *MOJO* named it reissue of the year, starting its review, "This is sooooo not shit."

Geoffrey Green, a singer-songwriter and English professor at San Francisco State introduced in Chapter 8, and **Kim Ruehl**, editor of the alt-country magazine *No Depression* and a music critic for folk.com, analyze whether *Self Portrait* is shit or not.

Bream: When *Self Portrait* first came out in 1970, it was reviled, it was ridiculed. Was that justified?

Green: It seemed justified, I think, to a lot of people at the time. But in light of Dylan's career arc since then, I don't think it was justified at all. I didn't feel it was justified at the time, but I especially don't feel that now.

Ruehl: It seems like it was just another instance of Bob Dylan being ahead of everybody else on this, whether he was conscious of that or not.

What's interesting is how many voices he sings in. He's going from rock 'n' roll to the blues to country to whatever "All the Tired Horses" he's going for with that. But his voice is so all over the place that it captured something of his influences and his interests and curiosities.

I don't know if we could say he sung very well on "Blue Moon." But he wasn't trying to sing it like Bob Dylan; he was trying to sing it like the song asks to be sung, which is to croon it. And same with "Copper Kettle." It sounds like a kid picked up your song and decided to figure out how to play it. It can almost come across as a statement of: You think you know me. You think you know what kind of music I should make. Well, here you go. Here's twenty-four tracks of proof that not only can you not predict what I'm gonna do, but you don't know what style—what I'm really about.

Green: I don't buy that the album, to Dylan, was a joke or a strategic career move to try and fend off the cult of personality. What impresses me is how so much of the album touches places he's been before and then places he will go to afterward.

It's kind of like a chronicle, like a travel journal, in a sense. He starts experimenting with these different arrangements and different musical styles and different genres of Americana.

Ruehl: Whereas a lot of artists just try to play the song straight, he's sort of been a champion of the idea that just because a song was recorded one way, one time doesn't mean that that's all the song can do. He's demonstrating that here with the two versions of "Alberta." This furthers the idea that a song means something different if you perform it in a different time and a different mood with a different style and different instrumentalists.

Bream: One of the theories on this album was that a lot of these songs were just warm-up takes for the other album that he was working on at the same time.

Ruehl: The one track you can really tell that on is "Woogie Boogie." It's sort of like somebody raised their hand and said, "We're done; let's move into what we're really gonna record." It's like that part before you start playing the real stuff, where you play something just to get a mood in the room and to get everybody warmed up.

It's hard to take seriously the venture that an artist like Bob Dylan would release an album just of warm-up tunes. There's nothing he's ever done that wasn't making some kind of artistic statement or challenging listeners in some way.

Bream: What do you think the thinking was behind the inclusion of the four Isle of Wight songs? The live tracks?

Ruehl: It ties into the past of Bob Dylan, and past and present. These are songs that are performed a little bit differently than they were recorded originally, and it's just part of his vision of the folk process.

Bream: If you look at the rest of the album, in some ways is this Bob Dylan's version of the list that Johnny Cash made for his daughter Rosanne of the essential American songs?

Ruehl: I think it's certainly not a comprehensive list of what he would probably consider the most important American songs. But it's not really your gateway Bob Dylan album. Unless you're really into weird music, it's not the first Bob Dylan album you really want to visit. But once you've discovered Bob Dylan, it's a great place to figure out what his deal is, and what has been fueling him for his whole career in terms of styles, artists, writers, and elements of music that are meaningful to him.

Bream: What's your impression of his singing on this album?

Ruehl: I don't get as much of an impression of him as a singer in a lot of his other work. He's a performer and a songwriter, but really the art of singing seems to be something he's exploring here. From the crooning to the stereotypical Bob Dylan singing—what people do when they do their Bob Dylan impressions. But there're a lot more styles and a lot more nuance in the singing on this record.

Opposite: Recording his album *Self Portrait* on May 3, 1969, in Nashville, Tennessee, *Michael Ochs Archives/ Getty Images*

Green: It's an experimentation with singing styles, but they're mostly in the service of the song. You could make the argument that "Gotta Travel On" is a kind of metaphorical portrait for the whole album, through musical styles, through forms, traditions, masks. Keep moving, like the Never Ending Tour.

Bream: There's a stereotype of the Dylan singing, the way he would punch the oddest words that you would expect. Here, it's a very conventional, almost very musical singing.
Green: *Another Self Portrait* [released in 2013] shows that he's capable of even more of that, as on "Pretty Saro." It reveals that the other kind of singing is a deliberate choice, as well. The idea that he could assume a more roughhewn voice, and then try to sing with more musicality, are native and interpretive dramatic decisions that he makes. Of course, his voice, or lack thereof, is paying the price for it now. But I think that he does sing quite well at the time.
Ruehl: The stereotypical Bob Dylan voice is not really thought of as a great singing voice. Like Geoff said, I think it is very intentional, but it's also nice to hear him actually singing in a musical way and know that he's capable of that.

Dylan has always heard other people's songs, explored other people's melodies, and worked other people's words into his work in a way to explore his own identity as an artist, and try and figure out if it's something he can use and what of it he can use. He did that certainly the most extensively with Woody Guthrie's work, but with Gordon Lightfoot and Tom Paxton covers, and Simon and Garfunkel and Eric Andersen. He seems to be doing it in a sponge-like way of trying to figure out, What is it about these other artists that works for me, and can I learn anything from that in order to make me a better artist? And can I learn from what doesn't work for me by singing these songs?

Bream: Where do you think *Self Portrait* fits in the Dylan canon?
Green: It's a more important album by far than critics originally thought it was, and a more revealing album. Again and again, Dylan is touring and recording and taking more diverse choices in his styles and music, and it's kind of like a portrait of American styles, from Zydeco to Calypso to reggae to blues, to everything. We can see that, really, for the first time in *Self Portrait*, that tendency to connect with the broadest sense of the folk process.
Ruehl: It certainly has a lot of depth, to understanding his entire canon, to understanding how everything connects and how we get from folk to rock to blues to whatever else he dabbles in. It's connective tissue, and I think it's a very important album for that purpose. I still don't think it's necessarily most listenable.

Bream: Why don't you think it's listenable? Or not most listenable?
Ruehl: It doesn't flow together well. It feels a lot like putting something on random play. You have to stop and really listen to it. It's not something you're gonna put on and just enjoy. It asks more of you as a listener, which is important and very valuable.
Green: When the album came out, I thought about it a lot, and then I didn't listen to it for a long time because most of the songs were sort of ingrained in me. Listening to it again in recent times, I do find it quite listenable, whether just for the musical choices or for the enigmatic and metaphorical aspects of the album. It's a good album to show people that Dylan doesn't sound always like the nasal parody of himself.

Bream: I think if you played some of these songs, people wouldn't know it's Bob Dylan, if you ask them to guess who is singing.
Green: That's absolutely true. They played "Blue Moon," I think it may have been at the end of an episode of *The Sopranos*, and I was watching it with a bunch of people and they didn't have a clue that it was Dylan.

Bream: Anything else to wrap this up?

Green: It's certainly a pivotal and quite revealing album into the seriousness of his art, even if he wants us to think of it as a joke and put-on in a frivolous gesture.

Ruehl: But the joke is that the jokes can be some of the most revealing, informative expression. Between *Self Portrait* and *Another Self Portrait*, there's so much that you could spend a career coming to understand Bob Dylan just through those two records. I think through the years that we'll understand it in a different way than we do now.

Green: We'll still be thinking about it, and that says something. Something significant.

Dylan made a rare European concert appearance at the Isle of Wight in August 1969, weeks after declining to play at the mammoth Woodstock festival near his own home. *Patrice Habans/Paris Match via Getty Images*

CHAPTER 11

NEW MORNING

with Robert Christgau and Colleen Sheehy

Released October 19, 1970

Producer: Bob Johnston

Recorded in Columbia Studio E and Studio B, New York

All songs written by Bob Dylan.

Session musicians: David Bromberg (guitar/dobro), Harvey Brooks (bass), Ron Cornelius (guitar), Charlie Daniels (bass), Buzzy Feiten (guitar), Hilda Harris (backing vocals), Al Kooper (organ/piano/guitar/ French horn), Russ Kunkel (drums), Billy Mundi (drums), Albertine Robinson (backing vocals), Maeretha Stewart (backing vocals).

Opposite: In Woodstock at his home on Ohayo Mountain Road in 1970. Dylan tried to avoid the topsy-turvy life in New York City. *Elliott Landy/Redferns/Getty Images*

The June 1970 album release of *Self Portrait* had reduced Dylan's critical stock to an all-time low. Coming out just four months later, *New Morning* was welcomed as a return to form, generally restoring him to the good graces of both critics and many listeners who had been disappointed with, or at least certainly perplexed by, *Self Portrait*. In retrospect, *Self Portrait* is regarded as more interesting and worthwhile than it seemed at the time, and *New Morning* is now seen not as the second coming some enthusiasts portrayed it when it was first issued.

What everyone can agree on is that *New Morning*, filled entirely with original material, was certainly a much different record than the covers-dominated *Self Portrait*. It also marked a return to New York as Dylan's base of recording operations. He cut the LP almost as quickly as he had done *John Wesley Harding* and *Nashville Skyline* in Nashville, however, and he laid down most of the tracks in Columbia Studio E during the first week of June 1970.

In the half-dozen years or so after his mid-1966 motorcycle accident, Dylan largely retreated from the public eye to focus on life with his wife Sara and young children, even as he continued to record and release records. Many of the songs on *New Morning* reflected his apparent domestic contentment, though by the time the sessions started, he'd moved back to New York City from Woodstock. More complex and less country-oriented than

Nashville Skyline, the material still steered clear of the topical lyrics and the more absurd word games he'd explored in the early and mid-1960s. "Day of the Locusts" was spurred by an incident away from home when Dylan accepted an honorary doctorate at Princeton University. But the LP's most popular tune was probably the straightforward love song "If Not for You," covered later by both George Harrison on his #1 debut solo album *All Things Must Pass* and Olivia Newton-John, who had a hit with it in 1971.

New Morning's reviews reflected not just critics' positive reaction to the record but also their relief that it wasn't another *Self Portrait*. "We've Got Dylan Back Again!" announced the headline to Ralph J. Gleason's commentary on the album in *Rolling Stone*, which hailed it as "the best thing new to come over the airwaves and out of the grooves in I don't know when." And as *Jazz & Pop* noted, "Dylan's voice is back to its *John Wesley Harding* level of clarity: no fakey country baritone here but no *Freewheelin'* whine either."

With fans perhaps feeling a bit gun-shy after *Self Portrait*, *New Morning* didn't fare quite as well on the charts as Dylan's LPs of the previous half-decade, though it made the Top Ten (and #1 in the UK). But while it seemed to herald a "comeback" of sorts, the singer would do little to capitalize on the renewed good will, appearing in concert on just a couple special occasions in 1971 and 1972, and not releasing another proper studio LP for another three years.

Robert Christgau, the dean of American rock critics, a long-time editor at the *Village Voice*, and the author of many books of rock criticism, looks at *New Morning* with **Colleen Sheehy**, director and CEO of the Plains Art Museum in Fargo, North Dakota; the co-curator of the exhibit "Bob Dylan's American Journey, 1956–1966" at the Weisman Art Museum in Minneapolis, Minnesota; and coeditor of *Highway 61 Revisited: Bob Dylan's Road from Minnesota to the World*.

Bream: Bob [Christgau], when *New Morning* came out, you gave it a grade of A-minus in your *Consumer Guide*. Are you still enthusiastic about it?
Christgau: As a matter of fact, I gave it an A and brought it down to an A-minus when I did the book. It's definitely the Dylan album I play the most. I'm really not a Dylan person. I don't really

Dylan talked with Coretta Scott King, widow of civil rights leader Martin Luther King Jr., after they were each given honorary degrees from Princeton University, on June 9, 1970. His appearance on campus inspired the song "Day of the Locusts." *William E. Sauro/ New York Times Co./Getty Images*

care what he has to say about the world. That is probably a prerequisite of liking this record as much as I do. Because this is definitely not one of his more prophetic records. That's one of the main reasons I like it. I like it because it's funny, because it's terse and bouncy and tuneful. And I like it because, in a general kind of way, it's a love record, and there really aren't a lot of those in his canon.

Sheehy: This is my favorite Dylan album. It's overlooked and underappreciated in his canon. I do like it for the reasons you mentioned, that he's not trying to make a statement. It's still the one I listen to the most. It's very joyful. I love his voice on it. He's singing in this full-throated voice, and he just conveys a sense of happiness that I want to go back to. I don't necessarily want to go back to his social/political critiques. I kind of read the album as a statement of gratitude.

Christgau: To who? Or what?

Sheehy: About being alive, about loving people, about the world. I think "Three Angels" and "Father of Night" are about that, about noticing things, about being thankful for the world as it is. I know "Father of Night" was based on a Jewish prayer.

Another thing I like about the album is he's using all these different musical styles—jazz, blues, folk, and that strong kind of beat-poet element on "Three Angels," "Father of Night," and "Dogs Run Free." To me, especially "Dogs Run Free" and "Three Angels," remind me of listening to Kerouac read with jazz accompaniment. There's kind of a freeness in his musical choices that I respond to. *Self Portrait* is crazy in its careening from one musical style to another and back. *New Morning* seems really coherent to me, even though it adopts these different styles.

Christgau: It's probably coherent because he ended up giving it to Al Kooper, who did the production. From what I read, Kooper determined what the music was going to be like, though Bob Johnston is listed as producer.

Sheehy: I do think *New Morning* is much well-crafted as a collection of songs. Dylan really disagreed with Al Kooper on some of them, and I think the alternate versions are on *Another Self Portrait*, some of the outtakes. Kooper was pissed off at Dylan at the end because Dylan wouldn't take his recommendations.

Christgau: The only one of the versions on *Another Self Portrait* that I think is any good at all is "If Not for You," which has the violin; I think that's sweet. But that's also an unruinable song. It is pretty straightforward and a wonderful song and doesn't have any parallels in Dylan's body of work that I can think of.

Bream: I think I read a quote from Kooper: "Bob changed his mind every three seconds."

Sheehy: It seems like a more disciplined album than *Self Portrait*. *New Morning* continues to be part of what is coming out of *The Basement Tapes* in the exploration of different musical styles and the simplicity of traditional music.

Christgau: *John Wesley Harding*, *Nashville Skyline*, *New Morning*, and then four years later *Planet Waves* all seem to me to be formally of a piece. These four records are collections of relatively brief songs, many of which have a pop sensibility or aura. Just in their compression and apparent simplicity. *New Morning* is musically the most accessible and straight-ahead of those four records. *John Wesley Harding* is austere, *Nashville Skyline* he puts on that crazy high voice—which I love but which is really strange.

Sheehy: Some of the other things about *New Morning* that interest me are its immersion in nature. All of the references to little birdies and little fishes and winter and spring, mountains and rivers. That beautiful simplicity of the lyrics and the emphasis on nature is a strong element in country music.

Bream: Speaking of nature, you didn't mention "Day of Locusts."

Sheehy: It's interesting that the locusts are singing for him. It's the human world that's kind of crazy and the locusts are affirming him. The locusts can be a deafening roar.

Christgau: Isn't it generally agreed that "Day of Locusts" is some sort of evocation of his Princeton degree? [In his book *Dylan's Visions of Sin* (2005)] Christopher Ricks says people assume it's this satire on academic life. Ricks says, "Careful now, to ridicule the ceremony would not only demean it but also one's self. But to rib it, fine. Comedy will save 'The Day of the Locusts.' It's a gentle ribbing of the situation." I like that reading because I do think of this as being essentially a humorous album.

I want to talk about my favorite song on the record, "One More Weekend." I regard it as a companion piece to "You Angel You." I think it's one of his two songs that are really about fatherhood. "One More Weekend" is about getting away from the kids and spending the weekend in bed with your wife. "You Angel You" is about loving your baby.

Sheehy: In "Sign in the Window," he says "a bunch of kids who call me 'Pa.'" There is a lot of fatherhood, and it ends with that song about father, heavenly father.

Another thing I like about the album is his phrasing. When I was working on the Dylan exhibit and got deeply into his music, I came to understand that it's really about the voice. In his recent albums, you see the phrasing. He's as good as Frank Sinatra.

Christgau: No, he isn't. No, he isn't. No, he isn't.

Sheehy: I really love how that comes out in "New Morning," on how he holds himself back on the first line: "Can't you hear the rooster crowing."

Christgau: It's quite possibly his best sung album in terms of conventional singing technique. I really enjoy the way he sings on this record in a way I often don't. It has more life to it. I do think it's beautifully phrased. Since the very beginning, he's been such an intelligent deployer of his voice.

Bream: People say "Went to See the Gypsy" was about Dylan going to see Elvis Presley.

Christgau: I think that's nonsense. Would someone like to look up to see if there was a Minnesota town near Hibbing while Dylan was there and figure out if he could have gone to see Elvis—and forget about Las Vegas for the moment.

Sheehy: I think he shows a lot of interest on other albums in gypsies, fortune tellers, and that more vaudeville level of entertainment that he's always enjoyed. There was a lot of vaudeville entertainment that went through Hibbing in his youth that he writes about in *Chronicles*. I don't take it literally. To me, the gypsy is some fortune teller who is going to tell you the meaning of life or what you should do.

Bream: What do you make of "Winterlude"?

Christgau: It's a goof.

Sheehy: I think it's another element of that playfulness and the different musical styles coming through from *The Basement Tapes* era. "Now I'm going to do a waltz with backup singers."

Bream: Earlier, Colleen, you said "Dogs Run Free" was very Kerouac.

Christgau: Maeretha Stewart [a Dylan backup singer], I think that's her track. To me, it sounds like Kerouac or a beat parody. I can't believe that he meant this as poetry. "If dogs run free, why not me, Across the swamp of time?, My mind weaves a symphony, And tapestry of rhyme." Do you really think he thought that was putting him up there with Keats or even Ferlinghetti? I think he thought it was a joke.

Sheehy: I have to say that when I was younger and first listened to this album, I thought this was a crazy song. Maybe I'm making this more profound than it is, whenever I'm looking at my dog and he's just sleeping and leading the dog's life. To me, it's also an extension of looking at nature and wanting to be part of it and wishing you could be a dog running free. I love "The Man in Me." Again, it's so exuberant. The la-la-la's, he's enjoying being a singer. I think there are a lot of gems on this album even if it's not considered one of his best.

Christgau: Me, too. I don't think there's a bad track on it. To me, I find "Three Angels" and "Father of Night" a little disappointing. I have a real resistance to any kind of religiosity. Somehow the tonal thing he does on this record doesn't work as well as some other places he does that. But I could also imagine changing my mind about that the next time I play this record. This is a record I'm going to continue to play.

Sheehy: I'll continue to listen to it. It's the one I sing along with more than any of the other records.

Opposite: Colleen Sheehy: "This [album] just makes me think about him as a father living in that rural environment, that he's maybe having an echo of his own childhood." *Elliott Landy/Redferns/Getty Images*

CHAPTER 12

PAT GARRETT & BILLY THE KID

with **David Browne and Evelyn McDonnell**

1. Main Title Theme (Billy) 6:07
2. Cantina Theme (Workin' for the Law) 2:57
3. Billy 1 . . . . .3:57
4. Bunkhouse Theme 2:17
5. River Theme. 1:30
6. Turkey Chase 3:34
7. Knockin' on Heaven's Door 2:32
8. Final Theme. 5:23
9. Billy 4 . . . . .5:04
10. Billy 7 . . . . .2:10

Released July 13, 1973

Producer: Gordon Carroll

Recorded in CBS Discos Studios, Mexico City, and Burbank Studios, Burbank, California

All songs written by Bob Dylan.

Session musicians: Byron Berline (backing vocals/ fiddle), Carl Fortina (harmonium), Gary Foster (recorder, flute), Carol Hunter (guitar/backing vocals), Booker T. Jones (bass), Priscilla Jones (backing vocals), Fred Katz (cello), Jim Keltner (drums), Russ Kunkel (tambourine, bongos), Bruce Langhorne (guitar), Ted Michel (cello), Brenda Patterson (backing vocals), Terry Paul (bass/ backing vocals), Donna Weiss (backing vocals).

Opposite: Director Sam Peckinpah created a part for Dylan as Alias in *Pat Garrett & Billy the Kid* after Dylan signed on to compose the soundtrack. *Gems/Redferns/ Getty Images*

In 1971 and 1972, little new music was heard from Dylan. The years were dotted with sporadic spurts of activity, none of which added up to anything close to an album. Recording-wise, there were the non-LP singles "George Jackson" and "Watching the River Flow" and the 1971 compilation *Greatest Hits Vol. II*, which featured just a bit of new material. His concerts were limited to a surprise appearance at the George Harrison–assembled benefit Concert for Bangladesh at New York's Madison Square Garden in August 1971, along with playing four songs at The Band's New Year's Eve show in the same city's Academy of Music.

Dylan still hadn't gotten a serious album project underway when writer friend Rudy Wurlitzer sent the script he'd penned for an upcoming film, *Pat Garrett & Billy the Kid*. After a demo Dylan cut for the title song was warmly received, the movie's director, Sam Peckinpah, invited the singer to not only compose the whole soundtrack but also to act in a supporting role. Dylan had been the subject of a couple documentaries, *Dont* [sic] *Look Back* (shot on his spring 1965 British tour) and the seldom-screened *Eat the Document* (filmed during the European leg of his 1966 world tour),

but had never acted in a feature. With little else on his plate, he and his family went to Mexico, where the western was being shot in Durango with illustrious stars such as Kris Kristofferson, James Coburn, and Jason Robards.

Relatively few people, and even relatively few Dylan fans, saw the final film, in which the musician played a sidekick to Billy the Kid (Kristofferson). Some of its commercial and critical failure was blamed on the studio taking control of the final edit from Peckinpah and making substantial cuts in its length. It would not be Dylan's final dramatic role in a feature film, but like his subsequent movies, it would fail to launch him into cinema stardom.

Much, but not all, of the music Dylan wrote and recorded for the movie was released on a soundtrack LP of the same name in mid-1973. Understandably, critics and fans weren't sure about whether to view it as a real Dylan album or something of a side project that wasn't quite part of his official canon. For one thing, much of the record was instrumental, with vocal-less tracks whose primary purpose was to accompany movie footage.

Though not quite a commercial flop, it wasn't a blockbuster either, just sneaking inside the Top Twenty. *Rolling Stone* panned it as "every bit as inept, amateurish, and embarrassing" as *Self Portrait*. Yet as with a good number of Dylan albums, its stock has risen in some quarters over the years, particularly among listeners who appreciate its haunting, dramatic flavor, whether on the instrumentals or the vocal numbers. And the most prominent of these, "Knockin' on Heaven's Door," gave Dylan one of his biggest hits, nearing the Top Ten in both the United States and the UK in late 1973.

A critical eye toward *Pat Garrett & Billy the Kid* is taken by **David Browne**, a contributing editor to *Rolling Stone*, former music critic at *Entertainment Weekly*, and the author of several music-related books, and **Evelyn McDonnell**, an assistant professor of English at Loyola Marymount University, former music critic for the *Village Voice* and the *Miami Herald*, and coeditor of *Rock She Wrote: Women Write About Rock, Pop, and Rap* (2014).

Bream: Do you view *Pat Garrett & Billy the Kid* as a soundtrack album, a proper Dylan album, an improper Dylan album, or what?
McDonnell: I view it as a soundtrack album. Without the soundtrack, it's really a failed album. It's eighty percent filler. But once you see the movie, it makes so much more sense.
Browne: I see it as a soundtrack as well. Okay, this is his first album in three years; I get that there would be a sense of disappointment. But, it is music for a movie. So I felt like we shouldn't judge it on the same terms as an album.
McDonnell: I did not see the studio version that [Sam] Peckinpah did. I saw the 2005 version. And then I also saw part of the 1988 [Turner Home] preview version. But I couldn't really tell that much difference between the two; I'm really not clear what the difference between those two was.

Bream: The key is that in the Peckinpah director's cut version, "Knockin' on Heaven's Door" is an instrumental.
Browne: The music supervisor wanted Dylan to add one more song to the movie, and he said, "We need it now." And Dylan came into the studio and played him "Knockin' on Heaven's Door" and the guy was like, "That's the worst piece of shit I've ever heard." It's now become a standard, pretty much.

Bream: What do you think of it as a soundtrack?
Browne: It's actually one of my favorite soundtracks of all time. Because it's an incredibly evocative, atmospheric record, even though a lot of it is instrumental. The acoustic instruments, the kind of folk-bluegrass rooted melodies, the incredibly haunting backing vocals, not just on "Knockin' on Heaven's Door" but "Final Theme" and all those

things—it works really beautifully as a piece. Even though a couple of the songs were repeated. I didn't actually see the movie for a couple years after I got the record, but I could almost sort of see it in my mind, pictures and things.

McDonnell: It works so well with the movie, and that is what he was writing it for. He wasn't trying to make it be a great album. He was writing songs for a contract.

Bream: Dylan has long had an obsession with outlaws in his work.

Browne: Billy the Kid was a killer, but there was a me-against-the-Man aspect to his whole story. It's also interesting that this really also fits in with all those other kind of revisionist looks back at the Old West: *Little Big Man* and Robert Altman's *Buffalo Bill*. There was an interesting, different take on what we saw in the history book. Dylan's music only added to that for me.

McDonnell: That's where "Knockin' on Heaven's Door" works so incredibly well. Because death is not glorified in this movie. It's all over the place. It's really horrible and it's tragic, too.

Bream: I'm not sure that Alias, Dylan's character, was in the original script, or if it was added.

McDonnell: It wasn't. He was created for Dylan, is my understanding. It's certainly a weird role to perform.

Browne: It definitely feels extraneous. Not too many pivotal things for Alias.

McDonnell: I don't think it adds anything to Dylan's career or to the movie.

Bream: Let's talk about some of the specific songs, or instrumentals. To me, "Bunkhouse Theme" is one of the sweetest things that Dylan has recorded.

Browne: It's just that really pretty, two-guitar piece instrumental. There is a pretty sentimental aspect to that, kind of a beautiful, simple—Russian baroque or something—quality to that piece of music. That really does stand out in his repertoire. You don't hear too many melodies like that.

McDonnell: The other thing about this album that must have been really disappointing to lead [*Rolling Stone*'s] Jon Landau to pan at the time, was how many instrumentals there are, how scant the lyrical content is, for a Dylan album.

Browne: "Final Theme" is a totally beautiful, haunting piece of music, driven by a flute. And that eerie, deathly backup choir. It's such a perfect way to kind of capture the mood of that movie, especially toward the end. And again, it has a feel to it unlike anything I think Dylan ever recorded. Kind of airy and expansive, and kind of a lonely feel as well.

Bream: What did you think when you listened to "River Theme"? It kind of presages the "Knockin' on Heaven's Door" melody.

Browne: Again, that's one of those songs, with those wordless backing vocals, that say as much, if not more, than if Dylan actually was singing.

Dylan's backup band at the Concert for Bangladesh included George Harrison (left) on guitar, Leon Russell on bass, and Ringo Starr on tambourine. *Bill Ray/ The LIFE Picture Collection/Getty Images*

McDonnell: When you think about it, he really only wrote how many melodies for this album? I really don't think he was phoning it in, because it was perfect for the soundtrack. You develop these themes and you want them to recur. They set certain moods and refer back to earlier themes and connect everything.

Browne: Maybe he was following the M.O. of the traditional orchestral movie score people who would go back to certain melodies throughout the course of the movie to kind of tie it all together. Or he was just lazy. Who knows?

Bream: I read somewhere that Dylan said that passages he had written for specific scenes ended up getting paired with different scenes in the editing process.

McDonnell: I think that got changed. People see it now the way Peckinpah intended it.

Browne: It is interesting how "Knockin' on Heaven's Door" has outlived the movie. Most people don't even remember the movie at this point, unless you're a hardcore Peckinpah fan or a hardcore Dylan fan. That song, which even was rejected by the music supervisor, has kind of outlived them both.

McDonnell: That's a song that could outlive Bob Dylan. There's people who know and love that song and don't even remember it's by Bob Dylan. I think it's one of the greatest pop songs.

Bream: It's also one of the simplest, both in terms of melody and in lyrics.

Browne: Which probably makes it one of the reasons it's survived. Nice simple melody; you don't have to navigate too much. I remember learning how to play that as a kid, and it is only like three chords over and over, I believe. It's very easy to play.

McDonnell: Again, I don't want to say he was phoning it in, but the fact that he didn't even come up with different titles for . . . [the songs whose titles refer to] Billy. It's just Billy 1, 4, and 7. Even [some other] titles, they're just "Bunkhouse Theme," "River Theme." I think in the creation of the music he wasn't phoning it in, but in the packaging of the music for the album, he probably could have.

Bream: On "Billy 7," it's one of the most different Dylan voices of all time. It's a lower voice.

McDonnell: I noticed that as well, and quite liked it, actually. Because I generally find Dylan's vocal range very limited and irritating. So I thought it was very emotional and had some depth it.

Browne: It's a perfect way to kind of wind down the record, in that it feels like taking things down, not just vocally. He could have ended the record with the "Final Theme," which is kind of a sad, mournful piece of music, but it's sort of beautiful and Western in its way. But the record ends on this real low-voiced, kind of a downer of a version of that same song we're hearing. Who knows if that was intentional? But it's sort of the capper on the end of the outlaw era, end of the rock star '60s thing to me.

Bream: *Pat Garrett & Billy the Kid*, **is it overlooked? Is it underrated?**

McDonnell: I would never buy this album for anyone or tell anyone to buy it, unless they were a fan of the movie or a fan of Bob Dylan. I don't think it holds up as a great work overall. So that's probably been rated just right. Because I don't think it was intended to be an album, so it has to be heard in the context of that movie, or of Dylan's career.

Browne: I'd probably go with underappreciated. I agree with Evelyn that I wouldn't necessarily go out and buy this for a non-Dylan fan or someone who is new to his work. But I do think it's underappreciated for what it is, which was a really interesting, evocative soundtrack album.

Opposite: Seldom seen onstage these days, Dylan sang five songs including "Blowin' in the Wind" and "A Hard Rain's a-Gonna Fall" at the Concert for Bangladesh, organized by George Harrison and Ravi Shankar, at Madison Square Garden on August 1, 1971. *Thomas Monaster/NY Daily News via Getty Images*

CHAPTER 13

DYLAN

with Daniel Durchholz and George Varga

1. Lily of the West (E. Davies/J. Peterson) 3:44
2. Can't Help Falling in Love
   (G. Weiss/H. Peretti/L. Creatore) 4:17
3. Sarah Jane (traditional). 2:43
4. The Ballad of Ira Hayes (Peter LaFarge). 5:08
5. Mr. Bojangles (Jerry Jeff Walker) 5:31
6. Mary Ann (traditional) 2:40
7. Big Yellow Taxi (Joni Mitchell). 2:12
8. A Fool Such As I (B. Trader) 2:41
9. Spanish Is the Loving Tongue (C. B. Clark) 4:13

Released November 16, 1973

Recorded Columbia Music Row Studios, Nashville and
Columbia Studio E, New York

Producer: Bob Johnston

Likely session musicians (none credited): Norman Blake
(guitar), Kenneth Buttrey (drums), Fred Carter Jr. (guitar),
Ron Cornelius (guitar), Charlie Daniels (bass), Dottie
Dillard (backup vocals), Pete Drake (steel guitar), Dolores
Edgin (backup vocals), Hilda Harris (backing vocals),
Millie Kirkham (backup vocals), Al Kooper (guitar/piano/
backup vocals), Russ Kunkel (drums), Carol Montgomery
(backup vocals), Bob Moore (bass), June Page (backup
vocals), Bill Pursell (piano), Albertine Robinson (backing
vocals), Maeretha Stewart (backing vocals).

For the first dozen or so years of his career, Dylan recorded for Columbia Records—an eternity in a business where artists change labels as often as today's pro athletes change teams. Columbia had almost dropped him from its roster when his debut album sold poorly, and he'd been tempted to leave for MGM in 1967, but the relationship had been a remarkably enduring one. But it came to an end, if only temporarily, in late 1973, when Dylan signed a two-album deal with the new Asylum label, founded by industry mogul David Geffen and high-powered manager Elliot Roberts.

It's not uncommon for labels to raid their vaults for unreleased material when major artists bolt to other companies. In Dylan's case, as his extensive *Bootleg Series* would prove in the CD era, there was an embarrassment of riches in the way of studio outtakes and live recordings, dating all the way back to when he signed with Columbia in 1961. So it wasn't a surprise when Columbia acted quickly to issue an LP of old previously unreleased material, even before Dylan was able to put out an album on Asylum.

Even by the standards of such exploitative projects, however, the unimaginatively titled *Dylan* was a shabby affair. Rather than issue material that fans already knew about and craved, such as his legendary May 1966 show at Manchester Free Trade Hall,

Columbia cobbled together nine outtakes from the *Self Portrait* and *New Morning* sessions. Not one of the songs was an original composition. Instead the tracks mixed traditional tunes with such unexpected covers as Joni Mitchell's "Big Yellow Taxi," Jerry Jeff Walker's "Mr. Bojangles," and the Elvis Presley hits "Can't Help Falling in Love" and "A Fool Such As I."

Dylan had no input into its compilation, and the disc was enclosed in his most rudimentarily illustrated cover. As Alan Rinzler wrote in *Dylan: The Illustrated Record* (1978), "No liner notes, no information about the actual recording dates, no credits or lists of personnel. The packaging seems cursory, almost vindictive in its throwaway obscurity."

Although critics were aware of the situation behind its release, *Dylan* was savaged in the press. Robert Christgau gave it an "E" in his *Consumer Guide*, and *Rolling Stone* dismissed it as "an inept package of a great artist's weaker moments, best left forgotten." It did creep up to #17 in the United States, even spawning a small hit single with "A Fool Such As I." Understandably, however, it's the only Dylan album never to be issued as a standalone CD in North America, at the request of the artist himself. (It does appear in the 2013 boxed set *Bob Dylan: The Complete Album Collection Vol. I*.)

Dylan's stay on Asylum would be short, and he'd be back on Columbia in time for his most revered album of the 1970s, 1975's *Blood on the Tracks*. By that point, *Dylan* was indeed virtually forgotten, though omnipresent in used record store racks, which remain the most likely place to spot a copy today.

Accepting the unenviable task of reviewing *Dylan* are longtime music critic for the *San Diego Union Tribune*, **George Varga**, and **Daniel Durchholz**, a St. Louis music critic and coauthor of several music-related books.

George Varga: "If *Dylan* was that bad, why was it okay to have it be available in other parts of the world?" *Michael Ochs Archives/Getty Images*

Bream: Do you think we should consider this an actual Dylan album, or should we just consider this product where the record label attached his name to it?

Varga: Columbia, I guess in a sort of pique, put out this *Dylan* album of outtakes that Dylan had no input into whatsoever—and was so inferior that Dylan himself didn't think they were of the standard to include on either *Self Portrait* or *New Morning*. That says something about their quality.

Durchholz: *Self Portrait* and *New Morning*—were done at a time when it seemed like Dylan had kind of lost his way artistically. I'm going with the standard theory that this was merely cobbled together. It's largely known as Columbia's quote-unquote "revenge" album against him for leaving the label. When he returned to Columbia, he had the *Dylan* album deleted. So it seems to me that he really was pretty intent on sinking that album and just trying to keep it out of everybody's mind because he disliked it that much.

Bream: The album went gold, so it did sell some.

Durchholz: But that was largely people buying it simply because it was a Dylan album. He was one of those—and is one of those artists—that a certain number of people will go out and buy no matter what it is, as long as his name is on it. The album did have a certain margin of success, probably right until people got home and put it on their turntables.

For his first tour since 1966, Dylan hit the road with Robbie Robertson and The Band, seen here in January 1974 at Madison Square Garden. *Gijsbert Hanekroot/Redferns/Getty Images*

If I transported myself back to 1973 and, oh, I just saw there's a new Bob Dylan album out, and slapped down my—$2.99 or $3.99—for it and brought it home, I might have felt pretty entirely ripped off. But by the time I heard it, it was completely understood that this was not really an album that Dylan wanted released, and I was more curious to find out, well, good Lord, why not? It turns out that I don't think it's as bad as it's regarded.

Varga: It's not as entirely awful as I recalled it'd be after not having heard it for many years, and there are actually some good things in it. Yet there are a few songs, like he belts the chorus to "Mr. Bojangles" in an increasingly, almost unhinged way . . . I have to think there was deliberate humor involved there. But that's the great Dylan enigma; you never know exactly when you're supposed to think one thing or the other.

Durchholz: His claim is that these songs were meant as like warm-ups in the studio, that they were not meant to be released. But I wonder about that, because these are finished tracks. They're not the kind of outtakes that we've heard from some of the other official bootlegs that have come out.

Bream: Which songs do you like? If any?

Durchholz: I don't know if I would say that I like it—I'm interested in his version of "The Ballad of Ira Hayes," which was, of course, most famously done by Johnny Cash. It was written by Peter LaFarge, who was a Native American folk singer that Dylan would have known from his Greenwich Village days. Dylan's version of it is not bad. It almost comes off, it's like a very spare arrangement of just kind of piano and organ, and it's almost like a spoken-word performance, except he sings the chorus.

Varga: I like the organ work on it. But the vocal inflections, they're almost too sincere, and if they're not, it's almost like an audio vat of corn chowder. "Sarah Jane" is a really enjoyable kind of country-rock, indie Americana song, and I'm surprised it hasn't been covered by the current crop of Americana bands, 'cause I think it would sound pretty fresh and people wouldn't know what it was. Despite the inane, giddy, la-la-la-la chorus, with what sounds like the female contingent from the Johnny Mann singers—and their appearance on several songs on the album—I'm just trying to figure out if this was Dylan being playful or perverse or both, and what the allure for him of that would have been.

Durchholz: On this record, he did actually play with some of the lyrics, and to what degree he could take credit for them, I don't know. I know he did on "Spanish Is the Loving Tongue." There's kind of a blatantly racist lyric in the original of that, about the girl—that song is kind of about a one-night stand with a Mexican girl. That was written by this cowboy poet named Charles Badger Clark and later set to music. And then Dylan changes the lyric. One of them was like, "She was Mexican, I was white, Like is not, It's better so," something like that, and he changes it. I forget exactly how he did it, but I think he's like a gambler in the lyric, and basically dispenses with that sort of racist lyric.

He did it kind of really awkwardly in "Big Yellow Taxi," in I guess the last verse, where the lyric says, "The big yellow taxi took away my old man." He says, "I heard the screen door slam, and a big yellow bulldozer took away the house and the land." Well, the screen door slam—I don't know what those lyrics have to do with one another, but I think he had to figure out something he could do there, instead of the old man being taken away.

Varga: "Spanish Is the Loving Tongue," I like that, 'cause we have rarely heard him croon so well. It's a song that I think you could play for the non-Dylan aficionado, that they might have difficulty even guessing it's Dylan. It's one of those instances where he takes on almost another voice that is so non-quintessentially Dylan that it takes on another realm altogether. And "A Fool Such As I," I think the boogaloo part is laughable, but the vocal is really very interesting. It's one of two songs on the album that I guess is Dylan paying homage to Elvis, but this is the more successful one.

If we go to "Can't Help Falling in Love," the song is kind of a near total failure, but it's all the more intriguing for that. I'm intrigued that, okay, let's take this song and give it a kind of dirge-like feeling; that's not the approach I think most people would have immediately thought of. His delivery is so earnest that it's both good and bad. Dylan did take a quite different approach, but I don't think it was aesthetically remotely successful.

Durchholz: The recording or cover version that Dylan has always said is his favorite of anybody else's is when Elvis covered "Tomorrow Is a Long Time." I wonder if in some vague sense, he was trying to offer a little bit of payback there.

I wanted to mention one of the other traditional songs, "Lily of the West," an old Irish American ballad that was actually kind of recast into an American song. Because in it the narrator travels to Louisville and falls in love with a woman who betrays him, and he kills the other suitor and then is convicted. So it's a very happy, happy little tune. Dylan alters the lyrics just a little bit in the way that's very typical for him, but is otherwise pretty true to the song. If I were to drop the needle on that and heard that song, I would have been ready for a pretty good ride with this album, because that one is maybe more characteristic of his work, even though he didn't write it.

Varga: It's a pretty song; it's kind of got a "Ghostwriters in the Sky" feel to it. The one problem is the female singers. They fit in very much with the tone of the music and the lyrics that he was doing in his born-again period. These female singers who were technically fine just seemed to be moonlighting from the *Lawrence Welk Show* or something. Maybe Dylan had an affinity for that, and this was one way of demonstrating that. But they're stumbling blocks. It's a strong opening song; it would have been a lot better without them, simply because they seem to have arrived from another planet to contribute their part. Then having "Can't Help Falling in Love" as the second track immediately dilutes the impact of having a pretty strong opening cut.

Bream: What is so bad about this album?

Durchholz: Dylan's fans look to him for like an absolute godhead. Like material that is just mind-blowing and lyrically so astute. With *Dylan*, you got completely the opposite of that. Nobody could really put it together as to why he would be covering those particular songs. In retrospect, it's not as bad as everybody thinks it is, but it's still definitely one of the lesser albums of his catalog. Maybe not exactly the worst, but it would be in the discussion, certainly.

Varga: You've got the out-of-character nature of the songs themselves. And it's hard sometimes to think that this wasn't a deliberate act of self-destruction. This stuff was really hokey.

Looking at the album cover, you could almost argue that Columbia Records was erasing Bob Dylan's image, that they were painting over him. Knowing what we now know about the whole context of him leaving the label, that does make a little bit of sense.

PLANET WAVES

with Jim Beviglia and Joe Levy

Released January 17, 1974

Producers: Bob Dylan, Robbie Robertson, and Rob Fraboni

Recorded in the Village Recorder Studio B, Los Angeles

All songs written by Bob Dylan.

Session musicians: Rick Danko (bass), Levon Helm (drums), Garth Hudson (organ/accordion), Richard Manuel (piano/drums), Robbie Robertson (guitar).

The careers of Bob Dylan and The Band had been intimately interwoven since late 1965, when Dylan chose the musicians—then known as the Hawks—as his backup group when he began to play electric rock onstage in earnest. The Band backed Dylan on his 1966 world tour; recorded *The Basement Tapes* with him in 1967; backed most of Dylan's rare concert appearances between 1968 and 1972, including the Woody Guthrie Memorial Concert in early 1968 and the Isle of Wight Festival in 1969; and were among the most prominent artists to record Dylan songs that he had yet to release himself.

Yet somehow Dylan had used The Band as his studio group for just a few sessions in late 1965 and early 1966, yielding just a couple tracks that found official release at the time. Band guitarist Robbie Robertson did play on *Blonde on Blonde*, and all five members made contributions to *Self Portrait*. But it wasn't until late 1973 that The Band finally entered the studio to record an album as Dylan's backup unit. Recorded in about a week in early November in Los Angeles, *Planet Waves* was the first Dylan LP entirely done outside New York or Nashville.

The sessions took place at a time when Dylan was ready to rev up his career again after a three-year period in which he had neither toured nor issued a conventional album of new material. Leasing a

Malibu house just up the coast from L.A., he rehearsed with The Band (whose Robertson had just relocated to Malibu as well) with the intention of going on tour for the first time since spring 1966. Dylan had just changed record labels, with Asylum wanting to issue a studio album before the extensive US tour in early 1974 and also record a concert album during the trek.

Since *Nashville Skyline*, Dylan's albums had gotten mixed reviews, even if the balance sometimes tilted toward the favorable (*New Morning*) or the hostile (*Self Portrait*). *Planet Waves* was no exception, especially because the hopes for the reunion of sorts were so high that they couldn't realistically be fulfilled. Straightforward and simple compared to the apocalyptic rock he'd performed with The Band on the 1966 world tour and *The Basement Tapes*, it nonetheless was a hit, becoming his first #1 album in the United States.

Wrote *New Yorker* critic Ellen Willis, "I think that the words on *Planet Waves* are meant mainly as filler—that Dylan is trying to get out from under his reputation as a poet and force us to concentrate on the music." Added Willis, "*Planet Waves* is unlike all other Dylan albums: it is openly personal. I think the subject of *Planet Waves* is what it appears to be—Dylan's aesthetic and practical dilemma, and his immense emotional debt to Sara."

Joe Levy, who was introduced in Chapter 8, editor at large of *Billboard* magazine and formerly executive editor of *Rolling Stone*, expounds on *Planet Waves* with **Jim Beviglia**, a journalist for *American Songwriter* and the author of *Counting Down Bob Dylan: His 100 Finest Songs* (2013).

Bream: Where do you stand on *Planet Waves*?

Levy: It's not in the canon, and there are fascinating reasons for that. One is that some people don't like it. The other is that it's the only studio record Dylan ever made for any label other than Columbia. It turns out it's a good record, and sometimes it's a great record. It's a rewarding record. It's a strange record. It's a record recorded in Los Angeles, written in New York, and it references the frozen Midwest. There's no other record where he actually goes into a recording studio with The Band and makes music that people are supposed to hear.

Beviglia: It's a bit of an odd duck because he's kind of trapped in between two themes in his career. There's the theme of *New Morning*, kind of the homebound guy who just wants to live out on the farm and raise children. Then there's also these songs with lyrics like "Dirge," "Wedding Song," and "Going Going Gone" which are a lot darker and sort of point toward the albums ahead, certainly *Blood on the Tracks*. The Band is sometimes utilized well, and sometimes it sounds like they're kind of

Dylan's forty-concert tour with The Band in 1974 resulted in the two-disc live album, *Before the Flood*. Michael *Ochs Archives/Getty Images*

on Band autopilot. There are times when this record is just fantastic, and there are other times when it's maybe just a little mediocre.

Levy: Dylan mediocre records are sometimes downright bad, and this one never is. I actually think The Band sounds great on this record. It's the only Dylan album where the playing of the musicians threatens to overwhelm the record and overwhelm the singer. You can hear him clearly, but these aren't always songs that foreground the lyrics. Thematically and musically, this record points to *Blood on the Tracks*, but it's a strange record. There are a lot of songs on it that want to be straight up love songs and undo themselves. The best one is "Something About You," which is a song about how awesome the woman he loves is. It's also a song that references marriage a lot from beginning to end in different ways, and suicide a couple of times. Clearly those are strange things to be talking about on the same record, and maybe at the same time.

Beviglia: There are times when The Band's music does overwhelm him. I'm not sure it's a good thing. It's not because The Band is playing badly, but I think that sometimes his lyrics and the music just sort of are at cross purposes. A lot of this was first take, second take. Sometimes that really helps a lot, and sometimes they could have really stood to look at a song closer.

You can hear in the album some tentativeness about which direction he wanted to go. It goes back to, "Am I still writing these songs about home?" and even those songs weren't completely committed to that idea. Then you have this much darker material. That's where I think the album is at its most interesting. On songs like "Dirge," like "Going Going Gone," you have Dylan at the kind of precipice of something and really looking into the abyss at times. The songwriting is much more complex in those songs than on other parts of the album. I also think those songs benefit from The Band maybe trying something a little bit different. In the case of "Dirge," where it's just Bob on piano and Robbie picking up an acoustic guitar, the music is just absolutely chilling on that song, just an absolute beauty.

Levy: "Dirge" is a kind of song, Dylan at the piano, that he hadn't necessarily released but he had done before and would do again. I go right to the opening track, "On a Night Like This," which is in the domestic mode that he has been in for a minute, which sounds great. It's on the fly here, a style on the lines of *The Basement Tapes*, in a much more professional setting.

Beviglia: I think it's *The Basement Tapes* maybe with these guys now with a little bit more studio experience where they could churn out something that sounds a little bit more polished but still has that backwoods vibe or basement vibe. It's a song on the surface about being in love and staying in this house and not wanting to go out, but you could look at it as maybe his way of saying, "Okay, I'm reconnecting with these guys again."

Levy: The idea of reminiscing, looking back, of going back to the beginning, is shot through this record. It goes so far to mention, "Growing up in old Duluth," where he lived until he was six years old.

Beviglia: Then there is his present, which is maybe most felt in "Forever Young," which is Dylan obviously writing about his son, Jakob. Dylan sort of looking ahead to this child growing up and what lies ahead of him. You have two different versions of the song on the album, which is typical quirky Dylan. You have the one that The Band really goes all out on. They give it a really tender reading with Levon Helm on the mandolin, Richard Manuel playing the drums, and, of course, Garth Hudson bathing the whole thing in that glow that only Garth Hudson could do. Then they have sort of the country-rock version following right after.

Levy: It is both lovely and maudlin at the same time. There is something self-taunting to me in this song. It may be written for his kids, and it may be his blessing to them. But it's

a taunt to himself, at thirty-two, about to go on tour for the first time since he's twenty-five, struggling to get enough songs written for a record.

He knows you can't stay forever young. You can say it twice, once slow and once fast, and it doesn't make it any more true.

Beviglia: What gets me about the song isn't so much the lyrics but certainly in that first version that ends Side One, it's the sort of almost desperation in Dylan's voice in the chorus, as if to say all these things I wish for my children, if it is indeed about his kids, I can't make them come true.

Levy: This is where anxiety enters the process for him in a way that it hadn't before. It is, in this case, a matter of trying to summon inspiration on demand. He doesn't have enough songs for the session. He goes back to New York to write. He has to get six of the tracks written, or eight tracks in six weeks, and he has to grind them out. Supposedly over the previous two years he hasn't been writing much at all.

Bream: Do you think that was compounded by being the first album under Asylum with a new contract?

Levy: I think the pressure is to get the record done to launch the tour. I do have trouble accepting *Planet Waves* as a rushed record that suffers from being rushed, since rushing is what works for him all the way down the line up until that point. I think it works here. This is an anxious record. In the world of rock 'n' roll, we love anger. Anxiety makes us twitchy, it makes us uncomfortable. That may be why it doesn't have the reputation it deserves.

Bream: Let's talk about "Wedding Song." Given the title and what it deals with, it bounces all over the place.

Beviglia: The lyrics, if you just read them on the page, they would sound like kind of a devotional love song and very sentimental almost. Then you put them with the music, which is Dylan on the acoustic guitar, a lot of minor chords, and suddenly it's sort of supercharged and gives them a vibe of this love that conquers all. Maybe there's something in that that's not actually going to happen—all these things that he's promising. He's singing so intensely as if he's trying to will it to stay in existence. Harrowing, that's the vibe I get from that song. I can't quite believe that he's all in on this, or that he thinks that it's going to last.

The song that really stands out the most is "Going Going Gone." It's one of the unheralded Dylan songs. He's this guy at the precipice of the next stage, and we don't know what that next stage is. Maybe it's a kind of good thing. He uses that kind of homerun call in the chorus to sort of signify it. That's the song on this album where everything comes together. You have The Band giving this really stunning performance. Robbie Robertson has some of his best guitar playing on this song, and it's really copacetic with the lyrics. I wonder what would it have been like if The Band had been backing *Blood on the Tracks*. That's what, to me, "Going Going Gone" sounds like.

Levy: This album musically points to *Blood on the Tracks*; it's just that that album is more simple. It's made with musicians who are terrified of the guy they're playing with. This album is not, and you can tell. These guys can stand, at this point in their careers, toe to toe with him.

Beviglia: "Going Going Gone" and "Dirge" those are the songs where The Band sounds least like The Band on this album. I always found it interesting that The Band at this point in their career kind of stop and essentially become Dylan's backing band again. There's not many of The Band's typical backing harmonies that they were known for. You have these great three singers at your disposal, and they're not in use at all. The Band gets their personality through on some of the more good-timey numbers, but the most interesting songs on the record are the ones where they sort of veer away from their comfort zone on "Dirge" and "Going Going Gone."

Levy: "Dirge" is a terrifying song to me. This is a mean song. It also has that really vicious line: "I can't recall a single thing you did for me except pat me on the back when I was on my knees." The opening line is "I hate myself for loving you." This is a tough song and one that, like "Going Going Gone," [is] quite riveting and quite stark. In some ways, these are songs that break apart the record. It does seem like a back-and-forth between different kinds of songs that might belong on a different kind of record about different kinds of people feeling radically different things. Yet to me that is what makes it such a fascinating and challenging album.

Bream: What did you think of Dylan's artwork on the cover?

Levy: It is the first Dylan album cover not about his face. With the possible exception of *Self Portrait*, every Dylan record is a picture of Bob Dylan. The cover art, as with a lot of things about this record, it's about shifting perspective. What are these three faces? Three ways of looking at the same thing? On an album with two to five different names [some written as subtitles by Dylan's hand on the cover] and two versions of the same song? All Dylan records are difficult to pin down; they're meant to be. This record is particularly difficult to pin down, and you could say it starts with this cover painting.

CHAPTER 15

BLOOD ON THE TRACKS

with Kevin Odegard and David Yaffe

Released January 20, 1975

Producer: Bob Dylan

Recorded in Columbia A&R Studios, New York, and Sound 80 Studios, Minneapolis

All songs written by Bob Dylan.

Session musicians (for New York sessions): Charles Brown III (guitar), Tony Brown (bass), Buddy Cage (steel guitar), Richard Crooks (drums), Paul Griffin (keyboards), Barry Kornfeld (guitar), Thomas McFaul (keyboards), Eric Weissberg (banjo/guitar).

Session musicians (for Minneapolis sessions): Bill Berg (drums), Gregg Inhofer (keyboards), Kevin Odegard (guitar), Peter Ostroushko (mandolin), Billy Peterson (bass), Chris Weber (guitar).

Although Dylan's commercial fortunes had suffered little in the half-dozen years before *Blood on the Tracks*' release, his critical reputation had taken a drubbing. Upon its appearance in early 1975, this record immediately stopped the clamor, and was not only greeted as a comeback of sorts but also as one of his best albums ever. Spare in production, it contained some of his most incisive songs about the peaks and valleys of romance, never more so in the hit single "Tangled Up in Blue."

Dylan's renewed vigor took real-life tribulations as its source. His marriage to Sara, honored by numerous homilies to the joys of family life in his songs of the late 1960s and early 1970s, was hitting a rough patch that would culminate in separation and, a few years later, divorce. Taking art classes with painter Norman Raeben allowed Dylan to, as he told *Rolling Stone*, "put my mind and my hand and my eye together in a way that allowed me to do consciously what I unconsciously felt. And I didn't know how to pull it off. I wasn't sure it could be done in songs because I'd never written a song like that. But when I started doing it, the first album I made was *Blood on the Tracks*."

Dylan would take two very different approaches to recording *Blood on the Tracks*, which combined tracks cut several months apart in two cities. Over the course of about ten days in September 1974, sessions in New York found Dylan in a somewhat unplugged mode, the recordings dominated by his voice and acoustic guitar. Versions of all ten of the LP's songs were cut during this time, but then he reconsidered his approach, remaking five of them in Minneapolis near the end of December, with different musicians and fuller arrangements.

"The lyrics were at the heart of the whole thing," remembers Kevin Odegard, who played guitar on the Minneapolis sessions. "Only 'Idiot Wind' went more than a couple of takes. But the driving force of the whole thing was that Dylan wanted to put this statement out there. He wanted to express himself artistically, and it was beyond music to us. It was great storytelling, and it was a thrill to sit around the fire and listen to Bob Dylan. You didn't wonder that he didn't want to do things twice. He did it perfectly well the first time."

Blood on the Tracks became his second #1 album, 1974's *Planet Waves* having been the first. Unlike *Planet Waves* and every other album he'd released between 1969 and 1974, however, *Blood on the Tracks* is now almost universally acclaimed as a classic that ranks among Dylan's finest work. The record, as *Rolling Stone* noted when placing it at #16 on a list of the 500 greatest albums of all time, featured "some of Dylan's most passionate, confessional songs. . . . He had never turned so much pain into so much musical splendor."

Discussing one of Dylan's greatest records is **Kevin Odegard**, a Minneapolis-based singer-songwriter and guitarist who played on *Blood on the Tracks* and cowrote *Simple Twist of Fate: The Making of Bob Dylan's* Blood on the Tracks (2005), and **David Yaffe**, a cultural critic and Syracuse University professor who wrote *Bob Dylan: Like a Complete Unknown* (2012).

Bream: Why does this album stand out?
Yaffe: *Blood on the Tracks* comes along—January '75 it's released—and this is like the decade of divorce. A lot of people are either having divorces or going through the final stages of the marriage that will blow up later in the decade. When you look at the divorce statistics and measure it with *Blood on the Tracks*, you think, wow, Dylan was really in sync with his times, to do a divorce album when he did. Anyone who's ever gone through a failed or a failing relationship can identify with the album.
Odegard: The album as a whole is, to me, the color of its cover: It's a fine red, complex and very expensive red wine. Total complex emotions, mixed tenses, metaphors. But everybody takes their own meaning away from all of these songs.
Yaffe: It had been a long time since he'd done an album that anybody thought was a classic. So nobody knew how to take *Blood on the Tracks*, and there was this immediacy of it that startled people.

There's a lot of out-of-tune playing on this album. Both the New York sessions and the Minnesota sessions have a lot of out-of-tune playing. I don't know if this is something that ever bothered you.
Odegard: Dylan never did more than one or two takes of anything. And there was never any mixing going on in Minneapolis. The only thing that he could remotely process

Dylan on *Blood on the Tracks*: "I can't understand why anybody would enjoy this kind of pain." *David Redfern/Redferns/ Getty Images*

was "Idiot Wind," and he'd get David [Zimmerman, his brother] for that. In New York, [engineer] Phil Ramone wasn't allowed to stop and start and really make suggestions. He had to capture this on the fly, just like [engineer] Paul Martinson did in Minneapolis. Some of that has to do with Bob's own instruments, and some doesn't. He's also more present on the Minneapolis sessions. He's playing organ, he's playing the mandolin, he's playing flamenco guitar on "You're a Big Girl Now." That's Bob.

Yaffe: That's funny. I would have never thought that. Wow.

Odegard: He asked Peter Ostroushko to play a part way, way, way up high on the neck of the mandolin, and Peter said, "I can't, it hurts my fingers." So Bob very nicely said, "Well can I borrow your mandolin?" And he wasn't tuning up between anything.

Yaffe: That probably explains the out-of-tuneness on that particular track. 'Cause that's the most startling out-of-tune playing, I think, is the mandolin on "You're a Big Girl Now," so that makes a lot of sense. That's Bob.

Odegard: That's Bob. That's not Peter.

Yaffe: It's just amazing to have such a great album that had just some basic problems with musicianship. It gets at something about the immediacy, too. That he had to get this down so fast that he wasn't gonna do something as pedestrian as tune a guitar or have the band tune it.

Odegard: You don't debate with Bob Dylan in the studio; you just don't do it. [Pedal steel guitarist] Buddy Cage tried it [in the New York sessions], and it didn't go well.

Yaffe: What do you make of the transitions between the New York sessions and the Minnesota?

Odegard: One school says it was too personal; Dylan backed away from the Minneapolis sessions. He depersonalized, he distanced himself from those very

Dylan was back touring with The Band in March 1975 at Kezar Stadium in San Francisco, where they shared a bill with Neil Young. *Alvan Meyerowitz/Michael Ochs Archives/Getty Images*

autobiographical details that he revealed in the New York sessions. He was afraid of the revelations that he was putting out there.

Yaffe: Then there's the story that he asked somebody for advice and then his brother David said, "No, it's not commercial enough; you need a band." Hence, the Minneapolis sessions.

Odegard: Bob had a band. He had Eric Weissberg, who was a great bandleader, and they did wonderful sessions together, but he threw everything out and just called [bassist] Tony Brown in. They did four out of the five New York songs in one night, with just Dylan and Tony Brown, and then they overdubbed. But David did say that, and he also offered the band to Bob, which is kind of where I come onboard.

Yaffe: Maybe some people liked the Minnesota versions because they had more anger in them. They like that aggressive; it makes it more rock 'n' roll. Whereas the New York sessions are more subtle emotionally. They sound more sad and resigned, and more melancholic, almost in a Hank Williams sort of way. Some people don't want to hear Dylan as a victim; they want to hear Dylan as the angry man of rock 'n' roll.

One thing that I prefer about the New York "Tangled Up in Blue" to the Minnesota "Tangled Up in Blue" is that I think his voice sounds more beautiful in the lower key.

Odegard: When Bob got to Minneapolis and he played "Tangled Up in Blue" in G, I thought it was just lame; I thought it was just layin' there, just another song. And I forgot where I was and suggested that he move it up a key.

Yaffe: Wow. So he belts it out even more.

Odegard: He had two really great musicians in the studio with him, [drummer] Bill Berg and [bassist] Bill Peterson, who are Dylan's equals in terms of creativity and artistry. They're great jazz musicians from a band called Natural Life in Minnesota. And Berg, in particular, just pushed and inspired Dylan, the things that he came up with. Playing "Tangled Up in Blue" behind the beat. His hi-hat lands at the very tail end of the beat, and puts a groove into the song that very few other drummers could ever come up with or duplicate.

Bream: What do you think is the significance of the title?

Yaffe: Kevin brought up the color on the record, which I hadn't thought about before. But, of course, that makes sense, that the color is related to blood. Is it too obvious to say he was spilling blood? I'm sure that's his title. That's not the title of some Columbia publicity person.

Odegard: I always imagined it was the blood that fell off the saddle. 'Cause the closest he comes to the title is "blood on your saddle" [lyrics in "Idiot Wind"].

Yaffe: *Blood on the Tracks* is all-encompassing. I think it takes a photograph of a very bloody stain where he spilled his own blood. Dylan was saying emotionally there's an immediacy to what I'm giving you; it's on the tracks. I'm spilling blood on these tracks— for you. Don't ask me what it means—listen. Everything is there; my insides are there. I've given you everything. And also, I think that you people that were trying to make me another messiah and then were disappointed when it turned out that I was a flawed person, I don't want to hear it from you either. This is my blood.

Odegard: Which was at once more intelligent and spiritual and creative than anybody else at that moment in recording history, or recorded history, had ever been able to succinctly state in an album title. *Blood on the Tracks*—here they are.

Yaffe: This is not Bob Dylan without tears. This is no-holds-barred Bob Dylan. This is not Dylan affecting something. This is Dylan feeling something. And trying to get it out there so fast, before the feeling goes. I think that's part of why these sessions were done so hastily, because he wants the feeling to be there, right, immediately.

Odegard: I can confirm that. You just captured exactly what the feeling of the session was. That's exactly what he said. He didn't want to slow 'em down, didn't want to interrupt.

He knows what he wants, and that's at the heart of what you're saying. He knew what he wanted, he rushed to get there, and it dissipates. If you're in the studio eight, ten, twelve hours, that feeling dissipates. We weren't there for more than three hours either night, the twenty-seventh or the thirtieth of December. Didn't go beyond that.

Yaffe: I don't know what to make of "Lily, Rosemary and the Jack of Hearts." It's hard to follow. It has a lot of verses; it's a long song.

Odegard: You're quoting David Zimmerman there. He said, "This is a long song. When you think it's done, it's not. Keep on playing." That was exactly his instructions to the band when that song started.

Bream: Let's talk about "Simple Twist of Fate."

Yaffe: Other than "Tangled Up in Blue," the one that he's performed live the most is "Simple Twist of Fate"—the title of your book. Why is it easier for him to do that one? I don't think he's done "Idiot Wind" since the '90s. He's definitely never done "Lily, Rosemary." "You're a Big Girl Now"—the last performance was in 1993.

Odegard: Is it because it's a song about Sara?

Yaffe: Right, right. He doesn't touch that. It's weird how popular this album is, and how he doesn't do many of the songs live very much. Obviously he does "Tangled Up in Blue." "You're a Big Girl Now," boy, these are brutal lyrics; they really are. If I was Bob Dylan, I would not want to sing that all the time. That's blood on the tracks right there.

Bream: David, as you said before we started, this is a depressing album. So how many depressing songs can you sing in one night?

Yaffe: "Lily, Rosemary and the Jack of Hearts," maybe it's related to divorce, but it's so much of this kind of allegorical cowboy mode that has a different mood than what you would expect from the album. Because you gotta let up somewhere. It can't be just constant. It's why that's there and "Up to Me" is not there.

Odegard: I see "You're Gonna Make Me Lonesome" as a happy song, just because of the way it ends. "I'll see you in the sky above, In the tall grass, In the ones I love." It's a nice song.

Yaffe: I remember an interview with Dylan in *Rolling Stone*, and the interviewer asked him if he was happy. And Dylan said, "Happy, what's that? Anybody can be happy." Then he said, "I don't really think of things in those terms. I think of being blessed or unblessed." And the interviewer said, "So, are you blessed?" And he said, "Well yeah, but not because I'm a big rock star." But yeah, happiness has never been a priority for Bob Dylan.

Bream: Anything else that you want to wrap up with?

Yaffe: I should say that even talking about this album is talking about an open wound. The fact that we can

Dylan worked with drummer Levon Helm and The Band on tour and for 1974's *Planet Waves*. By the end of the year, he was recording with a new ensemble of musicians—one in New York and another in Minneapolis. *Fred W. McDarrah/Getty Images*

David Yaffe: "If somebody's really looking for an album to speak to their soul [*Blood on the Tracks*] does that." *Ed Caraeff/ Getty Images*

sit around and talk about it, calmly, when this thing is still festering, it's part of just what makes it such a vivacious and deep and powerful work of art.

Odegard: I never listen to it intentionally. I would never put that on the turntable. I wouldn't do it. I just hear it when it comes on. It's in elevators and shopping malls, and it pops out of speakers here and there, but I never put this record on. I'm not a champion for what came out. I just happened to be there, that's all.

CHAPTER 16

THE BASEMENT TAPES

with Charles R. Cross and Joe Henry

Released June 26, 1975

Producers: Bob Dylan and The Band

Recorded in "The Red Room" in Bob Dylan's home in Woodstock, New York, and The Band's home, "Big Pink," in West Saugerties, New York

All songs written by Bob Dylan, except where indicated.

Session musicians: Rick Danko (bass/mandolin/vocals), Levon Helm (drums), Garth Hudson (organ/clavinet/accordion/piano), Richard Manuel (piano/drums/backing vocals), Robbie Robertson (guitar/drums).

These tracks were performed by The Band without Bob Dylan: "Orange Juice Blues (Blues for Breakfast)," "Yazoo Street Scandal," "Katie's Been Gone," "Bessie Smith," "Ain't No More Cane," "Ruben Remus," "Don't Ya Tell Henry," "Long Distance Operator."

With a double album just released and a tumultuous world tour just completed, mid-summer 1966 found Dylan at the apex of his pop stardom. As he'd broken so much new ground with his three mid-'60s electric rock albums, it seemed impossible to guess where he'd go next. As it turned out, for a while he didn't go much of anywhere. On July 29, 1966, a motorcycle accident near his Woodstock home put him out of commission indefinitely. Rumors circulated that he'd been maimed or even killed. For the next year and a half, there would be no new records or concert appearances—not an unusual gap for a major artist in today's world but an eternity in the 1960s.

Dylan had withdrawn from the music business, but unbeknownst to all but a few, he hadn't stopped *making* music. He continued to write songs at a fairly prolific pace, and for several months in mid-to-late 1967, he recorded quite a bit of material with most of the musicians from the Hawks, his backup band on that 1966 world tour. Taped in informal circumstances in his and the Hawks' homes, these tracks would eventually become known as *The Basement Tapes*.

The Hawks—Robbie Robertson, Richard Manuel, Rick Danko, Garth Hudson, and Levon Helm—would by 1968 evolve into The Band, a group that would become major stars in their own right. In 1967, however, they and Dylan were woodshedding in Woodstock, recording a mammoth body of material. Some of the songs were new Dylan compositions; some were written by him with members of the Hawks; and some were covers of vintage folk, rock, and country tunes. Oblivious to the psychedelia dominating rock music in 1967, the tone was homespun and down-to-earth, drawing on so many strains of roots music that it prototyped the style later labeled Americana.

For reasons that still remain somewhat mysterious, none of these recordings was released at the time. Some of the stronger tracks from the sessions, however, started to circulate among other musicians, and it wasn't long before some of the tunes started to get covered by the Byrds, Peter, Paul and Mary, Manfred Mann, and numerous other artists. The Band themselves re-recorded a few of the songs for their acclaimed 1968 self-titled debut album. Dylan, in contrast, would move on to different projects, though some of the actual Woodstock tunes started to get heard by fans when they crept out on bootlegs, 1969's *Great White Wonder* being the first of those.

Fascination with the recordings was so fervent that in 1975, a double album of highlights from the sessions was issued as *The Basement Tapes*, though there were overdubs on some songs, and a third of the tracks featured The Band without Dylan. The rest of the songs were finally heard on the 2014 six-CD box set *The Basement Tapes Complete*. It was the 1975 double LP, however, that introduced the most legendary unreleased rock music of all time to the world.

Diving into *The Basement Tapes* are **Charles R. Cross**, a Seattle-based music critic and author of several music-related books, and **Joe Henry**, a singer-songwriter and producer in Los Angeles, who was introduced in Chapter 6.

Bream: If *The Basement Tapes* album had come out in 1967 instead of '75, how do you think it would have been received?

Henry: [Critic] Greil Marcus tells the story about having gotten a hold of some tapes from the first four or five songs that had leaked out and sitting with friends and people both laughing out loud and weeping over it. I think it probably would have been received quite like that by a lot of people. If you can imagine it having been the follow-up to *Blonde on Blonde*, it makes perfect sense, even if it seems like a shocking departure from where he was.

Cross: The songwriting on this album, which is so extraordinary, would have been something people would have been talking about. Songs like "Tears of Rage" and "Odds and Ends," they're such unbelievable classics that his esteem would have only gone up.

Henry: *The Basement Tapes* certainly is a microcosm of everything that he was. You hear the strangest part of blues music, and some folk music, and ballads from the British Isles—everything that informed him at that moment. And really significantly deep wordplay, not unlike what many of the Beats were doing at the same time. Throughout The Basement Tapes—not just the official release but other stuff that so many of us have heard, where he's going back and doing old covers—he's revamping or playing on the vocabulary of really old, whimsical folk tales and ballads. In a way, he's sort of reassembling a new vocabulary for what he must be imagining is next. Yet when he has the next opportunity for an official session, he doesn't go back to even the strongest of those songs.

Bream: I think there was an interview in *Rolling Stone* in '69 where he said these were demos for songs not for him to record. So he viewed this as a songwriting session to offer these songs to other people.

Henry: I'm not sure I believe him. I think in that time he wasn't probably interested in recording them himself. But it's hard for me to imagine, with some of the material, that he really wrote it thinking that it was gonna be something he could pitch to Manfred Mann or Sonny and Cher, for that matter. He may have hand-picked a few to send out for other people, to keep his career in motion while he was in retreat, but I have a hard time believing entirely that he hadn't at some point disappeared into the music in the way that any artist must ultimately.

Cross: There were fourteen tapes that were kind of circulated. I tell the story in my Jimi Hendrix book of a publicist that worked with Dylan approached Hendrix and the word was "Bob really would like you to listen to these songs and maybe cover them." Bob was always very canny about publishing, and very aware of the fact that that was one of the main sources he had of income, beyond even record sales in those first few years, and even by 1967. Yet it's hard to imagine him letting go entirely of these songs and not going back and recording them at some point in some way.

Henry: I think that Bob may have begun by thinking that he was writing songs that he would pitch to others, but it sounds to me that something else takes hold. I think the work is much more expansive and strange than what he could have imagined ultimately was just going to serve as fodder for others. You hear the delight in which he is disappearing into that music that first fired his imagination as a teenager, at a moment when he was probably sick to death of his own voice and writing voice, much less the attention they were receiving. So he goes back to this very rich source that had turned him into a troubadour to begin with. It sounds to me like it's a form of liberation away from the celebrity aspect of the business he's gotten himself into and back into the joy and mystery of country and blues music.

Cross: It's also fascinating to look at the cover songs he did. He's going back and exploring songs by John Lee Hooker and Ian & Sylvia and Hank Snow, who he loved. If you listen to his radio show [on Sirius and XM, 2006–09], he'd rather talk about Hank Snow or Ian & Sylvia than he would Bob Dylan times a thousand-fold. In *The Basement Tapes*, it's almost like we're listening to Bob's radio show where he played old songs, but we're hearing him play them for really the first time. None of this stuff had really been released, or he hadn't played a lot of these songs in concert. So you're getting what Bob wants to explore and play. And it's fascinating that they're covering a Curtis Mayfield song, and that these sessions are encompassing all kinds of music, whether it's a Carter Family song, to a John Lee Hooker song.

Bream: One of the theories is that Dylan was trying to get out of his Columbia Records contract and sign with MGM. So they owed fourteen songs to Columbia, and *The Basement Tapes* actually just started out as trying to

Opposite: After years of working with The Band, Dylan returned the favor by appearing at the group's farewell concert dubbed The Last Waltz on November 25, 1976, in San Francisco's Winterland Ballroom. *Larry Hulst/Michael Ochs Archives/Getty Images*

end that contract with Columbia. And it obviously broadened into something bigger and more fun and more expansive.

Henry: I've heard that cited as well. But frequently you start things for one reason and they take their own life and run away with you.

Cross: There's this whole other story of what happens to those recordings—how they leak out, become an underground sensation and essentially inspire the first widely disseminated bootleg albums. That's a big part of *The Basement Tapes'* mystique—that you couldn't go in and buy it until 1975. And, of course, many of the fans jeered that the 1975 version was highly compromised in terms of what was done to the recordings and overdubs and cleaning things up.

Henry: You're listening to something that was supposedly never intended for public airing. It's like collected letters of a writer, personal letters after the fact. Or looking at Picasso's pencil-and-ink sketchbook. You evaluate it differently because nobody's put this forward as finished work, and thus you're liberated from the same kind of judgments. It's not only freeing to the artist but very freeing to a listener to approach it without the baggage of thinking that you're supposed to judge it as the next opus.

Bream: Let's talk a little bit about the sonic quality.

Henry: I think the tonality of the record is absolutely a part of its very unique and very powerful way under your skin, that you do feel like you're looking through a patina of burnished glass, peering into a cellar window, in a way. We see the limitations as part of what was most evocative about the experience.

Cross: If I remember correctly, the room was just twelve by twelve. These guys are right on top of each other recording this. They're literally inches away from each other's instruments, and you can hear some bleed on the record. But I think that's part of what adds to this, is the fact that they are so connected when they're cutting these songs. There's not a separation of somebody in an isolated booth not even looking at the other musicians.

Henry: Had the basement been bigger, it would have been more cavernous sounding. So the smallness of it provides some intimacy against the harshness of the square concrete bunker.

Touring in white face, Dylan brought his Rolling Thunder Revue to Madison Square Garden on December 8, 1975, to benefit the legal defense fund for Rubin "Hurricane" Carter, the prizefighter charged with murder. *Ron Galella, Ltd./ WireImage/Getty Images*

Cross: I think that unlike some of the other things that he did with The Band, certainly when he toured with them, this was kind of less a Dylan show and more a collaboration. You have this absolutely incredible band called The Band who can play anything. If you were gonna pick a band to have a collaboration with and kind of explore the roots of American music and folk and blues, you simply could not find a handful of better musicians.

Henry: It absolutely is a collaboration, but I don't think it's a collaboration on equal footing. I do think that The Band is following somebody who's driven by a vision, even if it's not a fully realized one.

It's interesting that Bob's comment when *The Basement Tapes* came out in 1975 was something like, "I thought everybody else had all that." It's a great example of sort of distancing himself from the work, as if it isn't his album. It's the album he's claimed least responsibility for, and yet I think it is more truly him than anything else he's ever released.

Bream: There seem to be two themes here: a search for salvation and deliverance.

Cross: Bob's greater interest in exploring the overt themes of religion in his work just a few years later makes more sense when you listen to all these songs. If there's one theme of Bob Dylan's work, it would be salvation. If "I Shall Be Released" isn't the song that's played at Bob Dylan's funeral, I'd be shocked. It ends up being a song that ties into that. All these songs on *The Basement Tapes* explore that, even the covers.

Bream: Do you want to talk about any specific favorite songs on the album?

Henry: "Tears of Rage" is as good as anything he's written to date. That's a just hair-raisingly beautiful and wildly emotional song.

Bream: Wouldn't that also be the first collaboration with someone else? Richard Manuel wrote that with him.

Henry: And "Wheels on Fire" with Rick Danko. Both up there on the top shelf of the songs that came out of that experiment.

Cross: "Tears of Rage," not only is that as good a song as anything he's written, but it's also as good a song as he ever sang. His vocal approach to many of these songs, there's a sweetness and a melancholy-ness to his voice that always really moved me and touched me. I felt like I was getting more of a window to the younger, more innocent Bob, rather than the at times jaded Bob of the *Dont* [sic] *Look Back* documentary.

Henry: I also think he sounds of completely indistinct age, not only on "Tears of Rage" but on a lot of this music. He just sounds a lot older than twenty-six. It's something that could have been happening at any time within a twenty-year period. It's disarming at times how free of time so much of that music seems to me, not only in terms of the age of the participants but of the time it was created. There is a melancholic weariness to all of it, even the most whimsical—"Apple Suckling Tree" or "Don't Ya Tell Henry," any of that stuff.

Cross: The motorcycle crash was never really what everybody quite thought it was, but there was a metaphorical and a spiritual crash that happened. These songs are the document of that, more than anything else he ever did.

Bream: Is this the first Americana album? Is this the blueprint for Americana?

Cross: I wouldn't say no, but the blueprint for Americana is Leadbelly and Woody Guthrie. But this is the first album that fits into that concept of quote-unquote "No Depression" music that is the Old Crow Medicine Show, where someone is exploring the roots of American folk and blues and trying to sort of move it into more of a rock genre.

Henry: Woody and Leadbelly, and the Bristol sessions that revealed the Carter Family and Jimmie Rodgers as emerging artists, might stand as the original Americana wellspring as far as recorded music. *The Basement Tapes* may well represent one of the first times that that legacy was consciously being built upon and expanded, where somebody was so consciously not only engaging a tradition but looking actively to expand upon it in a very conscious sort of a way.

Bream: It's obviously the Dylan album with the most mythology. It's the hardest to sometimes vet because of so many stories and myths about this album.

Henry: We don't really know the motivation here, because Bob has never truly addressed it. That's one of the most fascinating things about it, why we're pontificating on it. Because Bob has never really exactly explained what he was thinking, what the motivation was, how aware he was of all the things. We are left [with] the greatest Dylan mystery, simply to speculate on: Did Bob intend for this to come out? What was he thinking? Did he have any idea? We don't know. And that's one reason the story becomes part of Bob Dylan's myth. It's maybe one of the only parts left that is still a myth.

CHAPTER 17

DESIRE

with Nicole Atkins and Dan Wilson

1. Hurricane 8:33
2. Isis 6:58
3. Mozambique 3:00
4. One More Cup of Coffee (Bob Dylan) 3:43
5. Oh, Sister .4:05
6. Joey 11:05
7. Romance in Durango 5:50
8. Black Diamond Bay 7:30
9. Sara (Bob Dylan) 5:29

Released January 6, 1976

Producer: Don DeVito

Recorded at Columbia Studios, New York

All songs written by Bob Dylan and Jacques Levy, except where indicated.

Session musicians: Vinnie Bell (bouzouki), Ronnie Blakely (backing vocals), Eric Clapton (guitar), Mel Collins (sax/trumpet), Dom Cortese (mandolin/accordion), Yvonne Elliman (backing vocals), Erik Frandsen (slide guitar), Emmylou Harris (backing vocals), Luther Rix (congas), Scarlet Rivera (violin), Steve Soles (guitar), Terry Stannard (drums), Rob Stoner (bass/backing vocals), Howie Wyeth (drums, piano), Sheena (tambourine).

In the wake of the commercial and critical success of 1975's *Blood on the Tracks*, Dylan was more of a force in popular music than he'd been since the late 1960s, and more of a media presence than he'd been in almost ten years. This comeback of sorts was solidified by his Rolling Thunder Revue tours in fall 1975 and spring 1976, which found Dylan taking as many chances on stage as he had on his boldest records. Excerpts from two May 1976 Rolling Thunder shows would come out in late 1976 on *Hard Rain*, and recordings from the earlier leg would appear much later on the 2002 archive release *The Bootleg Series Vol. 5: Bob Dylan Live 1975, The Rolling Thunder Revue*. Between the tour's halves, Dylan issued *Desire*, his most acclaimed studio work of the 1970s other than *Blood on the Tracks*.

Unexpected collaborations have driven much of Dylan's most innovative music, and *Desire* would be no exception. Most of the songs were cowritten by Dylan with Jacques Levy, whose experience lay primarily in directing theatrical productions. Dylan had rarely composed material with songwriting partners, notable exceptions being some songs from *The Basement Tapes* penned with members of The Band. He'd also contributed lyrics to the Byrds' "The Ballad of Easy Rider," though it was principally written by Byrds leader Roger McGuinn. As it happened, however, Levy had already cowritten songs (including the single "Chestnut Mare") with McGuinn that appeared on Byrds albums and McGuinn solo releases. In 1975 Levy and Dylan met and began their own songwriting collaborations, Levy also helping with the staging of the Rolling Thunder Revue.

Another surprise addition to Dylan's team was violinist Scarlet Rivera, whom Dylan met by chance in Greenwich Village in mid-1975. Her gypsy-flavored playing was a key addition to the *Desire* sessions, mostly recorded in just a few days in New York in late July. Backing vocals by Emmylou Harris and Ronee Blakely also did much to flesh out the arrangements of songs that, with an average length of seven to eight minutes, were more epic in structure than almost anything Dylan had previously attempted.

Three of the tunes in particular were based on real-life characters, each causing more than their share of controversy. "Joey" was gangster Joey Gallo, and Dylan's portrait was sometimes criticized as too sympathetic. It was no secret that "Sara" was Dylan's wife, the couple now heading toward divorce. "Hurricane" was boxer Rubin "Hurricane" Carter, at that time imprisoned for murder. Something of a throwback to his protest songs advocating a cause (in this case justice for Carter), an edited version of the song became a Top Forty hit.

A #1 album, *Desire* was also a critical hit, with top UK music weekly *NME* naming it album of the year. If it's not quite as revered as *Blood on the Tracks*, it's close, *Rolling Stone* giving it the #174 position in its list of the 500 greatest albums of all time.

The praises of *Desire* will be sung by Grammy-winner **Dan Wilson**, a Los Angeles–based singer-songwriter and producer known for his work with Adele, the Dixie Chicks, and his own band Semisonic, along with **Nicole Atkins**, a singer-songwriter from New Jersey with three studio albums who is a fixture at an annual Dylan tribute concert.

Bream: Both of you seem very strongly drawn to *Desire*. Why?
Atkins: *Desire* is the only Bob Dylan record I like. I kind of grew up hating Bob Dylan. I couldn't understand why my friends liked him. I thought his songwriting was dumb, and I thought that his voice was annoying. Then I heard *Desire*, and it was a record that I grew up with. I always felt like whenever I listened to it, that I was in the room with some of the people that he made it with.
Wilson: I was a huge Dylan fan and had listened to everything but *Desire*, I think, when I first came upon it very late. It became my late-discovered favorite Dylan album.

What did your friends like about Dylan? What was the point of disagreement?
Atkins: I just felt that they always blindly dug him, like they would never say what was so great about it. I didn't get it until I heard "Romance in Durango," "Isis," "One More Cup of Coffee," and those sort of songs. They just had this drama that was like, "Wow, this may be the last song you ever hear before you die in a standoff."

Bream: I saw an interview with Jacques Levy, Dylan's cowriter on this album. He said Bob is not very good at linear storytelling, going from A to B to C to D. If you think about the narrative songs on this album, it's kind of a fascinating comment.
Wilson: My favorite song on the album is "Isis." That has the same shaggy dog story vibe as "Lily, Rosemary and the Jack of Hearts" from *Blood on the Tracks*. It's almost like this long series of setups for kind of humorous payoffs. When they finally get to the tomb and the casket is empty and there's nothing inside, and he throws his dead partner into the tomb and puts back the cover, then he says, "Then I rode back to Isis just to tell her I love her."

Dylan not only spearheaded a benefit concert to help the legal defense of imprisoned boxer Rubin "Hurricane" Carter in 1975, but he also wrote the epic song "Hurricane." Carter was tried for murder and convicted twice, but then the second conviction was overturned, and he was released from prison in 1985 after serving almost 20 years. *Blank Archives/ Getty Images*

Atkins: Listening to "Isis," I was just like holy shit, man, this song sounds like a party with a bunch of drinks in it.

The thing I like the most about that record is the fact that it sounded like friendship. It just sounded like a party with friends. Kind of like Bob Dylan was having fun.

Wilson: The lore that I have about it is that there was a lot of late-night jumping in cars and driving around New York, and that they found the violin player on one of these kind of bar-hopping, street-running nights.

Bream: He didn't even know if she could play. He liked her long hair and her mysterious gypsy look, and the fact that she was carrying a violin case.

Atkins: The violin—that is one of my favorite parts of the record, 'cause it sounds like a conversation.

Wilson: What does "Hurricane" mean to you?

Atkins: "Hurricane" is one of the first songs that made me cry. I was like, what is this about? Oh my god, this poor man. And I didn't know why. I found out. The songs on the record, especially like "Hurricane," just affected me more on an emotional, guttural level. That song made me feel like I was there and I was living a life that wasn't my own.

Bream: Dan, what did you think of "Hurricane"?

Wilson: When I first started falling in love with the record, I had really mixed feelings about it. It took me a long time to get used to the way Dylan said some of the words. There's a lot of things about the song that are really awkward. Like was I ready to hear Dylan sing "Rubin could take a man out with just one punch"? It's just such a non-Dylanish line. But like you said, Nicole, the story felt so real.

Atkins: When he says the words and then the violin comes in, it's like holy shit, now it's real. Like the violin is justice in court.

Wilson: She's like the truth at the end of every stanza.

Atkins: She makes you believe what he's saying.

Wilson: I think this is gonna sound kind of funny, but this is the first album that I loved that I heard a lot of mistakes on. Like there's a point in this song, in "Hurricane," where he sings the *n*-word and all of the guitarists lose their time 'til the next bar. It's like suddenly the word is so shocking to them that they all get off-time and they screw up for like an entire bar. The record, it's full of weird notes on different instruments and rhythmic kind of hiccups. *Desire* is like this crazy wild mess that's very lifelike.

Bream: "Hurricane" was one of my all-time favorite Dylan performances because it's so intense and urgent.

Wilson: Because he cared. 'Cause it's not propaganda, but he's sort of desperately trying to put what he feels is a true version of a story out there. It's like a "Lonesome Death of Hattie Carroll." Like the Jokerman is gone for a minute; there's no Jokerman about this song.

Bream: No, and he had participated in the protest rally, objecting to the imprisonment of Rubin Carter.

Wilson: He's believing in something. It's very different than the usual Dylan kind of, Is he fucking with me? Am I supposed to believe this shit? I like that part of Dylan, but that desperate urgency is very powerful.

Atkins: The thing that brought me to that song and also this record is, if you watch Western movies, or if you listen to Ennio Morricone and the way that he puts together songs, it puts you in a place. Every song on this record, especially "Hurricane," was like watching a modern-day Western movie. Every musician that was playing on it, even if it was like awkward or out of time, helped tell the story.

Opposite: That beige broad-brimmed hat turned up not only onstage during the Rolling Thunder Revue but also on the cover of *Desire*. *Jeffrey Mayer/ WireImage/Getty Images*

Bream: What do you think of "Joey," another profile of a real person?

Wilson: I used to skip over this song; I was really annoyed by it. Why do I care about this guy? He's probably a jerk. I watched *Mean Streets* and I watched those [Martin] Scorsese movies, and I was like, these people are not nice. They're not my heroes.

Atkins: I used to always skip over "Joey," too. We glamorize gangsters in Jersey like crazy, and I don't get that, as well. I always hated the chorus.

Wilson: "What made them want to come and blow you away?"—it was like, oh please. It's not like he's Mother Teresa or Martin Luther King [Jr.] or something.

Bream: Let's talk about "Mozambique."

Wilson: I always really enjoyed it. It's just kind of Dylan doing a fun, good-times party song. It's almost like you don't even need to know what Mozambique is. Is it a city? Is it a country? Is it a neighborhood in France? It's just so silly.

Bream: I almost got the impression that Dylan and Levy were trying to have a contest to see how many rhymes they could come up with for Mozambique.

Wilson: It's all about the wordplay.

Bream: Jacques Levy is really better known as a playwright and director.

Atkins: That record, it seems like a play. And I'm a huge Broadway lady. So maybe that's why I'm so drawn to it. Because it's so completely visual.

Wilson: These are also Dylan songs that went right to the concert stage perfectly, which isn't always the case with Dylan songs.

Bream: Let's talk about "Sara," one of the more direct songs that Dylan has ever written.

Wilson: I hate to confess, I have the same feeling about "Sara" musically as Nicole described about "Joey." It's almost a similar cadence. When he starts singing that chorus, I just feel a little bit detached from it. Do we need to know the back story to really love the song, and we just don't know it?

Bream: This song's writing is credited only to Dylan, as is "One More Cup of Coffee."

Wilson: I love "One More Cup of Coffee." That always sounded way more like a Dylan song to me than the other songs on the record. But with "Sara," I never really thought it sounds like a Dylan song. It sounded like it came from the wrong album or something.

Atkins: It was the last song on the album. It's like all these people died, and now my relationship is dead.

Wilson: My love of the record is very caught up in something that's super nerdy, which is I like the sound of it more than most Dylan records. The way the snare drum kind of reverberates, and every time he hits the back beat—even on "Sara," when the drummer hits the back beat, it sounds so serious and soulful.

Atkins: This is like an *Exile on Main Street* [by the Rolling Stones]. It's a record of place and people. Dylan was always such a solitary dude, and this record puts him in the room with friends.

Wilson: I feel like there's some times that none of them know the chords and it's all kind of a mess, and no one knows the song. Sometimes it pushes the music into the background.

Bream: Why do you think it's called *Desire*?

Atkins: This whole record sounds like desire. It sounds like sex and murder and want and travel. Those are all things that people desire. I always thought it was a perfect title for that record.

Wilson: For me, it's like an awesome title that I never even noticed. If I see the word somewhere, I probably think of this album.

STREET-LEGAL

with Janet Gezari and Alan Light

Released June 15, 1978

Producer: Don DeVito

Recorded at Rundown Studios in Santa Monica, California

All songs written by Bob Dylan.

Session musicians: Billy Cross (guitar), Carolyn Dennis (backing vocals), Steve Douglas (saxophone), Jo Ann Harris (backing vocals), David Mansfield (violin/mandolin), Alan Pasqua (keyboards), Jerry Scheff (bass), Steve Soles (guitar), Helena Springs (backing vocals), Ian Wallace (drums).

With two consecutive #1 albums (*Blood on the Tracks* and *Desire*) that got rave reviews, and two very different tours that generated the live albums *Before the Flood* (with The Band) and *Hard Rain* (with the Rolling Thunder Revue), the mid-1970s seemed like a golden era for Dylan. Behind the scenes, however, there was plenty of turmoil. His marriage to Sara, whose ups and downs were chronicled on some of the songs on both *Blood on the Tracks* and *Desire*, officially ended in June 1977. A 1978 movie shot during the Rolling Thunder tour, the four-hour *Renaldo and Clara*, was a costly commercial and critical flop. The construction of a mansion in Malibu was another huge drain on Dylan's finances.

The singer spent much of 1978 touring the world, making his first extended European jaunt since 1966 and playing in Japan for the first time. Recordings from two Japanese shows would form his third live album in five years, *Bob Dylan at Budokan*, in 1979. Before then, he'd record and release another studio album, *Street-Legal*, issued in June 1978.

On December 26, 1977, Dylan ran through some of the album's tunes at a rehearsal space he'd purchased in Santa Monica. That's where he'd record *Street-Legal*, characteristically, in one gulp over a week or so in April 1978. And as was often the case, there was a nearly complete turnover in personnel since his last album, though Don DeVito remained the producer. Notable additions to the backup crew included bassist Jerry Scheff, most famed for his work with Elvis Presley and the Doors; saxophonist Steve Douglas, one of Hollywood's most in-demand session players; drummer Ian Wallace, who'd been in King Crimson in the early 1970s; and backup singers Helena Springs, Jo Ann Harris, and Carolyn Dennis, who helped impart a gospel flavor that would be mightily amplified on Dylan's next few albums.

Since the beginning of his career, Dylan's records had elicited an extremely wide range of reactions, from worshipful ecstasy to frothing-at-the-mouth rage. In comparison, *Street-Legal's* reception was notable chiefly for the indifference with which many critics and listeners treated it. Wrote Alan Rinzler in *Bob Dylan: The Illustrated Record* (1978), "The overall effect is of someone kind of grim and depressed, forcing these songs out with a fatalistic attitude like: well here's the way it is for me now, not so hot, but still plugging." *The Rolling Stone Record Guide* (1979) was yet more nonplussed, simply observing, "*Street-Legal* is weird beyond immediate comment."

While it wasn't exactly a commercial failure, *Street-Legal* got a lukewarm reception in the marketplace as well, becoming Dylan's first album since 1964 (excepting the outtakes collection *Dylan* and the *Pat Garrett & Billy the Kid* soundtrack) to miss the Top Ten, if just barely. It did better in the UK, where it made #2 and got more positive reviews. Dylan spent most of the next six months touring, emerging the following year as a changed man both artistically and personally.

Janet Gezari, a professor of English at Connecticut College who has taught courses on Bob Dylan, and **Alan Light**, a music journalist in New York, former editor of *Spin* and *Vibe*, and author of several music biographies, turn their critical eyes toward *Street-Legal*.

Dylan, onstage in Oakland in 1978 in his *Street Legal* era. *Rolling Stone* called the album "weird beyond comment." *Ed Perlstein/Redferns/Getty Images*

Bream: When *Street-Legal* first came out, it was pretty much panned by everybody, but some people's opinions of it changed over the years. Do you think it's underrated, overlooked, subpar, or what?

Light: I think it's both overrated and underrated. There's stuff that's really stunningly good. There's stuff that's pretty terrible. I've always liked that there's a sense of ambition to *Street-Legal*; there's something that he's going for, even when he really misses the mark.

Gezari: I think that *Street-Legal* has been not just underrated, but oddly, peculiarly viewed. It was quite highly rated in Europe, and very, very badly reviewed in the United States, particularly by Dave Marsh in *Rolling Stone*, and by Greil Marcus. I think those reviews are just wrong. I think *Street-Legal* was the most completely successful album Dylan produced for a while. All of the songs on *Street-Legal* are first-rate.

Bream: A lot of people pointed out that it was strong lyrics, with very distracting arrangements. Some of the criticism was it was Bob showing his sort of showbiz side. There was a little Neil Diamond influence, a little Elvis Presley influence, especially in the arrangements.

Gezari: It would be hard to defend the production of *Street-Legal*. It was not a well-produced album.

Light: He really wasn't happy with the work that producer Don DeVito had done on *Desire*, but kind of settled, out of circumstance, to stay with him. They went through several drummers and ended up with somebody that he wasn't all that happy with. So I think that there was something that he had in his head that became increasingly difficult for him to actually execute.

Gezari: One of the early positive reviews that came out was Robert Palmer's, and he points to the fact that Dylan is in terrific voice on this album. His phrasing is magnificent. Some of the bitterness that I can pick up in Dave Marsh's review comes from feeling that these songs are opaque, that the lyrics are hard to figure out. Maybe that had something to do with the subject matter of *Street-Legal*. It is an album of songs about divorce. There are popular songs written about divorce, and there are popular songs written about breakups, failed relationships, but not popular songs written like these about the experience of divorce, which includes those complicated feelings of loss, feelings of vulnerability, feelings of anger, feelings of bitterness, and some pride also in resilience.

Light: "Changing of the Guards," it's always a song that I've struggled with. It's one that I still have no real sense of what's going on in the lyrics. In some ways Dylan does himself no favors by starting [the album] with that song and getting people back on their heels to say, "Listen, I have no idea what he's talking about."

Gezari: It doesn't make a lot of sense as a narrative. But the feelings in it are clear enough. So I feel as if I know what "Changing of the Guards" means, but I can't take somebody through the song stanza by stanza and explain every element in it.

Bream: "Baby Stop Crying" sounds like his closest attempt at a stone-cold R&B song.

Light: Certainly there's a lot of that old-time, old school R&B in here, [in] the centrality of the backup vocals in particular. Before going forward, one more question I want to ask Janet, is that this record certainly was attacked at the time [for] the representation of women. That in songs like "New Pony" and especially "Is Your Love in Vain," there is a hostility toward women that was coming out in a pretty visceral way in these songs.

Gezari: That is something it's hard not to think about. Especially in "Is Your Love in Vain" and "New Pony," which I think of as both sides of the same coin. On the one, the sentimental side. The other, the core side of the same bad ending, according to which women are seen as evil instruments to the well-being of some male figure.

Bream: Some people just came right out and said "Is Your Love in Vain" is sexist.

Light: When you get to "Can you cook, can you sew, can you make flowers grow," it's pretty.

Gezari: It's pretty awful, I agree. I don't even imagine that Dylan, in all of his moods, would like what it has to say. "New Pony" is in some ways more interesting because it is a

The man of many hats rocked Blackbushe Pop Festival in Hampshire, England, on July 17, 1978. *Express Newspapers/ Getty Images*

blues song. It's a raunchy but bitterer than usual, coarse blues song. I like it. I don't like the attitude toward women that it expresses, but I recognize that it's an attitude that belongs to a lot of songs.

Light: "Is Your Love in Vain" is really kind of a disaster, because that feels sort of more broad-stroke about what women are supposed to be, where "New Pony" still feels like it's directed at an individual.

Gezari: The album's also full of religion. "Senor" is certainly a religious kind of allegory. "Changing of the Guards" is a song you'd have to call apocalyptic. It sort of starts at a moment when there's a transformation. Sort of destruction of old ways of being in the world and an effort to find new ways of being in the world, and gospel is one of those new ways of being in the world that Dylan is beginning to explore and about to explore in a much more intense way.

There's plenty of gospel influence in *Street-Legal*, and there's a lot of influence of hymns and church songs, both songs belonging to the white church and songs belonging to the black church.

Light: What is clear is Dylan is at the absolute bottom, end of his rope. When you get to "Where Are You Tonight?" at the end of this record, and you get to him singing, "I can't believe it, I can't believe I'm alive. . . . Horseplay and disease are killing me by degrees"—you know, not just as an artist but as a guy, he has hit the wall. And you hear in these songs that he's hit the wall. You hear the anger; you hear the despair and the frustration.

Gezari: What do you think "Senor" is about?

Light: I think [it's] dreamlike. This notion of border towns and crossings and shifting cultures or cultural perspectives, all of that is in there. He used it very prominently in [his 2003 movie] *Masked and Anonymous*. As crazy as that film is, I think a lot of "Senor" shows up in that, that notion of this sort of apocalyptic border town, and how you navigate through unfamiliar territories, physical and emotional. I don't think there's another storytelling song on this album like this one. There's an ambition for melody and structure on this record. There are a few things that really don't work. "No Time to Think," the sort of sing-songy thing starts to drive me crazy after a while.

Bream: It sounds like it's an Irish drinking song.

Light: Yeah. He holds the waltz thing throughout, but that seems to sort of go on and on and reach a sort of drone at a certain point. But unlike some other Dylan records, I feel like there's a striving for melody on this record that's distinctive. The singing is strong, the performances are strong. There are Dylan records that feel kind of half-assed, and this never feels that.

Gezari: The lines in "No Time to Think" are really terrific. It's a song that relies on internal rhyme, and he just pulls off some amazing lines.

Light: There's some high-wire writing—writing in triples, triple rhyming, and then bringing things back for refrains. These were worked on.

Gezari: But it's also a song that feels as if it's not getting anywhere. It feels as if it could go on and on and nothing will change. It's got a kind of stasis to it.

"True Love Tends to Forget" is a song I like a lot. Again, I don't know what it is true love tends to forget. Talk about opaque lyrics.

Light: It works as a song, but I think it's certainly not one of the most focused-up and [with] clear conclusions to draw.

On a number of these songs, this notion of possession, and don't forget that I'm in charge, don't forget that you answer to me, comes up repeatedly. This is the mid- to moving into late '70s, and there's more equality issues coming to the table at that time. You get a feeling of discomfort from him, that those ways are changing.

Gezari: There are a number of Dylan love songs which are, I think, oppressive to women. That insistence on his ability to control a situation that is out of his control. At the same time, songs on *Street-Legal* are full of acknowledgment of the authority of the person he's contending against.

Light: If nothing else, this album has some major songs. Even "Changing of the Guards," however flawed, is a major song. "Senor" is a major song. I'm just so flat-out obsessed with "Where Are You Tonight?" as an astonishing piece of writing and an absolute cornerstone to the moment in his life. As the last song on a generally dismissed album, that is one of the real treasures of his work.

Opposite page: Janet Gezari: "In the liner notes to *Biograph*, [Dylan] says that [*Street-Legal*] was reviewed spitefully, and he's confused about that." *Jan Persson/ Redferns/Getty Images*

CHAPTER 19

SLOW TRAIN COMING

with Kevin J. H. Dettmar and Paul Zollo

Released August 18, 1979

Producers: Jerry Wexler and Barry Beckett

Recorded at Muscle Shoals Sound Studio in Sheffield, Alabama

All songs written by Bob Dylan.

Session musicians: Barry Beckett (keyboards/percussion), Micky Buckins (percussion), Carolyn Dennis (backing vocals), Tim Drummond (bass), Regina Havis (backing vocals), Mark Knopfler (guitar), Helena Springs (backing vocals), Pick Withers (drums).

Throughout Dylan's career in the 1960s and 1970s, the one constant was unpredictable change. The shifts from protest songs to personal ones, from acoustic folk to electric rock, from folk-rock to country-rock—none were moves that anyone saw coming. Of all his unexpected metamorphoses, however, none took his audience aback as much as his conversion to born-again Christianity at the end of the '70s. His new faith was not a purely personal matter, either, as the songs on his 1979 album *Slow Train Coming* clearly declared it for millions to hear.

Raised as a Jew, Dylan became attracted to Christianity in the final stages of his 1978 world tour, spending several months after its conclusion attending a Los Angeles–area Bible school run by the Vineyard Fellowship. When he recorded his next album in spring 1979, religious concerns were reflected in his new batch of songs, sometimes even in the titles, "Gotta Serve Somebody" and "When He Returns" being two examples. Gospel was an element in the folk, country, and rock from which Dylan drew throughout his career and would strongly influence both the material and production on the first album of his born-again phase, *Slow Train Coming*.

But while gospel was a significant presence, the LP did not abandon the kind of rock music that Dylan had played, more often than not, since first expanding into full-band arrangements in 1965. This time around, however, the rock would be of a more soulful, gritty sort than he'd played the past decade or so. To get a funkier sound, Dylan recorded in Alabama's legendary Muscle Shoals Sound Studio, where some of the greatest '70s rock and soul classics, including the Rolling Stones' "Brown Sugar" and the Staple Singers' "I'll Take You There," were cut.

Producing the sessions were Muscle Shoals keyboardist Barry Beckett and Jerry Wexler, who'd worked with many soul/R&B legends in the '50s and '60s as an executive at Atlantic Records. Other key contributors were guitarist Mark Knopfler, who'd just ascended to stardom as the chief force behind Dire Straits, and the Muscle Shoals Horns, who'd played on many soul and pop hits recorded in Muscle Shoals. As they had on *Street-Legal,* backup singers Carolyn Dennis and Helena Springs (here joined by Regina Havis) gave the tracks their strongest gospel spice.

Although Dylan's new material stirred its share of controversy—particularly when he played it in concert, to the exclusion of older classics many fans wanted to hear as well or instead—*Slow Train Coming* was both a commercial and critical hit. The record reached #3 in the United States and #2 in the UK, and "Gotta Serve Somebody" became his (as of this writing) final Top Forty hit. "The more I hear the new album—at least fifty times [in the past two months]—the more I feel that it's one of the finest records Dylan has ever made," bubbled *Rolling Stone* publisher Jann Wenner in the magazine. "In time, it is possible that it might even be considered his greatest."

Kevin J. H. Dettmar, a professor of English at Pomona College and the editor of *The Cambridge Companion to Bob Dylan* (2009), comes to Jesus on *Slow Train Coming* with **Paul Zollo**, senior editor at *American Songwriter*, a singer-songwriter and author of books on songwriting.

On stage in Paris, France, 1978
J. Cuinieres/Roger Viollet/Getty Images

Bream: How big a surprise was it when *Slow Train Coming* came out?
Zollo: It was a surprise that it was such a focused album and so beautifully recorded and rendered. It was also a huge surprise in terms of content, in that these are Dylan writing Christian songs, writing gospel songs.
Dettmar: I was in college and I was listening to punk. So I didn't hear *Slow Train Coming* until maybe even in the last decade. I knew it to be the first album of the quote-unquote "Christian" period. What struck me listening to it with that filter in place is how very ambiguously Christian it is. God's in there, although God had been in there in earlier albums, too, but it wasn't nearly as doctrinaire as I had feared it would be.
Zollo: He said he had an experience where Christ came to him, a typical, literal born-again experience, and that led him to go to a Bible college in Reseda, California, out in the San Fernando Valley of L.A. Everybody there studied the New Testament. So I think on one level, he was approaching it like someone would approach poetry or a different kind of literature, and really immersing himself in the new literature. And it was that which influenced his writing as much as the belief system, I think.

Dylan was swingin' like Sinatra in Toronto in October 1978. *Doug Griffin/Toronto Star via Getty Images*

Bream: What do you think producer Jerry Wexler contributed to this project?

Zollo: Very unusually, Dylan rehearsed all the songs. That's something he didn't like to do. Wexler wanted to just rehearse the rhythm section and record tracks without vocals, but Bob sang along every time they did a take, to the extent that Wexler said, "Bob, you're vocalizing too much. You have to hold off."

But they managed to find a chemistry that worked, and eventually did record tracks, and then remarkably got Dylan to come and overdub a lot of the vocals, as opposed to singing in the studio with the band. That, with the great musicians and with Wexler's vision, resulted in an album of great focus, and a very clear, beautiful sound.

Dettmar: Inviting Jerry Wexler and inviting Mark Knopfler to be part of the production, you don't do that if you're not looking for something rather different in the studio.

Zollo: Dylan said he didn't want to write these songs; he said these songs started to come out of him. He knew that his audience, and the world in general, would be baffled or even offended if he did these songs, so he wanted Carolyn Dennis or Helena Springs or another vocalist to do 'em. But then he realized, "No, these are my songs and I'm going to sing them." So I think he realized he's gonna need a special approach. He was really impressed by Jerry Wexler's work with great soul artists like Aretha Franklin and Percy Sledge. And apparently he'd heard Knopfler at the Roxy [club] with Dire Straits in Los Angeles. He was really impressed with Knopfler's clean, beautiful guitar lines. Then he wanted to do it at Muscle Shoals and use the Muscle Shoals horn section. That shows he had a very specific sound vision in mind for this.

Bream: Let's talk about Mark Knopfler's contributions to this album.
Zollo: I think Knopfler really plays off of Dylan's vocal in a great way, adding a lot of passion and grace to the lyrics, which are very pointed.
Dettmar: [To] go after Knopfler, it's one of the foundational decisions about the album. It suggests that he already, before the songs are even in place, recognizes that the blueprint for this album is something quite different.
Zollo: I agree. This was a very focused session, outside of Los Angeles, outside of his comfort realm, with musicians he hadn't worked with before.

These songs were all written at one time, on one subject, basically, and were very focused and were part of a collection. I think he was always thinking of these songs as a group. They're all biblical songs in some way.

Bream: Do you think a lot of this is the impact of Wexler being a real old-school pro?
Zollo: With Dylan, his job became: how do I make a record around this guy doing it like this, using Dylan's methods, which are never orthodox, and somehow creating an album anyway? Wexler said, "No, no, I don't want you to sing, Bob." I don't know of any other producers who ever did that with him. So clearly Wexler's working methods help keep the album focused.
Dettmar: It's hard to imagine anybody else being able to get away with that, too. He was very well established, very senior.

Bream: Let's talk about "Gotta Serve Somebody."
Dettmar: There's a way in which if it were a political song, rather than a song of faith, it's still true. That what you gotta serve is a boss or ideology or what have you. I'm kind of struck by how many of the songs—I don't mean this as a criticism at all—are ambiguous enough that they sort of both are but aren't insistently about faith issues. Sometimes, like in "I Believe in You," he's actually using the idiom of a pop song to talk about religious matters.
Zollo: The whole song is the same equation over and over: you may be this, you may be that, but at some point you're gonna have to make up your mind. And he's giving us basically two choices.
Dettmar: Those two choices are in that one repeated line: "It may be the devil or it may be the Lord."

Bream: What did you make of the line when he says, "And you can call me Zimmy," which I thought was kind of a sense of humor there?
Zollo: He's always used humor, and famously changed his name from Zimmerman to Dylan, and people accused him of being a liar in some ways, that he was hiding something. Here he's saying, "You can call me Zimmy, you can say I'm a Jew, you can say who I am or where I came from; it's not gonna change anything anymore." That name, at this point, is secondary to the bigger equation, which has to do with God.

Dettmar: It's based on a comedian called Ray Johnson who had this shtick. There was a Bud Light commercial: you can call me Ray, and you can call me, whatever. Dylan actually says, "You may call me R. J., you may call me Ray." So it like morphed into this quotation from a Bud Light commercial.

Bream: Let's talk about "Precious Angel."
Zollo: This is a song to a woman, a precious angel under the sun. He wrote a love song. Clearly that person was bringing this new understanding to Bob, the idea of, shine your light on me.
Dettmar: There are lots of songs in the history of pop that use the metaphor of an angel to talk about the girlfriend. The love object is an angel as she would be in "Teen Angel" or whatever pop song, but also sort of a spiritual actor who helps to connect him or remind him of beings outside of the earthly realm. He wants to kind of re-sacredize that metaphor that has become thoroughly secular through pop history. In the first verse, there are a couple of really bad lines or at least kind of unprocessed, fundamentalist speak like "now there's spiritual warfare." Some of that vocabulary just feels a little bit half-digested.
Zollo: It's about acceptance of belief and how a human deals with faith and ideas of belief. This song to a woman, it's the most overt Christian message of any of these songs. He's talking so specifically about Christ in this one.

Bream: "I Believe in You," is that a secular song? A spiritual song? Both?
Dettmar: Both, definitely. There's the song called "I Believe in You" on Neil Young's *After the Gold Rush*, which is 1970, though it's hard to believe that Dylan wouldn't know it. The Neil Young song is talking about a very human belief in another fallible human being. Dylan sort of takes that and says humans aren't worthy of belief; belief is for God. And the song kind of changes halfway through. You start out assuming that he's talking to a lover, and it kind of gradually, imperceptibly morphs into being God.
Zollo: I thought this song was directed to God from the first line. "They ask me how I feel, if my love is real." "If my love is real" makes it seem secular, but right away he says, "They want to drive me from this town, they don't want me around, because I believe in you." Which seems to me pretty clear that he's talking about his main belief in Christ. It just has such a beautiful melody and an unusual form in that there's no chorus. I think this one really sums up musically kind of the ecstasy he was feeling connecting with this new belief.

Bream: Let's talk about the title song "Slow Train."
Zollo: He's always been such a genius at showing us imagery and getting us to feel certain ways by showing us pictures, and this idea of the slow train coming, I think that was the ideal metaphor. It's like more than twice as long as a normal pop song. It's expansive brilliance.
Dettmar: Part of what people criticize the Christian albums for is that it was becoming a little too black and white again. But "the enemy I see wears a cloak of decency" in "Slow Train" sounds like mid-to-late '60s Dylan in a way. That kind of arch-political suspicion, bordering on paranoia. It doesn't feel like the vibe of the album overall.

That tendency to preach or to judge in earlier songs, it becomes a kind of Christian triumphalism here. But he doesn't see himself as being part of the problem he diagnoses. He's standing outside of it and sort of proscribing and judging. And people bridle at that.
Zollo: He already said, "The times they are a-changin'." And this, he was saying we're living in end times, or that the change is imminent. Previously the change was the cultural change and how America was changing. This is about the change coming to mankind.

Bream: This could lead us to the next song, "Gonna Change My Way of Thinking."

Zollo: "Change My Way of Thinking" is one song on the album that seems like it was written to himself, where a "Precious Angel," they're written out to the world, or "Slow Train."

Dettmar: There's a way in which the song suggests it's all about my own initiative and commitment and discipline, and that's not really the Gospel, with a capital *G*. That is about how you can't pull yourself up by your own bootstraps and the rules don't work, and you're gonna need something outside the system to save you.

Zollo: Part of this was Dylan getting this Christian and biblical imagery into a song which is the blues, and fusing the Bible and blues in a way that hadn't been done before.

Bream: "Man Gave Names to All the Animals" seems to have his first hint of reggae in one of his songs, but on the other hand, it seems to have kind of an eastern European, almost Jewish melody in there as well.

Zollo: The key is E minor and that is kind of almost a klezmer-like melody. And very simple. It's almost like a blues or a chant that repeats. Some people consider it may be Dylan's worst song. A lot of Dylan lovers just don't think this song should have been included. I'm not a biblical scholar, but this is an Old Testament idea, right; this is about the origin of the earth.

Some critics called this Dylan's Neil Diamond phase. After all, they did have the same manager, Jerry Weintraub.
Keith Baugh/Redferns/Getty Images

Dettmar: I just think it's bad writing. It could've been on Dylan's kids' album. If you were Dylan's age, there's something kind of fun about it. But it's just paper thin.

Zollo: It'd be a good song for the Sunday school class or the Bible class. I thought it was such an odd choice, on such a serious album, to include this song.

Bream: Let's talk about "When He Returns," which I guess in some ways seems most overtly about a messiah.

Dettmar: It seems like this has to be the closing track in some ways. I don't know how the album could return to any kind of equilibrium after this, because it is the most overtly doctrinaire song.

Zollo: My understanding is that he always intended it as the final track. He knew nothing could quite follow this song. It's stark. And I think musically, the one most like traditional gospel, too. For Dylan to summon up the passion and the ability to sing it as purely as he does is pretty remarkable.

This one's not ambiguous at all. "He's got plans of His own to set up His throne, When He returns." That's completely against the Jewish idea that the messiah never came the first time. This is very clearly Christian and waiting for the second coming.

CHAPTER 20

SAVED

with Wesley Stace and Ahmir "Questlove" Thompson

Released June 23, 1980

Producers: Jerry Wexler and Barry Beckett

**Recorded at Muscle Shoals Sound Studio
in Sheffield, Alabama**

All songs written by Bob Dylan, except where indicated.

**Session musicians: Tim Drummond (bass),
Regina Havis (backing vocals), Jim Keltner (bass),
Clydie King (backing vocals), Spooner Oldham
(keyboards), Fred Tackett (guitar), Mona Lisa Young
(backing vocals), Terry Young (keyboards).**

Slow Train Coming ended the 1970s on a high note for Dylan, selling well and garnering a lot of critical praise. Its hit single, "Gotta Serve Somebody," was honored with a Grammy Award for best male rock vocal performance, Dylan's first solo Grammy. In concert, things were bumpier, the singer getting flak both for declining to play his classics and extensively espousing his newfound beliefs in between song raps. And Dylan, gravitating toward the packed concert schedules that would dominate his professional activities for decades to come, was touring a lot, playing nearly eighty North American shows from November 1979 to May 1980.

During a break in the schedule, he fit in five days of recording in Muscle Shoals, Alabama, again to lay down his first album of the 1980s, *Saved*. Few Dylan LPs of the 1960s and 1970s had been similar to their predecessors, but *Saved* would in some ways be an exception. It was not only recorded in the same studio as *Slow Train Coming* but also used the same producers, Jerry Wexler and Barry Beckett. As even the title announced, it too would be informed by Dylan's religious interests and carry a gospel feel in much of its material.

Yet there were differences between the albums as well. Dylan enlisted entirely different musicians. Unusually for Dylan, he'd already played and refined the material in concert with these same musicians. If gospel had been a factor in *Slow Train*, on *Saved* it was even more upfront, both in the compositions and the arrangements. Somewhat controversially, the original cover depicted the hand of Jesus Christ reaching down to touch the hands of believers, though it was replaced in later pressings by a painting of Dylan in performance.

The biggest difference of all, however, was in its commercial and critical reception. *Saved* was not a hit, becoming his first album to miss the Top Twenty since 1964 (though, as was often the case, it did better in the UK, where it reached #3). Reviews were not nearly as positive either, both at the time and in retrospect. Michael Gray was especially pithy in *The Bob Dylan Encyclopedia* (2006), dismissing it as "the nearest thing to a follow-up album Dylan has ever made: a *Slow Train Coming II*, and inferior."

"I think *Saved* was badly reviewed because it's probably Dylan's last hundred-percent religious album," speculates singer-songwriter Wesley Stace, aka John Wesley Harding. "I think the old theology, rather than the record, is being badly reviewed. It does feel as though Dylan has written himself slightly into a corner. That slow train has been coming for ages, and then we get to *Saved*, and it's the past tense. He's already been saved."

Getting *Saved* is the task of **Wesley Stace**, a singer-songwriter who has released seventeen albums under the name John Wesley Harding and written four novels under his own name, and **Ahmir "Questlove" Thompson**, drummer for the Grammy-winning group The Roots; leader of the band for *The Tonight Show Starring Jimmy Fallon*; producer who has worked with Elvis Costello, Amy Winehouse, John Legend, and others; and author of the memoir *Mo Meta Blues: The World According to Questlove* (2013).

Bream: Ahmir, why do you feel so strongly about the *Saved* album?
Thompson: For some reason, I'm always attracted to what I later find out to be the most critically slogged work of someone's career. *Saved* came out when I was nine years old. In the 1980s, my parents became born-again Christians. So suddenly all they listened to was WZZD, this AM gospel station that played contemporary gospel music. *Slow Train Coming* and *Saved*, they were just bombarded into my head. He sang in such an animated voice. Dylan was like my favorite Muppet that never was.

Stace: I was at the King's School, Canterbury, in England. I knew a lot of what was in the Bible from studying, but also 'cause it was all around us. I didn't quite buy *Saved* the day it came out, but I bought it pretty soon afterward. And I was very, very receptive to its music.

At the time, even though I realized that it was being badly reviewed, I felt quite defensive of him. I felt quite like, no no no, give this guy a chance. There were songs in which he was saying stuff like, "Are you thinking for yourself or are you in with the pack?" And that appealed to me, too. Plus I've always thought it's a smokin' album musically. I love hearing that band play. Though it's not quite as neat and tidy as *Slow Train Coming*, it's a pretty exciting record.

Bream: *Saved* is the first time I'm aware of, other than in the early years when he did a couple folk songs in coffee houses, where he had played all these songs live before he recorded them.
Stace: So they had the arrangements already worked out on the road. They go to exactly the same people who made the previous

Dylan was chillin' at the 1980 Grammy Awards where he won his first solo Grammy for best male rock vocal performance for "Gotta Serve Somebody." *Ron Galella/WireImage/Getty Images*

The gospel according to Bob Dylan at Toronto's Massey Hall in 1980.
Peter Noble/Redferns/Getty Images

album like ten months earlier. He's back in the same studio, and he leaves four days later. I can't think of another one where you have an album made that quickly, with that exact number of songs. Everything he recorded at the sessions is on the record.

I think it's got two or three spectacular moments on it. There's that bit in "Saved" when he goes, [singing] "Saved by the blood of the Lamb, Saved," and then he just leaves it. He goes, "And I'm so glad" . . . and he just goes "How glad," and the backing singers, instead of him, go, "So glad." It's kind of like he's in a frenzy. It seemed like it's him demanding of the backup singers, and it reaches a little fever pitch.

Thompson: Just the whole gospel tradition of the Baptists' call and response and the moaning. I remember it well as a kid, but I didn't even draw a comparison to that, that he was really paying homage to the Southern tradition of fire and brimstone and gospel sound.

This particular album, I know it better than his whole catalog. I saw nothing wrong about it. [Critic] Robert Christgau voiced the average concern of Dylanologists, which was that no one wants to be preached to. It was a turn-off with the whole gospel, the soul sisters in the background.

Stace: But a key difference between *Slow Train Coming* and *Saved* is that on *Slow Train Coming* those gospel singers are given these very organized parts. On this album, they're just testifying and wailing. They're just freaking out and loving Jesus.

Slow Train Coming was a very successful album. *Saved* was not a successful album. He's already been saved, and he's offering some pretty stark choices to the listener. I can see that they are ideological problems, because just a few months before he made this album, or maybe a couple weeks afterward, he's preaching to people in his audience about how homosexuality is a legal thing. And how homosexual politics is ruining San Francisco. I don't dispute for a second there are problems with it, but what I don't really care about is whether it is therefore kind of cool or uncool to like the music.

I think to this day that the harmonica that he plays on "What Can I Do for You?" is the best Dylan can possibly be. The harmonica playing on that song was amazing. "Pressing On" has always been kind of my favorite song on the album, and then you get Dylan slaving away on the lead guitar. I think it must be Dylan because I can't believe that neat and tidy Fred Tackett would be playing that. And I've always loved "A Satisfied Mind." It just sounds like it's one of those great studio moments where he starts playing a song and everybody goes, "Oh yeah, we know that one; let's just play."

Thompson: I liked "Solid Rock." I wasn't at a place where I was digesting him as a poet or a prophet, a wordsmith or a genius. But this was the sort of thing that you don't hear in terms of gospel music. Compared to the other gospel that was also played on this radio station, songs like "Solid Rock," or even "Pressing On," aren't boring, mundane gospel music like the other contemporary gospel stuff.

Bream: Ahmir, how does this stack up as a gospel album?

Thompson: I see none of these tunes as gospel records. From a sonic point of view, I find a lot of contemporary Christian gospel music to be not that exciting, almost on a very yacht-rock level. I always felt that Dylan's Christian records—even with *Slow Train Coming*—it's an R&B record.

Stace: I could see why what Dylan was offering to this world, that I knew nothing about, could perhaps be very well served by the musician fervor of *Saved*. Because when Tim Drummond and Jim Keltner are playing the bass and drums together, that is a pretty exciting thing to hear. I love the bass and drums on "Saved" and on "Solid Rock." And although it will never be the greatest Dylan album, it's one that, at the time in my life that it hit me and ever since, I've been getting rewarded by in various ways.

I have no problems with its points of view. Dylan said all kinds of bizarre things in songs that I don't agree with. I also feel that Dylan was basically saying mostly kind of the same things for most of his career, but finding different linguistic language envelopes—discourses, I guess, is the phrase—to wrap himself up in. One was the kind of country/homey one that was *Nashville Skyline*; one was the crazy, druggy, kind of surreal one that was the mid-'60s; and one was the protest one. I see the biblical one as really the same kind of thing but using the language of the King James Bible, which was very familiar to him, and kind of tweaking little phrases this way and that.

I liked Bob Dylan being a Christian; I don't dislike it. I'm an atheist; I don't really care. I just like hearing him sing sometimes, and he does it pretty well on this album.

At that time, I was fifteen and very much thought I was thinking for myself by deciding that I liked *Saved*, when everybody else was saying it was shitty. If Bob Dylan released *Saved* today, it would be a beloved record, and probably proclaimed one of the greatest of his career. They'd be like, "This is a great old American poet. Listen to him sing like a bird, and his band playing, and he made it so quick and it's all about God. God love Bob Dylan; he's our savior."

When I was listening to Dylan singing "What Can I Do for You?" it really made me think, that's crazy, to hear this confident, on-his-own, out-on-a-limb artist going, "What can I do for you?" That really moved me when I was listening to *Saved*. To have had the weight of the world on your shoulders, and then just to go, "Fuck it, I give in for a little bit. I'm gonna listen to you. You can tell me what to say."

Bream: What did you think of the album cover?

Stace: It's a bloody record. He's saved by the blood of the Lamb, and the record has a bloody hand in every bit of that record. It's like the inside sleeve is red. Everything's red. His hair is red on the inside sleeve. And the cover, so offensive or weird or heavy to people, that it was actually withdrawn and replaced with a lesser sense of image.

Thompson: That imagery of the hand touching the people, that used to creep me out as a kid.

Bream: What are your favorite songs on *Saved* and why?

Thompson: "Solid Rock" was my favorite. Any of the more fire-and-brimstone, uptempo—"Saved," another one. I was drawn to the adrenaline. Hearing those songs, it was just energetic; it didn't sound like regular gospel music.

Stace: I love "Saved." But it's actually the tender songs that are very interesting. I really like "Covenant Woman," which is a little bit like "Precious Angel," and sung perhaps by the same person or something.

People just read *Saved* as though it's the album after *Slow Train Coming*, and of course it is that, but also it isn't just that. It's also part of Bob Dylan's ongoing life.

CHAPTER 21
SHOT OF LOVE

with Daniel Durchholz and Don McLeese

Released August 10, 1981

Producers: Bob Dylan, Chuck Plotkin,
and Bumps Blackwell

Recorded at Rundown Studios in Santa Monica,
California, and Clover Studios in Hollywood

All songs written by Bob Dylan.

Note: "The Groom's Still Waiting at the Altar," originally
the B-side to the single "Heart of Mine" and included
on the cassette release, was later inserted as track six
to the ten-track compact disc in 1985 and has been
included in all subsequent pressings.

Session musicians: Carolyn Dennis (backing vocals),
Steve Douglas (saxophone), Tim Drummond (bass),
Donald "Duck" Dunn (bass), Jim Keltner (drums), Clydie
King (backup vocals), Danny Kortchmar (guitar), Regina
McCrery (backing vocals), Carl Pickhardt (piano), Chuck
Plotkin (drums), Madelyn Quebec (backing vocals),
Steve Ripley (guitar), Willie Smith (organ), Ringo Starr
(drums/tom-tom), Fred Tackett (guitar), Benmont Tench
(keyboards), Ron Wood (guitar), Monalisa Young (vocals).

Opposite: Dylan's Christian crusade continued at Poplar
Creek amphitheater outside Chicago on June 10, 1981.
Paul Natkin/WireImage/Getty Images

As the 1980s got underway, Dylan was, for the first time since very early in his career, neither a hot commercial property nor looked to by critics and other performers as a cutting-edge artist. Punk, new wave, funk, and disco, none of which Dylan tapped into, were the major trends of the late 1970s and early 1980s; rap was on the horizon. *Slow Train Coming* had been a big hit while incorporating gospel music and religious themes, but 1980's *Saved*, with a similar if modified approach, hadn't been nearly as popular. And his tours of the period were criticized for their absence of songs from his pre-born-again phase.

On his West Coast tour in late 1980, Dylan started to admit a few classics from the past such as "Blowin' in the Wind," "Like a Rolling Stone," and "Mr. Tambourine Man" into his set again, though the shows remained dominated by his recent compositions. By the same token, his next album, *Shot of Love*, broadened its focus from Christian-gospel material to a wider canvas. Songs with a religious bent remained present, as the title alone of "Property of Jesus" confirmed. Yet there were also love songs and, in the oddest turn of all, a tribute to controversial comedian Lenny Bruce.

In addition, *Shot of Love*, unlike *Slow Train Coming* and *Saved*, would not be cut in Alabama's Muscle Shoals Sound Studio. Instead, the sessions took place in spring 1981 in Hollywood's

Clover Studios and Dylan's own Rundown Studio in nearby Santa Monica. While the core of *Saved*'s band was still backing Dylan up, others lent a hand as well. The production team changed, too, Dylan acting as co-producer with Chuck Plotkin, who had worked with Bruce Springsteen.

Shot of Love did not arrest Dylan's declining fortunes, peaking at #33 in the United States and faring better in the UK, where it made the Top Ten. That didn't stop leading British rock critic Nick Kent from slagging it as "Dylan's worst album to date" in the *New Musical Express*. "What we have on *Shot of Love* is journeyman's work," offered Lester Bangs in the *Village Voice*. "The trouble is that the material doesn't deserve more than a perfunctory reading. Most of the songs are sufficiently nondescript and inconsequential, you'll find yourself sitting around playing the name-that-stolen-riff game."

The critics "wouldn't allow the people to make up their own minds," complained Dylan in the liner notes to the 1985 *Biograph* box set. "All they talked about was Jesus this and Jesus that, like it was some kind of Methodist record. I don't know what was happening, maybe Boy George or something but *Shot of Love* didn't fit into the current formula. It probably never will. Anyway people were always looking for some excuse to write me off and this was as good as any."

St. Louis music critic and author **Daniel Durchholz**, introduced in Chapter 13, refuses to write off *Shot of Love* with **Don McLeese**, former music critic at the *Chicago Sun-Times* and the *Austin American Statesman*, senior editor at *No Depression*, and a professor at the University of Iowa, where he teaches a course on journalism and Bob Dylan.

Bream: Is this the end of the Christian trilogy, or the beginning of his move back to secular music, or a little of both?
McLeese: Obviously a little of both. When it came out, it was perceived as just another Christian album because we didn't know where he was going next. But it's obvious that some of those songs, particularly the love songs, can be read in either way. "Lenny Bruce" certainly isn't a conventional Christian hero, though Dylan paints him as some sort of martyr dying for our sins. I think it's different in retrospect than it was at the time. At the time, it was like, "Well we have lost Dylan; he's gonna be making these Christian albums forever," and you either put up with them or you don't. I love parts of all of these three albums and consider each of them to be better than some of the more highly regarded secular albums.

Durchholz: They've definitely gained a lot of strength in retrospect than they had when they came out. Some of these records have some of his most didactic songs and some of his worst singing. It was so weird for the guy who made many of us question authority in the first place, suddenly finds himself in a place where he was submitting to authority and basically telling everybody else that we had to do the same or basically go to hell. With *Shot of Love*, it took a while for everybody to realize that he was coming out of that a little bit, because there certainly are a lot of songs on the record that still lend themselves to that Christian phase. The way this record worked out, it does turn out to be a little of both.

McLeese: I think of this as kind of the [drummer] Jim Keltner album. In terms of a groove, it's an amazingly rhythmic album. Danny Kortchmar is very, very good on guitar on here. We associate him with all that laidback L.A. stuff, particularly the James Taylor stuff, but Kortchmar does a real job carrying this album.

One of the problems of lumping these three albums together is if you listen to *Slow Train Coming*, it is all Old Testament. It's all the God of wrath and judgment. *Shot of Love* is a real New Testament album, just the emphasis on love rather than judgment. Within

Dylan wanted Europeans to get "saved," as evidenced by his performance in Toulouse, France, on June 21, 1981.
DANIEL JANIN/AFP/Getty Images

this so-called spiritual phase or born-again phase or whatever you want to call it, there's real movement from the first album to the third album. Very different in tone.

Some of these songs are just going through my head all the time: "Heart of Mine," "Watered-Down Love," "The Groom's Still Waiting at the Altar," which they didn't even consider good enough to put on the album the first time through. What I remembered about this album was the framing. I remembered "Shot of Love," just how strong that was out of the box, and I remembered "Every Grain of Sand," which I think even at the time people thought this ranks with the top ten Dylan songs ever. So how can a guy have gone so far off track and still come up with an "Every Grain of Sand?" Nobody has written more great album closers than Bob Dylan.

I also think you can tell from listening to this album that Bob Dylan was listening to Bruce Springsteen. [Producer] Chuck Plotkin had worked with Bruce, and so there was a sound that was similar. Bob Dylan was listening to reggae. Bob Dylan was listening to Bob Marley. Bob Dylan had abdicated being at the center of the culture. People's attention went elsewhere. Dylan was aware of it, and I think this was one way of dealing with it. Not that one becomes a Christian because one is no longer topping the charts, but the fact that there are other values out there; there are other things my music can be used for. And I think that Dylan just occupied a different place in society.

Bream: Let's talk about "Property of Jesus," which seems to be a putdown for the nonbelievers.

McLeese: I guess it's a putdown, but I don't think it's any more caustic than, say, "Like a Rolling Stone" is. Dylan has had a certain amount of contemptuousness in his music, even before the so-called born-again phase. It's obviously drenched in irony—"You got something better, you've got a heart of stone." To me, it isn't the most ringing defense of Christianity. It's preaching to the choir, basically.

Durchholz: When Dylan picks an enemy, whether it's whoever he's addressing in "Positively 4th Street" or "Thin Man" or "Like a Rolling Stone," he's gonna come after you with guns fully blazing, and that's what he does here. But because religion is so overtly the topic of the song, and most of the album or part of the album, it comes off as being one of his more both righteous and self-righteous songs, sort of more of a piece with the songs that you find on *Saved*. But musically, it's a really strong track.

McLeese: It's got a great groove; it's got the call-and-response with the gospel chorus.

Bream: Let's talk about the title cut, "Shot of Love," which Dylan described as his, quote, "most perfect song—defines who I am spiritually, romantically, and whatever else."

McLeese: I don't think he would say that today. He must have said that sometime around the release of the album. I like the song. I also like the way that even though the shot of love is spiritual love, it could also be secular love. It's really got some punch to it. Structurally, it's a lot like "Gotta Serve Somebody." But "Gotta Serve Somebody" and that whole album, that was Old Testament; that was the God of wrath and judgment. This was New Testament. This is the God of forgiveness and love.

Durchholz: It's got the secular kind of love in there, too, where he's "And I don't wanna be with nobody tonight, Veronica's not here, Mavis just ain't right." Who I think possibly to be Mavis Staples.

McLeese: This doesn't exalt spiritual love on the one side and then put secular love someplace else. Somewhere it's all mixed together as love. I think that's the difference between this album and the two preceding ones.

Durchholz: I don't know how this happened, but he was casting about for producers, and somehow on this particular track he winds up in the studio with Bumps Blackwell, who produced Little Richard, among others. This track is really strong musically, and maybe for that reason, maybe from just being inspired.

Bream: Let's look at "Heart of Mine," which seems to be almost his most overt love song in years.

McLeese: It's Dylan at his most sophisticated in the structure of the song, in the chord changes, in the piano playing, which almost reminds me of Thelonious Monk—it is so angular. People tend to think of Dylan as three chords and borrowed folk melodies and stuff like that, and I think that "Heart of Mine" really shows a more sophisticated musicality than he is sometimes given credit for.

Durchholz: It's a really lively track, and part of the reason might be that he was just having fun with this. This is the track that got re-recorded for the album because Ringo Starr happened to be there. You got Ron Wood, you got Ringo, you got Duck Dunn, you got Smitty Smith playing the organ. It's kinda one of those things where the musicians were just getting together and jamming and having fun. And it's a little messy.

Also, in terms of it being messy, "Heart of Mine" has got a really bad mixed metaphor. There's one line where he says, "You can play with fire, but you'll get the bill." That's not exactly Dylan at his finest in terms of writing. And also, it's very clichéd—"if you can't do the time, don't do the crime."

Bream: What's "Lenny Bruce" doing on this album?

McLeese: "Lenny Bruce" is not only one of Dylan's strangest songs ever, it's many levels of strangeness. It's a song about a murder. Lenny Bruce is cast as a Jesus-like figure, but nobody would have confused Lenny with Jesus.

You can understand Dylan identifying with Lenny Bruce, but on one of his so-called Christian albums, Lenny Bruce is the thumb that sticks out.

Durchholz: The lyrics contain so many strange non sequiturs. That Lenny Bruce never won a Golden Globe, never made it to Synanon. Maybe it was kind of a throwaway that ultimately stuck. But it does feel like it has some deeper meaning, when he's saying stuff like "He was an outlaw, that's for sure, More of an outlaw than you ever were." I have a feeling that he's talking about himself in this song, or talking to himself. There's certainly lines that would refer to Dylan. "They stamped him and they labeled him like they do with pants and shirts. He fought a war on a battlefield where every victory hurts."

He was in this really curious place throughout this whole record and the process of making this record, whereas he seemed to be kind of still in this Christian phase, but also working his way out of it, for whatever reason.

McLeese: It could well just be that he said what he had to say. Perhaps he had been able to reconcile in his mind the secular and the spiritual in the way that he hadn't with *Slow Train Coming*. It was like, "If I don't sing songs that are specifically about serving God, then I'm not doing my job here on earth," or something. By this album, he was having some fun. He was loosening up, and he was blurring those distinctions.

Bream: What do you make of the album cover?

Durchholz: It's one of his worst album covers, after *Saved*.

McLeese: To me, it looks like a Roy Lichtenstein, and Lichtenstein had all these flashy cartoon-type graphics. It's certainly an album cover unlike any other of Dylan's. And it is explosive, and it does give a sense of that energy, particularly of the title cut. And in some ways, it's pretty playful. You look at this, and this looks like it's a real jolt to the system. Whether one finds it aesthetically pleasing or not, it definitely sticks out within Dylan's catalog.

Opposite: Copenhagen, Denmark, 1981.
Jan Persson/Redferns/Getty Images

CHAPTER 22
INFIDELS

with William McKeen and Paul Zollo

Released October 27, 1983

Producers: Bob Dylan and Mark Knopfler

Recorded at The Power Station in New York

All songs written by Bob Dylan.

Session musicians: Alan Clark (keyboards), Sly Dunbar (drums), Clydie King (backing vocals), Mark Knopfler (guitar), Mick Taylor (guitar), Robbie Shakespeare (bass).

There was never an official announcement or anything of the sort, but 1983's *Infidels* marked a return of Dylan to secular music, or at least material without overt Christian themes. Religious references had never been absent from his work and would continue to appear in the future. But on record, at least, most listeners viewed this as the end of his "born-again" phase, which had lasted three albums: 1979's *Slow Train Coming*, 1980's *Saved*, and 1981's *Shot of Love*.

In 1982 Dylan had one of the quietest years of his career, at least in terms of professional activity. There were no officially released new recordings, though he worked on an unreleased album of duets with backup singer Clydie King. His only live appearance was a brief cameo at an antinuclear rally. More than at any other time since beginning his career, he seemed in danger of slipping into irrelevance. When he started working on *Infidels* in New York in spring 1983, he'd use collaborators that put his tracks more in tune with the sound of 1980s popular music.

Coproducing was Mark Knopfler, now a superstar as the figurehead of Dire Straits; he had already played guitar with Dylan on *Slow Train Coming* and would double as a guitarist on the *Infidels* sessions. Also on guitar was Mick Taylor, who'd been a vital part of the Rolling Stones from 1969 to 1974. The biggest departure was the recruitment of Robbie Shakespeare on bass and Sly Dunbar on drums; as Sly & Robbie, they'd become Jamaican reggae's top rhythm section and production team. But while the sound on *Infidels* was slicker than it had been on Dylan's previous outings, it was hardly glossy. Having learned from *Slow Train Coming* that Dylan would move on to something else after two to three takes, Knopfler recorded the band live, even though studio technology was making that method of operating increasingly infrequent on rock recordings.

With more secular songwriting that even admitted political commentary of sorts on the slightly controversial "Neighborhood Bully" (which was widely interpreted as a pro-Israel statement) and "Union Sundown," *Infidels* was often hailed, not for the last time, as "the best Bob Dylan album since [fill in the blank]." *Blood on the Tracks* was the record *Rolling Stone* filled in that blank with, praising *Infidels* as "a stunning recovery of the lyric and melodic powers that seemed to have all but deserted him."

When outtakes from the *Infidels* sessions eventually circulated, some critics carped that some of the material passed over for release was as good or better than what was selected for the album, particularly in the case of "Blind Willie McTell" (which did finally get issued in 1991 on the first *Bootleg Series* installment). But while it didn't return him to the top of the charts, *Infidels* sold better than his final two Christian-themed LPs had and brought him in the MTV era with his first two videos, for "Sweetheart Like You" and "Jokerman." The album's more important purpose was restoring Dylan's credibility as a contemporary artist who still had much left to say.

With a few things to say about *Infidels* are **William McKeen**, professor of journalism at Boston University and the author of *Bob Dylan: A Bio-Bibliography* (1993), and singer-songwriter and journalist **Paul Zollo**, who was introduced in Chapter 19.

Bream: This was hailed as sort of a return to secular music for Dylan. Do you agree?

McKeen: On one level, it appeared that way, but I think there're a lot of his religious beliefs in the songs.

Zollo: Anytime you try to pin Dylan down, it's always a mistake. To say this is a Christian album and now this is a return to Judaism, this is secular, it never applies. It's all of the above. He's still talking about Satan, which is a very Christian idea, in "Man of Peace." And he's always blending both Testaments, and Christianity and Judaism, with all the other ancient religious symbols.

McKeen: And he blends in some Rastafarianism. That's what "I and I" comes from, I meaning self and God together.

Zollo: Without a doubt it's one of the best-sounding Bob Dylan albums, due in part to Mark Knopfler, who mostly produced it, though he didn't get to mix it 'cause he went on tour, and it got mixed by the engineer. But he assembled just an amazing band. It's one of the cleanest-sounding Dylan albums. Dylan recorded it the way he always did; he

William McKeen: "*Infidels* was probably where he started 'to look to lines from movies to sort of kick off his inspiration.'" *David Mcgough/DMI/The LIFE Picture Collection/Getty Images*

He may have been in his Christian period, but the bard from Minnesota was still welcomed into the Songwriters Hall of Fame on March 15, 1982. *The LIFE Picture Collection/Getty Images*

sang live with the band. But he actually was willing to come back and do some overdubs and sing some vocals over, which he had never done before. He used to regard that as sort of sacrilege, to even consider that.

I think he was inspired by playing with such great musicians, and his singing was focused, soulful, and great. *Infidels*, to me, is one of maybe the greatest frames ever for Dylan's songs. Part of it is that they had such sensitive guitarists and musicians. Dylan said so himself when he talked about Knopfler, that he played those leads without getting in the way of the words too much.

McKeen: I think back on the gospel trilogy, particularly *Slow Train Coming* and then *Saved*.

He's got so much to say, he can barely pack it all in the songs on *Infidels*. Whereas in *Slow Train Coming* and *Saved* he was kind of saying the same thing, not necessarily over and over, but without a lot of complexity.

"Sweetheart Like You," it's got that sort of angry political statement in the middle. It's got the reference [to] the father's house with many mansions. Then just to piss off even more people, he says, "A woman like you should be at home, that's where you belong." He's attacking, or at least irritating, everybody with that song, but yet it's a great song.

Bream: Let's talk about "Neighborhood Bully."
Zollo: It's striking that so many great American songwriters—from Irving Berlin to Harold Arlen, Gershwin on—have been Jews, but rarely write about the Jewish experience. And Dylan rarely has, but this, he embraces it head-on, and I think brilliantly. And it's so relevant to consider what's going on right at the moment. "The neighborhood bully just lives to survive, criticized and condemned for being alive. He's not supposed to fight back, supposed to have thick skin. He's supposed to lay down and die when his door is kicked in. And he's the neighborhood bully." I don't think it's ever been written about in a more powerful way.
McKeen: I was aware of the political overtones in "Neighborhood Bully," but the thing I like is the way the band cooked on that song, the slide guitar and everything like that. That's one of the reasons *Infidels* was so satisfying. It's a very interesting album on a lyrical level, 'cause there's so many things going on, lots of wordplay and lots of songs that appear to be a bunch of different ideas put together. At the same time, you can kind of tune that out and just enjoy the music.

There is so much great craft in this album. This seemed to me to be an effort to nonaggressively get back the old audience, 'cause a lot of the audience left him during the gospel years. I think he was deciding that he needed to be a little bit backed away from spiritual music. And the way to do that was to make this real blasting piece of rock 'n' roll that struck me as kind of a *Highway 61* sort of album, in terms of the whole sound.
Zollo: Unlike the previous albums, which reflected his faith and his conflicting ideas about faith, he talks about himself on this album. "Don't Fall Apart on Me Tonight," there's that great line about "You feel like you're stuck inside a painting, hanging in the Louvre." That shows how Dylan's been framed and is considered iconic, and how strange it is to be a man and yet be an icon or be a myth.

Bream: Let's talk about "License to Kill."
Zollo: It's remarkable, and it has one of his most unusual and mysterious lines. So many of these lines, we can draw 'em to ancient mythology or books of the Bible. "Man has invented his doom, First step was touching the moon." That's a foreboding line that our technology and our ability to reach the moon has led to our ultimate doom.

Bream: Do you think he was referring to wasting our time with space travel?
Zollo: I don't know if it's space travel specifically, or just that we are devoting our attention in the wrong direction. We're putting so much effort toward certain technologies that aren't gonna help man, where we're ignoring others.
McKeen: We have such a hard-on for technology that we're forgetting about our humanity. I don't think he would ever be so unsubtle as to just make it a shot at the space program. [He] kinda predicts how we are today, where you walk around and you see everybody staring at this little device in their hand and not talking to each other.
Zollo: This is also a song about sending soldiers overseas to kill people and giving them license to kill, and then "burying them with stars and selling their bodies like they do used cars." There's nothing too obvious about this song. He's covering a lot of bases.

Bream: Let's talk about "Union Sundown."

Zollo: Bob proudly came from the tradition of Woody Guthrie. Folk music and unions went hand in hand. But he looked at how the unions had shifted, so it's a sundown on the union. It's about greed.

McKeen: A terrific piece of rock 'n' roll, brilliantly played and all that—but when you think about the lyrical context of it, and where he came from, I thought it was a very brave statement to make. Because he knew it was gonna offend so many people. I recall some critic saying, "Well he sounds like a cranky conservative." I thought, *Well not really, he just sounds like Bob Dylan.*

Zollo: It could be a very boring folk song if not done right, but he made it rock, which makes it great.

"Union Sundown" is very much about today, as is "License to Kill." "Neighborhood Bully" about Israel. None of it seems dated. Even when he wrote very timely songs, he infused them with a timelessness, so those songs still last.

When I consider that we started with, "Is it a secular album?" The song "Man of Peace," I think, could have been on any of the Christian albums; it would have fit right in. It's a very Christian song about how Satan can come as a man of peace.

Bream: "Don't Fall Apart on Me Tonight" sort of continues the Dylan tradition of having a quieter, softer song to close the album, and also one that kind of gives a hint at what might come next.

Zollo: Again, it's directed toward a woman, a love interest. "Just a minute before you leave, girl"—it starts so conversational. Just like, you got a lot of nerve to say you were my friend. But right away he gets into Dylan territory, and even slightly Christian: "But these streets are filled with vipers, who've lost all ray of hope. It's not even safe no more, in the palace of the Pope." Written not long after the Pope had been shot. So right away he starts with a very narrow focus and widens it.

McKeen: Whenever I run into one of those assholes who says Bob Dylan can't sing, I think this is one of those songs I'd put on and say, "Oh yeah? Well listen to this." 'Cause I think the singing on that song is masterful.

Zollo: People think of him for his explosive poetry, but this is such an intimate lyric. And the sense of regret in this song—"Maybe I'd have saved some life that had been lost, Maybe I'd have done some good in the world, instead of burning every bridge I crossed." So much regret, thinking that he hasn't accomplished much. Or his idea that "I made shoes for everyone and I'm still barefoot." This idea that he's accomplished so much and yet he's still destitute in some ways.

Bream: What about "Jokerman"?

Zollo: I always felt that "Jokerman" was about himself, that he's the Jokerman, similar to the Tambourine Man.

McKeen: I always thought that the Jokerman was Jesus.

Zollo: It's a Cubist song in that you can see it from many angles, and it has many different aspects and reflections. "Jokerman" probably encompasses a multitude of people and personalities.

Bream: Anything else you want to say about *Infidels*?

McKeen: I'd give it an eighty-five 'cause I can dance to it.

Zollo: It's lost none of its power for me, unlike a lot of albums from the past that I listened to. Maybe his best-sounding studio album of all time. And his genius is just so reflected throughout every one of these songs. Even given the exclusion of some famous ones, I think it remains one of his greatest albums.

Opposite: Dylan schmoozed with singer and TV star Dinah Shore at the 13th Annual Songwriters Hall of Fame induction dinner. *Bettina Cirone/IMAGES/ Getty Images*

CHAPTER 23

EMPIRE BURLESQUE

with Alex Lubet and Don McLeese

1. Tight Connection to My Heart
   (Has Anybody Seen My Love) 5:22

2. Seeing the Real You at Last 4:21

3. I'll Remember You 4:14

4. Clean Cut Kid 4:17

5. Trust Yourself 3:29

6. Emotionally Yours 4:30

7. When the Night Comes Falling from the Sky . . . 7:30

8. Something's Burning, Baby 4:54

9. Dark Eyes 5:07

Released June 10, 1985

Producers: Bob Dylan and Arthur Baker

Recorded at Delta Sound Studios in New York, Cherokee Studios in Los Angeles, and the Power Station in New York

All songs written by Bob Dylan.

Session musicians: Roy Bittan (keyboards), Peggy Blu (backing vocals), Deborah Byrd (backing vocals), Mike Campbell (guitar), Chops (horns), Alan Clark (synthesizer), Carolyn Dennis (backing vocals), Sly Dunbar (drums), Howie Epstein (bass), Anton Fig (drums), Bob Glaub (bass), Don Heffington (drums), Ira Ingber (guitar), Bashri Johnson (percussion), Jim Keltner (drums), Stuart Kimball (guitar), Al Kooper (guitar), Queen Esther Marrow (backing vocals), Vince Melamed (synthesizer), John Paris (bass), Ted Perlman (guitar), Madelyn Quebec (second vocals), Richard Scher (synthesizer), Carl Sealove (bass), Robbie Shakespeare (bass), Mick Taylor (guitar), Benmont Tench (keyboards), Urban Blight Horns (horns), Little Steven Van Zandt (guitar), David Watson (saxophone), Ronnie Wood (guitar).

The early- to mid-1980s were among the less active periods of Dylan's career. He took a near-total break from live performance between late 1981 and his mid-1984 six-week European tour, on which he shared bills with Carlos Santana. It wasn't his most prolific era for writing and recording, either, but he kept at it, starting work on his follow-up to *Infidels* shortly after the European tour ended. *Empire Burlesque* would be among Dylan's most drawn-out album productions, spanning both coasts and more than six months.

In the first two decades in which Dylan recorded with other musicians in the studio, he'd generally favored working mostly or exclusively with one or two groups of players. *Empire Burlesque* was more typical of the way in which many rock records had come to be constructed by the mid-1980s, however, in its use of a large crew.

Work commenced in July 1984 at New York's Delta Sound Studios and would continue at several other facilities in New York and Los Angeles. The album was mostly produced by Dylan himself, but in the biggest departure of all from his previous work, he engaged Arthur Baker to produce the final session and extensive overdubs in March 1985. Baker was hot for his work on dance records and Afrika Bambataa's "Planet Rock," as well as dance remixes of hits by Springsteen and Cyndi Lauper.

Unsurprisingly, some listeners and critics saw *Empire Burlesque* as Dylan's attempt to make his sound more contemporary. It wasn't just fans who had mixed feelings about the approach; longtime associate Jim Keltner "was very, very disappointed" to find his drum track replaced with a drum machine on "Trust Yourself," as he acknowledged in Howard Sounes' biography *Down the Highway: The Life of Bob Dylan* (2011). Dylan's use of dialogue from vintage movies in his lyrics did not go unnoticed, and overall the record had a lukewarm response, missing both the US Top Thirty and the UK Top Ten. Even a positive *Time* magazine review was qualified in its praise, calling it "a record of survival and a tentative kind of triumph."

Dylan did not tour in the album's wake, though he kept his profile up in 1985 with performances at the Live Aid and Farm Aid benefits; a guest appearance on the "We Are the World" single raising funds for Ethiopian famine relief; and playing on Artists United Against Apartheid's protest single "Sun City." He also released videos for four songs from *Empire Burlesque*. And at the end of the year, Dylan's career-spanning five-disc *Biograph*, mixing highlights of his catalog with unreleased material, became the first such archival boxed set for a major rock artist.

Don McLeese, a veteran music critic, professor, and author introduced in Chapter 21, explores *Empire Burlesque* with **Alex Lubet**, a singer-songwriter and professor of music at the University of Minnesota in Minneapolis, where he teaches classes on Bob Dylan.

Bream: Don, you interviewed Dylan about this time.
McLeese: He was about to embark on this tour with Tom Petty and the Heartbreakers. Originally they were only going to go to Australia and New Zealand. He said that he was going to New Zealand because he wasn't sure the people in the States were even that interested in him anymore. This would have been after *Empire Burlesque*, and him perceiving that it had not been this huge breakthrough. It had not lived up to whatever expectations were. And I think *Empire Burlesque* is a fascinating album, just because of the way that it shows Bob Dylan trying to figure out what a Bob Dylan album should be like.

Bream: What do you think set this album apart from other Dylan albums?
Lubet: The production style is extremely different. It comes in the cluster of albums that people tend not to like so highly, with *Down in the Groove* and *Knocked Out Loaded*. It's quite different from those albums in that it doesn't have cover songs on it. For me, there are potentials on the album, and I think, what could have been done to have allowed it to live up to some potentials? There are lyrics that even I could have written. But I think there are some genuinely really good songs, some of which are masked by the production, some of which actually managed to eat through the production.
McLeese: We're still coming out of a disco era, so there is an emphasis on rhythm throughout at least half of these tracks. Booming drums that you associate so much with arena rock of the '80s.

There is a real attempt here to make a big album, a big Bob Dylan album. You've got one former Rolling Stones guitarist on it, you've got one current Rolling Stones guitarist on it, you've got members of the Heartbreakers on it. You've got this big sound. You've got "When the Night Comes Falling," which I think everybody wanted to see as a big Dylan song, like the old big Dylan songs. The highs are higher than they are on *Infidels*. But I also think that it's much more of a grab-bag album. It doesn't necessarily seem like these songs flow together or cohere together. The highlights go in different directions, whereas *Infidels* is all of a piece.

Dylan's comments at the Live Aid hunger benefit for Ethiopia in July 1985 sparked Farm Aid, a benefit for US family farmers, where he joined Tom Petty and the Heartbreakers on September 22, 1985 at the University of Illinois. *Paul Natkin/ WireImage/Getty Images*

Opposite: The man in the long black coat rocked London's Wembley Stadium in July 1984. *Michael Putland/Getty Images*

Lubet: *Infidels* has one band; it was recorded in a coherent set of sessions. This album apparently took more studio time than any other album Dylan's ever made, or close to it. It also had more overdubs, I think, than just about any other album that Dylan has ever made. Genre-wise, it's kind of all over the place.

McLeese: I don't think that we can divorce the recording process from the time. Anything that was aiming for arenas was that big, elaborate, overdubbed, computerized sort of sound. I think Bob Dylan was honestly trying to make a place for himself in that world, while still being Bob Dylan.

Lubet: I think people need to cut him a little slack on being interested in other music that was happening around him and wanting to be involved with it, instead of looking at that as being some kind of sellout. Although he's moved past the born-again lyrics, there're certainly elements of that sound that stayed with him for a while; I'm thinking, in particular, of the backup singers.

McLeese: The backup singers and the organ. Definitely. There's a lot of gospel on this album.

Lubet: I think of him as also trying to be kind of a soul man. There are a couple of songs where he really wants to be a soul singer. One of my very favorite Dylan songs is on this album, and it's one where the production more or less works. It's "Emotionally Yours." It's not a heavyweight song, but it's a beautiful love song.

Dylan does some great singing on the album, too. He's right there with his inflections and his occasional Minnesota drawl. Unfortunately, the remixing really hurts that.

McLeese: On this album, you do have the soul singer singing against the syncopation. You have "Clean Cut Kid," which probably could have worked as a bluesy shuffle on *Highway 61*. You have "Dark Eyes," which is a totally different voice from Dylan, and it's totally different than anything on the album. It upholds Dylan's long tradition of using that last song not only as a strong summary but a jumping point for something that might come next.

Perhaps this song serves as a critique of what some people have seen as these excesses of what has come before.

Bream: Are you convinced by this album that Dylan has returned to secular music?
McLeese: Those who make that absolute distinction between secular and spiritual are totally missing the boat on Dylan. Even this album, which sets itself out as a secular album, if you look at the lyrics to the opening song on the album, it's "Never could learn to drink that blood and call it wine." So here's Dylan remarking specifically on the Christian ritual of communion. There are other instances throughout here where he's bringing that stuff up. And maybe not affirming it, maybe breaking with it there, but at least invoking it.

The sound of this album, thirty years down the road, is problematic. There are some songs on here that are beyond redemption. If I never listened to "Never Gonna Be the Same Again," that'd be fine. But there's other stuff there that's really crisp. "Clean Cut Kid," that works. "Trust Yourself," which also has to be heard as some sort of commentary on the so-called born-again period; that works. It's got a gospel chorus to it, it's got an uptempo rhythm, it's got very straightforward lyrics. Cuts like that are timeless on here.

I get the feeling that Bob Dylan saw this world out there that he was preparing to reenter. He was trying to reach a younger audience that hadn't necessarily got into the myth of Dylan, and many of whom, if they thought of him at all, thought of him as a religious crank. He's working with a hot remix guy, and he's teaming up with Tom Petty and the Heartbreakers, which was just great. The interplay was very similar to that with The Band. He had to experiment with this and see how far he could capitulate and still be Bob Dylan. And that's Arthur Baker, videos, synthesizers, and

having every track on the album have kind of a different backing band and perhaps a different feel.

These days, Dylan would not make another album like *Empire Burlesque*. Dylan has refound himself and discovered what process works for him.

Lubet: That production goes along with songs that have more chord changes, and sometimes more complex forms, than a lot of earlier material. Some of the songs have wonderful melodies and wonderful chord changes, and they don't match up with the lyrics. There's kind of a musical complexity about *Empire Burlesque* that backfires for many, many people, but he shows that he knows a lot of stuff that people didn't necessarily think that he had.

Bream: "Emotionally Yours" and "I'll Remember You" are two of the most direct songs on the album.
Lubet: I would rank "Emotionally Yours" much, much higher than "I'll Remember You." They are very direct. To pull "Emotionally Yours" out of his output and say that this is a very, very simple love song is to me unfair. "Make You Feel My Love," for instance, is also a pretty simple but wonderful love song.
McLeese: It's among the more conventional songs, but I think that there's a lot of songs on here that are really direct, and then some that aren't. I mean "Clean Cut Kid" is very direct.

Bream: He's sung a lot of antiwar songs over the years, but that one is specific about the Vietnam war.
Lubet: Absolutely.

Bream: Some people point out the passages from "Dark Eyes" came from a Humphrey Bogart movie and something from a Star Trek dialogue.
Lubet: There are movie references other places in the album. In a way, this album kinda kicks off that wave of Dylanology where people start looking really hard to find the borrowings.
McLeese: He's always been a magpie. I don't know where the melody from "Dark Eyes" is from, but I'm sure you could find it pretty quickly, and I'm sure that Dylan didn't write it.

Bream: I saw Bob Christgau's statement about *Empire Burlesque*, and he said, "It's the best Dylan album since *Blood on the Tracks*, but I wish it were a bigger compliment."
McLeese: We have to acknowledge that *Empire Burlesque* had very mixed reviews. In Britain, they didn't like *Empire Burlesque* at all. Michael Gray still says it's just a piece of rubbish. *Rolling Stone* praised it to the heights. Dave Marsh, former *Rolling Stone* music review editor, thought it was brain-dead. A lot of it depended on your expectations; each of us had to ask for ourselves, "What do we want from a Dylan album at this point? What can we expect from a Dylan album? What will we settle for in a Dylan album?"

CHAPTER 24

KNOCKED OUT LOADED

with Gary Graff and Joel Selvin

1. You Wanna Ramble (Little Junior Parker) 3:14
2. They Killed Him (Kris Kristofferson) 4:00
3. Driftin' Too Far from Shore (Bob Dylan) 3:39
4. Precious Memories
   (traditional, arranged by Bob Dylan) 3:13
5. Maybe Someday (Bob Dylan) 3:17
6. Brownsville Girl (Bob Dylan/Sam Shepard) . . . 11:00
7. Got My Mind Made Up (Bob Dylan/Tom Petty) . . . 2:53
8. Under Your Spell (Bob Dylan/Carole Bayer Sager) 3:58

Released July 14, 1986

Producer: Bob Dylan

Recorded at The Church Studios in London, Skyline Studios in Topanga Canyon, California, and Sound City Studios in Van Nuys, California

Session musicians: Mike Berment (steel drums), Peggie Blu (background vocals), Majason Bracey (background vocals), Clem Burke (drums), T-Bone Burnett (guitar), Mike Campbell (guitar), Carolyn Dennis (background vocals), Steve Douglas (saxophone), Howie Epstein (bass), Anton Fig (drums), Lara Firestone (background vocals), Pamela Quinlan (background vocals), Milton Gabriel (steel drums), Keysha Gwin (background vocals), Don Heffington (drums), Muffy Hendrix (background vocals), April Hendrix-Haberlan (background vocals), Ira Ingber (guitar), James Jamerson Jr. (bass), Dewey B. Jones II (background vocals), Phil Jones (conga), Al Kooper (keyboards), Stan Lynch (drums), Steve Madaio (trumpet), Queen Esther Marrow (background vocals), Larry Mayhand (background vocals), John McKenzie (bass guitar), Vince Melamed (keyboards), Larry Meyers (mandolin), Angel Newell (background vocals), Herbert Newell (background vocals), John Paris (bass),

Bryan Parris (steel drums), Al Perkins (steel guitar), Tom Petty (guitar, backing vocals), Crystal Pounds (background vocals), Raymond Lee Pounds (drums), Madelyn Quebec (background vocals), Cesar Rosas (guitar), Vito San Filippo (bass), Carl Sealove (bass), Patrick Seymour (keyboards), Jack Sherman (guitar), Daina Smith (background vocals), Maia Smith (vocals), Medena Smith (background vocals), Dave Stewart (guitar), Benmont Tench (keyboards), Annette May Thomas (background vocals), Damien Turnbough (background vocals), Ronnie Wood (guitar), Chyna Wright (background vocals), Elisecia Wright (background vocals), Tiffany Wright (background vocals).

In February 1986, Dylan began his first tour in some time with concerts in New Zealand, Australia, and Japan. Backing him were Tom Petty and the Heartbreakers, stars in their own right and the most highly regarded backup unit he'd employed since he'd worked with The Band. They would tour North America for a couple months in the middle of the year, as well as playing on some of Dylan's next album, *Knocked Out Loaded*, much of which was recorded in the break between tour jaunts.

In the middle of all this, Dylan secretly got married to Carolyn Dennis, one of his backup singers since 1978. The marriage didn't become public knowledge until 2001 when Howard Sounes reported it in *Down the Highway: The Life of Bob Dylan*. The author also explained that the couple had a daughter, Desiree, born in January 1986, but had divorced in 1992.

But, in 1986, fans were paying more attention to Dylan's new songwriting collaborators because *Knocked Out Loaded* had a mixture of Dylan compositions, Dylan collaborations, and cover tunes. One song apiece was written with Petty, playwright Sam Shepard, and, in the most unlikely pairing, hit pop songwriter Carole Bayer Sager. His trio of cover choices was as wide-ranging as his choice of writing partners, including bluesman Junior Parker's "You Wanna Ramble," country star Kris Kristofferson's "They Killed Him," and the traditional gospel hymn "Precious Memories."

It's not uncommon for albums to be cobbled together from numerous sessions that might not all have been intended for the final record. *Knocked Out Loaded*, however, was for a Dylan record an unusual patchwork, taking one track from November 1985 sessions in London; three, all covers, from spring 1986 recordings made in Topanga Canyon near Los Angeles; and a final song, "Got My Mind Made Up," done in Van Nuys (also near L.A.). Most unusually of all, three outtakes from *Empire Burlesque* were retrieved to fill out a disc that, at thirty-six minutes, wasn't exactly one of Dylan's longer outings.

The impression was that the final result lacked coherence and identity, although the eleven-minute collaboration with Shepard, "Brownsville Girl," was often singled out as a highlight on an otherwise uninspiring collection. Even Dylan conceded to *Rolling Stone*, "It's all sorts of stuff. It doesn't really have a theme or purpose. . . . If the records I'm making only sell a certain amount anyway, then why should I take so long putting them together?"

His indifference was echoed by *Rolling Stone*'s review, Anthony DeCurtis finding the album "ultimately a depressing affair, because its slipshod, patchwork nature suggests that Dylan released this LP not because he had anything in particular to say but to cash in on his 1986 tour. Even worse, it suggests Dylan's utter lack of artistic direction." Adds longtime San Francisco Chronicle rock critic Joel Selvin, "We're used to Dylan and his indifferent recordings, but this was egregiously indifferent."

This "egregiously indifferent" album will be discussed by **Gary Graff**, a veteran music critic from Detroit who writes for *Billboard*, the *New York Times*, and other publications, and the "egregiously indifferent" commentator **Joel Selvin** himself, the longtime music critic of the *San Francisco Chronicle* and author of numerous music-related books.

Bream: When *Knocked Out Loaded* came out, what did you think of the album?
Graff: I didn't find it awful, but I was expecting something really good. I thought the guy was in a groove, and I thought the potential was there for an upper-echelon Dylan album. When I saw him play with Petty and the Heartbreakers, he was really inspired, and I figured that had to be wearing off or making its mark on him in the studio. What we got felt like an odds and sods.
Selvin: Other than "Brownsville Girl," it just seemed instantly forgettable. Until I got this assignment, I don't think I'd listened to the record since I put it back after reviewing it.

Graff: "Brownsville Girl" is more memorable as an event than a piece of music. It's kind of engaging as a piece of music, but I think "kind of" is the operative term there.

Selvin: It's not his most successful epic. But it stood out as something that was like at least on his pay grade.

Graff: I hate the vocal performances. The material is just terrible.

Selvin: It doesn't hold up at all. You gotta wonder what sort of impetus there was behind it. It doesn't feel like an album that had to be, at all.

Graff: It had actually begun life as kind of a Chicago blues album. "You Wanna Ramble" being indicative of, I guess, of where he was going with that. He started out doing that, and then somewhere along the line just decided not to, and instead came up with this.

The only unifying thing is the use of female backing singers. They're not just doing background vocals, they are kind of responsive and complementary to what he does. That may be its sole conceptual success.

Selvin: How did you like the children's choir on "They Killed Him"?

Graff: I thought it was hokey. I think "They Killed Him" is a really good Kris Kristofferson song, but this thing Dylan did with it on this album, it's so Teflon and kind of polished and slick. There's no emotional resonance to it.

Selvin: We're accustomed to Dylan tossing off songs without any great conviction. In this case, this is just like there is no real sincere vocal performance on the album. He just doesn't even inhabit the songs at all. You mentioned the Chicago blues thing. That's surprisingly flaccid and weak. Everything's lined up on the line, and they have that heavily compressed drum sound. This feels like the most uncrafted of his albums, and there's just no sense of there being any artistic motivation behind it.

Graff: Maybe the one he sounds most committed to is this "Driftin' Too Far from Shore," which is like his '80s dance-pop moment—and the song he's performed the most from the album over the years, which is another thing I find kind of shocking and egregious, too, 'cause it's obviously garbage.

Selvin: I thought the vocal performance on that was overly mannered. It's essentially just an old hymn book thing that he redecorated.

Graff: I think Dylan spent a good deal of the '80s uncharacteristically trying to please people. "Driftin' Too Far from Shore" is another example of trying to fit in. Once he came back from the born-again period, I think on many of the albums there are all sorts of nods that Dylan wanted to belong and was looking for a way to be part of the mainstream rock discussion of the time. Dylan was eager to please, or trying to find a way to please more than he had in the past.

Selvin: Clearly he was out of touch with that gestalt he'd been on top of. It had been taken away from him by people like Tom Petty. When he was doing the *Infidels* album, which was his first sort of post-Christian thing, he was taking direction from the Bill Graham Management people, and they were trying to steer him into some sort of radio-friendly thing, as if they knew. They kept pointing to the recent success of Santana, who'd been on the charts with "Winning." You know, "Gotta do something like that, Bob."

He lost touch with his inner creative geography. He was productive but guilty of plagiarizing, rewriting, recycling, indifferent, sloppy work. Those are all the things that make Dylan so fascinating to us; he can encompass these tremendous achievements and also do hack work. He's out of touch with himself as an artist, as a musician. He has no sense of self.

Bream: Do you think that's why maybe he leaned on people like Carole Bayer Sager, which seems like such an outlier for him as a song collaborator?

Selvin: As I understand, the story on that is that Carole Bayer Sager wrote the title. And she was surprised to find out that she was a collaborator on a Dylan song.

Opposite: Joel Selvin: "My sense of the Petty collaboration [on tour] was that Bob was holding on for dear life up there."
Ebet Roberts/Redferns/Getty Images

Graff: More than a songwriter, I really think Carole Bayer Sager is a craftsperson in music. With my theory about him being eager to please at this point in his career, it would make sense that he would say, "Okay, this is somebody who's hitting the home runs now. Maybe I ought to, one way or another, see what she's doing, and try to understand that."

Selvin: This song was a product of him meeting her at a party and overhearing this title. With all due respect, Gary, I don't see Dylan being fascinated by a slick pop songwriter like Carole Bayer Sager. This is a gal who wrote "A Groovy Kind of Love" and collaborated with her husband Burt Bacharach on those horrible Neil Diamond records. I don't see her striking a chord with Dylan.

Graff: The Petty collaboration "Got My Mind Made Up," is another great disappointment on this album. We all thought that, after being together on tour, they could have come up with something better.

Bream: If you look at the vast array of musicians he has, from Clem Burke from Blondie and Anton Fig from Letterman and Ron Wood and Dave Stewart, it's like he's trying everyone who had a minute or two of success in the '80s.

Graff: But it never seems like he really got their flavor, except maybe for "Driftin' Too Far from Shore." Even then, it had the approach, but he never really got the flavor. You listen to that keyboard part and it's like, couldn't you have gotten an engineer or somebody who knew how to really get that sound that the Eurythmics had or the Thompson Twins had, or whatever it was Dylan was trying to get there? It sounds like he wanted it, but didn't want to go get it.

Selvin: Lot of raw tracks, very few overdubs, highly compressed drums, and a lot of EQ on the guitars. A real sort of standard rock band demo from the era. No imagination. If you're gonna try and dial in that kind of a sound, you'd think he'd spend some time mixing it. And it's very clearly not well mixed.

Graff: It sounds recorded rather than produced.

Selvin: Knocked off. And not with any great imagination by the musicians involved, who've all played on much more interesting records and should know better than playing that kind of hackneyed, rote stuff.

Bream: One arrangement that sounds different to me is "Precious Memories."

Selvin: Oh, the bogus reggae thing. That was already a bad cliché. He tried that reggae thing again with "People Get Ready," the Curtis Mayfield song that he did on the movie soundtrack to *Flashback* [1990] with Dennis Hopper. He was fascinated by it. But this is like ten, fifteen years too late to be cool.

Graff: It's almost like he didn't have any better idea about how to arrange it.

Selvin: Mediocre idea, poorly executed.

Bream: Is this the worst Dylan album?

Selvin: Bob's made a lot of bad albums. That's okay. Bad albums are a product of trying to do great albums. Bob Seger's probably never made a bad album; he's never made a great one either. He makes a lot of good albums. Whether this is the worst Dylan album or not, there's plenty of competition.

Graff: I certainly think this is in the bottom ten. I don't know if it's the very worst, but it's definitely down there. It's not an album that gets returned to or will get returned to. If it wasn't for "Brownsville Girl" and Sam Shepard being involved in it, I don't think it's an album that would ever be commented upon.

Opposite: Gary Graff: "There's no engagement and no conceptual unity to *Knocked Out Loaded*." Ebet Roberts/ Redferns/Getty Images

CHAPTER 25

DOWN IN THE GROOVE

with Stephen Thomas Erlewine and Alan Light

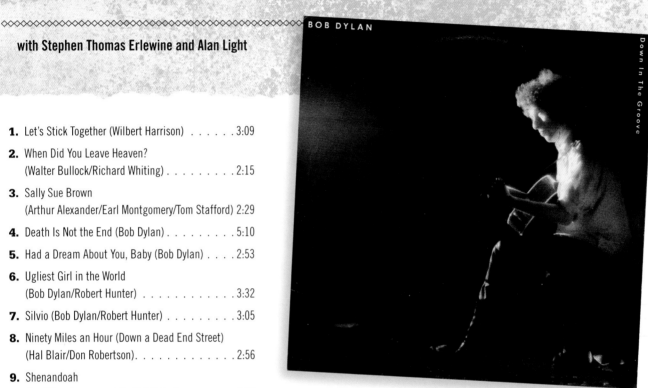

BOB DYLAN

Down In The Groove

1. Let's Stick Together (Wilbert Harrison) 3:09

2. When Did You Leave Heaven?
   (Walter Bullock/Richard Whiting) 2:15

3. Sally Sue Brown
   (Arthur Alexander/Earl Montgomery/Tom Stafford) 2:29

4. Death Is Not the End (Bob Dylan) 5:10

5. Had a Dream About You, Baby (Bob Dylan) 2:53

6. Ugliest Girl in the World
   (Bob Dylan/Robert Hunter) 3:32

7. Silvio (Bob Dylan/Robert Hunter) 3:05

8. Ninety Miles an Hour (Down a Dead End Street)
   (Hal Blair/Don Robertson). 2:56

9. Shenandoah
   (traditional, arranged by Bob Dylan) 3:38

10. Rank Strangers to Me (Albert E. Brumley). 2:57

Released May 30, 1988

"Death Is Not the End" produced by Bob Dylan and Mark Knopfler; otherwise, production credits not given

Recorded at Townhouse Studios in London; Sunset Sound Studios in Los Angeles; other unknown studios in Los Angeles; and (for "Death Is Not the End" only) The Power Station in New York

Session musicians: Michael Baird (drums), Peggie Blu (background vocals), Alexandra Brown (background vocals), Eric Clapton (guitar), Alan Clark (keyboards), Carolyn Dennis (background vocals), Sly Dunbar (drums), Nathan East (bass), Mitchell Froom (keyboards), Full Force (background vocals), Jerry Garcia (vocals), Willie Green Jr. (background vocals), Myron Grombacher (drums), Beau Hill (keyboards), Randy "The Emperor" Jackson (bass), Steve Jones (guitar), Steve Jordan (drums), Danny Kortchmar (guitar), Bobby King (background vocals), Clydie King (background vocals), Pamela Quinlan (background vocals), Larry Klein (bass), Mark Knopfler (guitar), Brent Mydland (vocals), The New West Horns (horns), Madelyn Quebec (keyboards, background vocals), Kevin Savigar (keyboards), Robbie Shakespeare (bass), Stephen Shelton (drums, keyboards), Paul Simonon (bass), Henry Spinetti (drums), Bob Weir (vocals), Kip Winger (bass), Ronnie Wood (bass).

Whether Dylan was in an artistic slump in the mid-1980s is a matter of opinion, but whether or not his songwriting pace had slowed is not. *Knocked Out Loaded* in 1986 had a lower percentage of original material than any Dylan album since *Self Portrait* (and, if you count it, the 1973 outtakes collection *Dylan*). Only four of the ten tracks on his next album, 1988's *Down in the Groove*, were original songs, and two of them were penned with a collaborator. *Down in the Groove* also continued his commercial slump, failing to make the US Top Fifty.

A reliance on outside material was not in and of itself an indication that Dylan would not be able to summon a well-received album. He'd manage that feat with an entire record of covers, after all, just five years or so later with *Good As I Been to You*. *Down in the Groove*, however, has been viewed by many as lacking focus and, like *Knocked Out Loaded*, featured a supporting cast of thousands. In addition to using many musicians rather than a set band, most of the record was drawn from combined sessions in London in August 1986 and Los Angeles in spring 1987, Dylan reaching all the way back to the *Infidels* sessions to retrieve "Death Is Not the End."

As for what *wasn't* unusual about *Down in the Groove*, the covers Dylan selected reflected his extremely wide influences and tastes. Early rock 'n' roller Wilbert Harrison's "Let's Stick Together" had, when redone by Harrison as "Let's Work Together," been a hit in 1970. "Rank Strangers to Me" had been popularized by famed bluegrass duo the Stanley Brothers; "Shenandoah" had been an oft-performed traditional folk song for more than a century; and "Sally Sue Brown" (with guitar by ex–Sex Pistol Steve Jones) made early soul singer Arthur Alexander the only songwriter covered by Dylan, the Beatles, *and* the Rolling Stones. For two of the four original tunes, Dylan collaborated with Grateful Dead lyricist Robert Hunter, with members of the Dead performing on the tracks as well. Furthermore, artist Rick Griffin, another Dead associate, was commissioned to do cover art, but Columbia Records rejected his creation.

Coming on the heels of an album that had pretty much flopped, *Down in the Groove* put Dylan in his deepest trough as a recording artist. This didn't stop him from continuing to work on other projects during the sessions and after its release, including acting in the film *Hearts of Fire* (and contributing material to the soundtrack); a tour in July 1987 with the Grateful Dead, which generated the live album *Dylan & the Dead*; and, just before *Down in the Groove*'s release, recording an album as part of the supergroup the Traveling Wilburys, with Tom Petty, George Harrison, Jeff Lynne, and Roy Orbison. By the end of the 1980s, Dylan would rediscover his songwriting muse for his next solo album, which also regained some of the audience and critical acclaim his previous records had lost. And, in 1988, he received the ultimate recognition with his induction into the Rock and Roll Hall of Fame.

Getting into the groove of this record are veteran music journalist **Alan Light**, introduced in Chapter 18, and **Stephen Thomas (Tom) Erlewine**, music editor of allmusic.com.

Bream: When *Down in the Groove* came out, it was pretty resoundingly ripped.
Light: I don't think that time has made anybody especially more receptive. If you expect that anything that he does is interesting in a grander context or scheme of all the work together, it fills in and connects the dots a little bit within that.
Erlewine: While acknowledging that it's kind of a mess, you can see what he's working through. It also seems to begin some of the themes that he would explore later on, in the '90s and into the new millennium, through the Never Ending Tour, which really did start as promotion for *Down in the Groove*. But I kind of like the mess aspect of it. In certain places it's reconnecting to a more stripped-down sound after *Empire Burlesque* and *Knocked Out Loaded*. It feels like he's trying to figure out where to go, and I like the

raggedness of that. There are some appealing moments on it for me, including the two Robert Hunter songs, which aren't great, but they're enjoyable.

Light: There's a sense of grabbing at straws a little bit, and sometimes it clicks. The end of this record, [with] "Ninety Miles an Hour," "Shenandoah," and "Rank Strangers," is when this record finally kind of settles into something. Those were the kind of songs that then started, within a few years, turning up in the set list at the show. It's certainly a footnote of a record.

Tom, I'm curious about your thoughts about the Robert Hunter songs. In general a lot of people do kind of like them, and obviously Bob likes 'em enough that he kept 'em in the set for a long, long time. I've never cared about either of those songs, but they're maybe the most significant things on here.

Erlewine: I enjoy them on the level of being a throwaway. I prefer "Silvio" to "Ugliest Girl in the World" because it's kind of light and silly and has a little bit of a relaxed vibe. And I like the hook on it. Sometimes I can be a sucker for a hook over a lyric, and that would be the case with "Silvio." It actually gets stuck in my head. It's one of the songs on the record where he seems to be having fun singing it. Sometimes, like with "Sally Sue Brown," he almost gives a little bit of energy in the vocal and backs off a little bit. It's halfway there, whereas "Silvio" feels like it's a bit of a committed, up-tempo performance. I have problems with Hunter as a lyricist in general. But they kind of feel like workmanlike songs. I like the modesty of them.

Light: There were a few times around this period where Dylan, with any interview he did, was really expressing this sense of I don't have it in me. He was saying, "I've written a lot of songs. There's a lot of songs that are still around to be examined. Everybody thinks that's what's most important to me, and it's just not."

Erlewine: This record really reflects that. He has only one song that's totally credited to him, "Death Is Not the End." "Had a Dream About You, Baby" is also his, but "Death Is Not the End" is the only one that's really gotten covered by other people as well. It's so heavy on covers, it does suggest that there's a certain fatigue with writing.

Bream: Let's talk about the other Hunter song, "Ugliest Girl in the World."

Light: That seems like a one-liner stretched way too thin as a song. I think maybe [it] was funny as a title or an idea, and then to have to slog through the full lyrics of it, it's a bit of a chore. It's going for a lighter touch and becoming pretty tiresome pretty quickly. There's not a lot of songs that seem to be written in Bob's world that are sort of punchline-out like that.

Erlewine: I like it a little bit better than Alan, but I would never claim to have it be one of my favorites. I don't like it as much as "Silvio." Dylan is a really funny writer, and he can be a funny singer. He knows how to phrase a joke. What makes this kind of awkward is that the punchline is there for us, but there's not really any big delivery in the joke itself. But I kind of like the feel of the recording. It kinda gets that Dead feel a little bit, just enough to give it a little bit of a pulse for me. But it's the kind of song that you also forget about. The fact that it's not executed as well as it perhaps could have been also suggests the creative dry spell that he was in.

Bream: "Death Is Not the End" was an outtake from _Infidels_.

Light: I've never loved it. I find it sort of plodding and too static to really work. Somebody has to bring up the Nick Cave cover, which I think is pretty interesting, to find more menace and threat in that song than the sort of more weary tone that Bob gives to it.

Erlewine: The recording of this is a little bit dreary. It crawls along a little bit, and feels like it could be a little bit fuller. The song isn't bad, though.

Opposite: Dylan collaborated with Grateful Dead lyricist Robert Hunter on two songs on _Down in the Groove_. *BERTRAND GUAY/AFP/Getty Images*

Light: I remember reading that Dylan had brought Full Force into the studio [for "Death Is Not the End"], and seeing Steve Jones and [Clash bassist] Paul Simonon were on the record ["Sally Sue Brown"]. It's like there were these opportunities to shake things up and do something different with these arrangements, and then none of that happened. They just ended up being these sort of workmanlike, lackluster arrangements. Hearing one of the Sex Pistols and one of the Clash coming in, okay, maybe it's gonna go to that garage-punk direction. And it doesn't go anywhere near that direction. That could be anybody else playing those instruments on those songs.

Similarly, having Full Force come in and sing some backup harmonies—that could be his regular backup singers or some other session guys. You don't get any sense that there was any particular interchange. If there's a regret about this record, if it was gonna be this kind of odds-and-ends thing, at least it could have maybe been more experimental, given some of the tools at hand.

Bream: Speaking of strange—Eric Clapton on guitar, Kip Winger on bass for "Had a Dream About You."
Light: The Kip Winger credit is only topped maybe by the Randy Jackson credit on "Ugliest Girl in the World" and "Under the Red Sky," right? That's when it really just seemed like, okay, we're opening the doors and whoever wants to come in can. I don't know which is stranger, to bring in these sort of more outlier players, or to then not do anything at all with them.
Erlewine: It just becomes sort of anonymous session men. Maybe that's the sound he was trying to go for. Or maybe he was kinda checked out, too.
Light: To the defense of this record, that version of "Rank Strangers"—with just the guitar and that sort of loud, kind of swooping bass part that's sort of playing the lead—is a really interesting arrangement and sound for that song. There's a mood and a feel, not just to the way that he sings that song, but actually the way that track sounds and then it kind of ends. I don't know if it's purely the bass playing alone, but it feels like the bass playing alone. That's a pretty compelling recording, particularly as an end to this album.

"Shenandoah" done as a pretty straight folk song was pretty surprising to hear at this moment, and felt like this was not the kind of thing that he was gonna do again. Obviously he went on to do it quite a lot again, but at that time he hadn't done anything comparable to that for a long, long time.

Bream: *Rolling Stone* in 2007 called this the worst Dylan album.
Light: It's been named that, yes. Once you're really a fan and student of his career, it's the part that is so mystifying to the rest of the world, which is why we find the bad records so interesting. Because they do still tell a part of the narrative. And once you see what's before and after, even the ones that are lyrically flawed or hugely flawed, they're still important in one way or another.
Erlewine: The term "worst" almost loses meaning because the entirety becomes more interesting than the specifics of the record. It's fun to see how the bad albums are bad, or what they represented at a certain time.
Light: The other thing about this record, it's really short. Like thirty-one minutes or something. So how much damage can you do?

Opposite: Onstage, Dylan played with Tom Petty and the Heartbreakers, but in the studio for *Down in Groove*, he grooved with members of the Rolling Stones, Grateful Dead, the Sex Pistols, the Clash, and Winger. *Peter Still/Redferns/Getty Images*

OH MERCY

with Eric Andersen and Tom Moon

Released September 18, 1989

Producer: Daniel Lanois

Recorded at Studio on the Move in New Orleans

All songs written by Bob Dylan.

Session musicians: Malcolm Burn (keyboards/bass/tambourine), Willie Green (percussion), Tony Hall (bass), John Hart (saxophone), Daryl Johnson (percussion), Larry Jolivet (bass), Daniel Lanois (lap steel/dobro/guitar/omnichord), Rockin' Dopsie (accordion), Cyril Neville (percussion), Alton Rubin Jr. (scrub board), Mason Ruffner (guitar), Brian Stoltz (guitar), Paul Synegal (guitar).

The chilly commercial and critical reception accorded to 1986's *Knocked Out Loaded* and 1988's *Down in the Groove* had in some respects left Dylan at the lowest point of his career. But he continued to work, evolve, and move toward a point where he could reestablish his standing as a leading singer-songwriter. In the wake of the *Down in the Groove* album, he initiated what came to be known as the Never Ending Tour, which has seen him average about one hundred shows a year since 1988.

While the stage has generally seemed to be Dylan's greatest zone of comfort, in 1989 he also recorded what is often regarded as his most elaborate studio production, *Oh Mercy*. The album was also his first of entirely original material since 1985's *Empire Burlesque*, and Dylan details numerous factors that helped him rediscover his songwriting muse in his book *Chronicles* (2004). That such a seasoned composer could tap into his skills again was not a shock, but given his general aversion to slick studio technique, his choice of producer for the material was.

In the mid-1980s, Canadian Daniel Lanois entered the top ranks of producers working on albums by Peter Gabriel, Brian Eno, Dylan's old buddy Robbie Robertson, and especially superstars U2, whose *Unforgettable Fire* (1984) and *The Joshua Tree* (1987) he'd coproduced with Eno. Dylan had gotten to know U2 after making a guest appearance with the band at a 1987 concert and writing (and performing on) a track on their *Rattle and Hum* (1990) album, "Love Rescue Me." On the recommendation of U2 singer Bono, Dylan took on Lanois for the *Oh Mercy* sessions.

Upon meeting Lanois, as Dylan wrote in *Chronicles*, "Over the course of an hour or so, I knew I could work with this guy, had a conviction about him. I didn't know what kind of record I had in mind. Didn't even know if the songs were any good." But by the end of the sessions, Dylan continued, "The record satisfied my purposes and his." Cut in New Orleans in early 1989, it was, in the estimation of Dylan scholar Clinton Heylin, "one of the most un-Dylanesque albums in the man's oeuvre." As Heylin added in the same critique (in 1997's *Bob Dylan: The Recording Sessions, 1960–1994*), "*Oh Mercy* is the product of a way of thinking that takes as its starting point *Sgt. Pepper*, not *John Wesley Harding*."

While *Oh Mercy* wasn't a huge hit, it was a significant commercial rebound, making the US Top Thirty and the UK Top Ten. If not commonly cited as one of Dylan's best records, it's certainly now regarded as his best of the 1980s. Both *Q* and *Rolling Stone* listed it among the finest fifty albums of the decade, and while Dylan would not work with Lanois again for quite some time, the collaboration helped the musician enter the 1990s on a high note.

Disclosing their notes on *Oh Mercy* are **Eric Andersen**, a well-traveled singer-songwriter who has released twenty-five albums and has known Dylan since the 1960s (Dylan recorded Andersen's "Thirsty Boots" on *Another Self Portrait*), and **Tom Moon**, a music critic for National Public Radio and formerly for the *Philadelphia Inquirer*, and the author of *1000 Recordings to Hear Before You Die* (2006).

Eric Andersen: "When the lyrics and meanings are strong, the music can lose them, but at times when they are weak with throwaway lines, to set up another zinger, the music carries the song." *Richard Corkery/NY Daily News Archive via Getty Images*

Dylan's Never Ending Tour started in 1988—and it's still going. *Ed Perlstein/ Redferns/Getty Images*

Bream: *Oh Mercy* **was hailed as the great comeback album. Do you think in retrospect it is that great, or was it just because it came after two lesser albums?**

Moon: It's somewhere in the middle in terms of comeback with regard to his commercial fortunes. But as a pivot to what comes after, it's really important. It's one of those records that really set up what his thinking was for the later records. It's like the first glimpse of what became the touring band for the Never Ending Tour and that kind of writing.

Bream: Let's talk about some of the songs. Let's start with the opening track, "Political World."

Andersen: It's one of those prescient songs. I can only go by the lines, when you talk about men committing crimes, and crime don't have a face— that could apply to a lot.

Moon: This is not the first or the last one of these songs he writes. "Everything Is Broken" is almost another one. He has this way of being very dark and almost having a jaundiced viewpoint, to the point where you think he's close to being over the line, but he never is over the line. He ends up being like the truth teller whose acid way ends up being the way in. You listen to him because you don't understand how someone could be that bitter and also be that spot-on.

Andersen: I don't think it's bitter. It's just an insightful song. He's not making judgments; it's just what he perceives.

Bream: In *Chronicles***, Dylan said "Political World" was an update of "With God on Our Side."**

Andersen: I don't think it's correct. With "God on Our Side," there is a moral judgment saying that people behave this way because they believe God is on their side. "Political World" has nothing to do with that. This is just like a laundry list of observations that are true.

Moon: I tend to agree with Eric. I'm not sure that the songs are as parallel—or I don't see the parallel that he sees.

Andersen: I've made some notes about some points I want to discuss. New Orleans was and still is important to Bob. *Oh Mercy* does not include any city specific imagery of places but more the haunted moods he brought to the setting—his own memories of "smoke on the water, it's been there since June" mixed with other mists and myths. These tales are always aided and abetted by Lanois' spooky, sparse, swampy Acadian production touches.

Oh Mercy cries out with self-doubt, longing, pain, compassion, and unseen truths— almost a kind of morality play. We may not know all the personal details of his life, naming names and who is who, but we do know the intimate circumstances. His songs are brutally honest. From pain, he doesn't flinch. This album reflects a personal midnight hour of darkness—his hours of darkness—traversing the wasteland of an exposed soul. It would take a lot of guts to write this kind of confession.

He can demonstrate a lot of sweetness, too, but he knows how to take responsibility for bad outcomes like "What Good Am I?" People suffering from "The Disease of Conceit." The songs reveal a humble human vulnerability that questions permanence itself—either human or otherworldly. I know Bob; he's been very friendly to me and has been my friend. I didn't have any idea how he keeps returning to these subjects with no answers. "Disease of Conceit" and "What Good Am I?"—extremely moody. Extremely touching. Very few people reach those points. On those two songs alone, he deserves some kind of gold stars for it.

Moon: Lots of critics do not like "Disease of Conceit." What some people found troubling about that song particularly, especially in the context of something like "Everything Is Broken," was that here, on some parts of this record, he's very disciplined about sort of lashing together the music and the lyrics. He's got a very clear cadence running through it, and a melodic framework that he's poured his thoughts into. And with that, that tune has a little bit less of a melodic structural core.

Andersen: "Disease of Conceit" is a genius song. Think of any dictator or any religious leader.

Moon: "What Good Am I?" and some of the other ones are closer to pure genius. I think "Disease of Conceit" poetically is genius, but I find merit in the criticism that says it kinda drifts.

Andersen: I disagree with you entirely. I think it's one of the best of two or three best songs on the album. "Everything Is Broken" and "Teardrops Fall"—they seem to me the weakest songs.

Moon: I disagree with you about "Everything Is Broken."

Andersen: That's a total laundry list. That's saying the sky is blue; it's rained outside, the curb is wet; the store is open; a car stopped at the red light.

Moon: It is. Yet it is so artfully put together, and sort of looks ahead to the later work in the sense that he's got this very simple eight-bar or twelve-bar structure—it's kind of a blues, actually—and he's just gonna riff. I think "Everything Is Broken" works because it's not a huge laundry list. It's a very tight little thing. It's a great commentary.

I don't think you could say this about a lot of the work that happened in the '80s from Bob, but when you hear "Everything Is Broken" now, it sounds like now. There's this kind of dire imagery of stuff breaking, and the groove is like this sort of very New Orleansy, Monster Mash, almost jokey, like creepy-crawly kind of groove that has a wink in it, as a lot of this record does. If you listen to it without listening to the words, it sounds like a party.

Andersen: It has kind of a happy party, kind of an R&B thing. Lanois uses a lot of the tremolo guitar in it.

Moon: Right at the edge of distortion, where it sounds like it could be some sort of studio thing from the '50s.

Andersen: Two songs I like very much are "Most of the Time" and "Man in the Long Black Coat." He has this thing with sort of these unresolved love affairs. Like "Most of the Time"—well I got my life together most of the time, but then he always comes back saying, "I don't care if I ever see her again." He gets weak, most of the time. That's a beautiful song.

Moon: The organ playing in that, there's a wonderful vibe.

Andersen: "Man in the Long Black Coat" has the mystery, the real feeling of the body, the woods in the swamps . . . Spanish moss, mangroves, bald cypress.

Moon: People in a small town talking about a person, which I think is very interesting. It's very much a short story in itself, where they didn't leave a note. It's like whisperings and murmurings in the town square of this shadowy figure.

Andersen: He obviously seduced and took her. And there's no body ever found. She just took off. But it's like a vanishing scenario, worse than suicide, almost more shocking since no body's ever found. And he keeps going back to this note. I found that pretty far out.

Moon: I like the groove of that, too. The band, it's like they could be playing behind an Allen Toussaint record from the mid-'70s.

Andersen: Well, it's New Orleans. I found this to be a very mystical, mysterious song, and you wonder. . . . "Somebody out there is beating a dead horse." I would guess that as him beating the dead horse, a perplexing memory, and the situations he gets into that he always comes back to. I think it's self-revelatory.

Moon: I could also hear it as his comment on people trying to sort of parse every line of his work. To him, it's like this is a dead horse as well.

Andersen: I'm not doing that. This is a narrative, and the guy is maybe watching and it could be his girlfriend. At the end, she splits with the guy. I love this thing where she asks him to dance. . . . "At the old dance hall on the outskirts of town, He looked into her eyes when she stopped him to ask, If he wanted to dance, he had a face like a mask." Very ominous. Slow dance of life they're talking about here. So she disappears—no note, no nothing—and whoever the narrator is tried to understand what happened.

Moon: You go out of "Ring Them Bells" where it's religion and he's calling out the saints, and we're in church, and then suddenly we're in this sort of much more murky scene with this stranger in "Man in the Long Black Coat." What's the intentionality of this sequence?

Andersen: Two of the major things in your sequencing [in general] are the key, one song to the next, and the rhythm, one song to the next, considering also the length. I don't know here; you'd have to ask them. But I think "Ring Them Bells" is a beautiful song.

Moon: One of the things that struck me when I came back to this record was how disciplined these verses are. Like when you listen to [2012's] *Tempest* and [1997's] *Time Out of Mind*, there are times when you get along to about the fifth verse and you're like, okay, I get it.

Andersen: Lanois rode his ass like a donkey. He made him do new vocals.

Moon: Everything I know about him, if he had extra verses that he believed in, they'd be there. Yet here, it's like these are perfect, crystalline, three-and-a-half minute, four-minute things.

Andersen: That's Lanois. He's the one who put his foot down. He played hardball. He smashed a guitar in the studio, he was so pissed off at Dylan.

Bream: Why do you think it's called *Oh Mercy*?

Andersen: When you look at the nature of the songs, it is so riveted with self-doubt. They're so overwhelmed by forces outside himself that he can't control, including "Everything's Broken," "Political World," all these songs. I think the inner plea would be, that's what we need right now. When you think about what's happening—with Ebola in Texas . . . a world war with Islamic nations—oh mercy is about all you're gonna get. Mercy is a last resort, when you don't have the power to do anything about things that are out of control, if you have no power over it. Bob being very religious, I think it's a no-brainer, the obvious title.

Moon: It goes back to these songs being very introspective and looking at points in the past where he encountered pain or created pain, and stuff that's unresolved.

Andersen: He did all those religious albums, and he was really into it. It was Bob not writing about this inner world, looking out, like he usually does. These were the albums writing about something—not about him, about something else. He did these albums and he was not convinced. He goes into *Oh Mercy* filled with self-doubt about the

Creator, about his life, his relationships—everything, as far as I can tell, has just gone to shit. Exploded, in some ways. But he has the balls and the courage and honesty to write about it. So when you have this album with so much doubt and pain, *Oh Mercy* might be a last breath. There's nothing to turn to, he realized. Nothing.

We're very lucky to have a guy like him. Somebody going out there in the wilderness and coming back and reporting, who doesn't need to do that. And he doesn't stop. Sometimes in the darkest hours of the night, in the most terrifying places, he writes when there's no mirrors. It's like being blindfolded on the Autobahn and driving 120 miles an hour. He's not afraid.

Dylan jammed with George Harrison at the third annual Rock and Roll Hall of Fame induction ceremonies on January 20, 1988 in New York City. The Beatles, the Beach Boys, the Drifters, the Supremes, and Dylan were enshrined that night.
Ron Galella/WireImage/Getty Images

CHAPTER 27

UNDER THE RED SKY

with Gary Graff and Paul Metsa

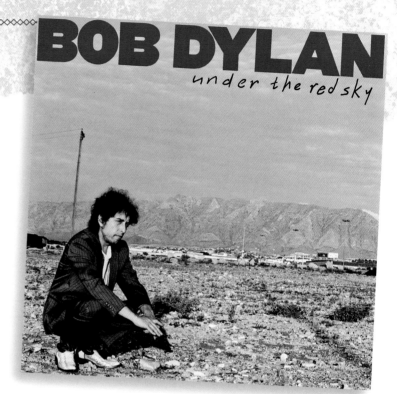

1. Wiggle Wiggle. 2:09
2. Under the Red Sky 4:09
3. Unbelievable 4:06
4. Born in Time 3:39
5. T.V. Talkin' Song. 3:02
6. 10,000 Men 4:21
7. 2 X 2 . . . . 3:36
8. God Knows 3:02
9. Handy Dandy 4:03
10. Cat's in the Well. 3:21

Released September 10, 1990

Producers: Don Was and David Was

Recorded at Oceanway Studios in Los Angeles; Culver City Studios in Culver Studio, California; and The Complex in Los Angeles

All songs written by Bob Dylan.

Session musicians: Kenny Aronoff (drums), Sweet Pea Atkinson (backing vocals), Rayse Biggs (trumpet), Sir Harry Bowens (backing vocals), David Crosby (backing vocals), Paulinho Da Costa (percussion), Robben Ford (guitar), George Harrison (guitar), Bruce Hornsby (piano), Randy Jackson (bass), Elton John (piano), Al Kooper (keyboards), David Lindley (slide guitar), David McMurray (saxophone), Donald Ray Mitchell (backing vocals), Jamie Muhoberac (organ), Slash (guitar), Jimmie Vaughan (guitar), Stevie Ray Vaughan (guitar), Waddy Wachtel (guitar), David Was (backing vocals), Don Was (bass).

Dylan has made numerous records hailed as "comebacks" in his career, going all the way back to *Blood on the Tracks* (and maybe *John Wesley Harding*). Yet he's never been one to ride the wave of those comebacks for long, or to stick to apparent winning formulas that made those comebacks succeed in the first place. If he'd wanted to do so after *Oh Mercy* restored a good measure of his public acclaim, the logical thing to do would have been to continue working with that album's producer, Daniel Lanois. Dylan would indeed work with Lanois again, but not until 1997, instead collaborating with a much different production team for *Oh Mercy*'s follow-up.

Recorded in early 1990 in Los Angeles, *Under the Red Sky* was produced by Don and David Was, with Dylan also getting a credit under the pseudonym Jack Frost. Don and David Was (unrelated despite their use of the same pseudo-surname for stage purposes) had experienced considerable success in the 1980s as the core of the eclectic band Was (Not Was). Don Was also had just produced a Grammy-winning, chart-topping comeback album by Bonnie Raitt, *Nick of Time*. The *Under the Red Sky* sessions employed a number of musicians with impressive resumes, including Stevie Ray Vaughan, George Harrison, David Crosby, Elton John, Bruce Hornsby, and David Lindley.

Received with an odd mixture of praise and disdain upon its release, *Under the Red Sky* was at times hailed for its earthier R&B elements, but others dismissed it as an underwhelming disappointment after *Oh Mercy*. Perhaps the harshest critic of all, albeit a decade and a half later, was Dylan himself, who told *Rolling Stone* in 2006: "At the same time I was also doing [a Traveling] Wilburys record . . . then I'd go down and see Don Was, and I felt like I was walking into a wall. He'd have a different band for me to play with every day, a lot of all-stars, for no particular purpose. Back then I wasn't bringing anything at all into the studio, I was completely disillusioned. I'd let someone else take control of it all and just come up with lyrics to the melody of the song." There were, Dylan summarized, "[t]oo many people in the room, too many musicians, too many egos, ego-driven musicians that just wanted to play their thing."

Coming as it did between an acclaimed comeback and a shift to traditional folk material for his next two albums, *Under the Red Sky* is one of the least discussed records in Dylan's catalog. Undeterred by the album's reception, he continued his newly adopted nearly-one-hundred-shows-per-year pace unabated. A second album by the Traveling Wilburys also appeared in 1990, but Dylan wouldn't release another album of original material until 1997.

Discussing *Under the Red Sky* are **Gary Graff**, longtime Detroit music critic and author introduced in Chapter 24, and **Paul Metsa**, a Minneapolis-based singer-songwriter who, like Dylan, grew up on Minnesota's Iron Range and authored the memoir *Blue Guitar Highway* (2011).

Bream: Some people have called this album a triumph, some think it's a turkey, some are in between. Where do you stand on that?

Graff: It's certainly not the pariah of Dylan's catalog that a lot of people would like to call it, but it's a flawed and, at times, very indifferent kind of album.

Metsa: There're three, maybe four really great songs. "Born in Time" is amazing. I like "God Knows." "Handy Dandy" is as close to "Like a Rolling Stone" that we've ever heard since "Like a Rolling Stone" was put out. But really what attracted me to the record was the song "Under the Red Sky," which is probably one of my top ten favorite Dylan songs.

Graff: I would concur on three of those four. I find myself with "Handy Dandy" going back and forth a lot, partly because it does feel like kind of a cheap version of "Like a Rolling Stone," and some of it, to me, does sound kind of goofy. I think the biggest mistake Dylan made, or that maybe Don Was made on the album—whoever made the decision—was starting this album with "Wiggle Wiggle."

Metsa: To start the record with that, as opposed to, let's say, "Under the Red Sky," speaks to the perversity at times of Dylan's mindset in terms of his own material.

Graff: Part of the back story of *Under the Red Sky* is he dedicated it to Gabby Goo Goo, who was his then four-year-old daughter. So you can see "Wiggle Wiggle" being the starting track as a very personal kind of choice. But to have this weird toss-off nursery rhyme, with this phenomenal group of players playing it, just set the thing off completely on the wrong foot.

Metsa: This is, I think, Dylan sitting around in the morning, taking care of the kid until mom or his daughter or whosever kid this was comes home. I don't have to love everything he does, but as a songwriter, I enjoy where he finds these little glimpses of inspiration. If he's reading the nursery rhymes to whoever, and that turns into a song—whether the song works or not, I still find that's a fascinating way to find your inspiration.

Graff: You hear the kind of inspiration you're talking about in other songs here, too. "T.V. Talkin' Song" plays to the badder grandpa. Even "2 x 2" might, although we're talking a ganja-smoking grandpa in something like that. "Under the Red Sky," you could see that as being almost a lullaby. You can only imagine him trooping in, trouble at home, trouble on the other record [by the Traveling Wilburys], feeling bad about the record industry, and here he has to walk into a studio to make a new record, and maybe not only to make a new record but to be making it with one of the hottest producers in the record industry at the time. Don Was was the darling of the industry part of the record industry. Every label wanted him to take their veteran artist and do a Bonnie Raitt on 'em. I'm sure Columbia felt the same way about him working with Bob Dylan. Even though Don, who I've known for a long time, was doing this totally for all the right reasons, from a creative perspective. Bob Dylan is one of his boyhood heroes. Don did not go into this wanting to make Bob Dylan's *Nick of Time*. He went in wanting to make the album that Bob Dylan wanted to make. Part of the problem was Bob Dylan didn't know the kind of album he wanted to make at the time.

Metsa: That record lacks a certain cohesion. It seems like there was the same group on a song or two or three, but the rest were sliding the quote-unquote "session parts" through.

Graff: You wonder, too, if in the choice of session players, if (A) some of these people didn't have compromising photos of Don Was, or (B) he owed them favors, or (C) he wanted to work with them in the future. 'Cause you look at all these people and you wonder how many weren't saying to him, "Oh dude, you're working on a Dylan album; get me on it, get me on it."

Metsa: I remember when I was reading about it being recorded and it said Slash is going to be doing a Bob Dylan record. I thought, whoa, okay. This is not your father's Oldsmobile.

Graff: And it's funny, 'cause what Slash plays on, you can't even tell it's Slash. Which, I think, all power to Slash for that. I don't think we wanted to hear a Guns N' Roses tilt to anything on this album. But there's a lot of people on this album who belong there. George Harrison—Dylan had been working with him intimately in the Wilburys.

Metsa: "Under the Red Sky"—I didn't realize that was George Harrison. My god, what a gorgeous slide guitar solo.

Graff: One thing you can tell from many of the performances on the album is how seriously the people who Don Was brought in did take playing on the album. You got Stevie Ray Vaughan at some of his most restrained but his most beautiful playing. And to have him in tandem with [his brother] Jimmie, you can tell that those two guys listened to quite a few of the records that Dylan did with The Band.

Metsa: The other thing that I loved about the song "Under the Red Sky" is the accordion. When I listen to that song, I hear Doug Sahm and Augie Meyers, who go way back with Dylan. There's a couple other tunes where he's playing accordion, I'm going, "My god, would I love to see him play that in concert."

Bream: Speaking of "Under the Red Sky," Dylan once explained that it's about his hometown.

Metsa: I'm not sure, overtly, if I felt an Iron Range connection. It kind of has that polka beat. It's really upbeat, and with the accordion, it certainly can conjure images of a picnic in a park on the Iron Range in the summertime. It's a very optimistic sounding song, which I really enjoy. Gary, I'd like to ask you, but I think pretty much throughout the record, Dylan's voice is in pretty good shape.

Graff: I think that's a production aspect, too. Don Was pushed Dylan's voice to give it a presence that Dylan probably wouldn't have had on his own. He really allowed it to be out front. He really allowed the voice to drive the songs—which was refreshing to hear, and I do think he sings very well on the album.

Opposite: David Crosby joined Dylan's all-star cast on *Under the Red Sky* along with Elton John, George Harrison, Stevie Ray Vaughan, Slash, and Randy Jackson of *American Idol* fame. *The LIFE Picture Collection/Getty Images*

Metsa: It's a great vocal performance all the way through. And I like the harmony vocals; there are a couple of tunes that David Crosby sang on that were really great. I could've used hearing a little more Crosby.

Graff: Crosby and the Was (Not Was) guys—Sweet Pea Atkinson, Sir Harry Bowens, and Donald Ray Mitchell—those guys brought out something, too. Dylan had already done things with female soul backing singers, but it was nice to hear him with a male soul backing cushion behind him like that, too.

Metsa: What's your take on the "T.V. Talkin' Song"?

Graff: That's another one that, like "Handy Dandy," I go back and forth with. Sometimes I find that I really dig it, and it feels like Bob's got something to say, and sometimes I listen to it and I'm like, "What are you going on about here?" I like some of the impressionism of it. There's sometimes I get to the end of that song and I feel like he didn't say anything.

Metsa: It's probably one of my least favorite songs on the record. I give him kudos for trying to make a bit of a political statement, trying to get a little bit of that quasi-rap thing that he's been doing for years. But to me, the first time I heard it, I'm like, this is Dylan's answer to Stephen Stills doing "Black Queen." I think Dylan listened to Stills doing Dylan, and so it's like what we're hearing is really Dylan being influenced by a couple of generations of himself through another artist.

Graff: The one we haven't talked about yet is "God Knows," which for me is the class of the album. You wonder sometimes if Don and David Was didn't look at that song and say, "Well where are the other nine of these?"

Metsa: My favorite tune on the record is "Born in Time." I think it's one of his top fifteen. It's kind of that Bing Crosby meets Jack Kerouac by way of Chet Baker or something

Bream: Let's talk about "Cat's in the Well."

Metsa: I was not a big fan when I first heard it, but now that I've heard it, oh a dozen times over the last twenty years in concert, it's a barnstormer. That song really works on the level of "I need a good rocker, one that I can end the night with."

Graff: When you listen to it in the context of the album, it does feel like a toss-off kind of ending. Especially after something like "Handy Dandy," which has a little more emotional weight to it. You think about him bookending the album with "Wiggle" and "Cat's in the Well." Clearly, he wanted to start light, end light.

Bream: Where does "Wiggle Wiggle" rank in your Dylan canon rating?

Metsa: He wrote seven hundred of them [songs]. Maybe somewhere between five hundred and six hundred. It certainly is not my go-to Bob Dylan song.

Graff: I think about how much a song that has been so summarily dismissed has been discussed. This thing is the standard bearer for mediocre Dylan.

In *Musician* magazine, Paul Nelson called *Under the Red Sky* "a deliberately throwaway masterpiece." *KMazur/WireImage/Getty Images*

CHAPTER 28

GOOD AS I BEEN TO YOU

with Ron Loftus and George Varga

1. Frankie & Albert
   (traditional, arranged by Mississippi John Hurt) . 3:50
2. Jim Jones (traditional, arranged by Mick Slocum) 3:52
3. Blackjack Davey (traditional) 5:47
4. Canadee-i-o (traditional) 4:20
5. Sittin' on Top of the World (traditional) 4:27
6. Little Maggie (traditional) 2:52
7. Hard Times (Stephen Foster) 4:31
8. Step It Up and Go (traditional) 2:54
9. Tomorrow Night (Sam Coslow and Will Grosz). . . 3:42
10. Arthur McBride
    (traditional, arranged by Paul Brady) 6:20
11. You're Gonna Quit Me (traditional) 2:46
12. Diamond Joe (traditional) 3:14
13. Froggie Went a Courtin' (traditional) 6:26

Released November 3, 1992

Producer: Debbie Gold

Recorded at Bob Dylan's garage studio in Malibu, California

As his fiftieth birthday passed, Dylan became regarded more as a living legend—or, less charitably, a fossilized relic—than a vital singer-songwriter plugged into the contemporary zeitgeist. His highest-profile activities of the early 1990s had more to do with honoring his past achievements than creating new work. In February 1991, he received a Lifetime Achievement Award at the Grammys, performing a shambling rendition of "Masters of War"; the following year, an all-star concert by him and others at Madison Square Garden honored the thirtieth anniversary of his recording career. In the interim, 1991's *The Bootleg Series Vol. 1–3* box set began a still-running series of official compilations of previously unreleased recordings from his vast archives.

Dylan *was* very much an active musician, but at this point, more on stage than in the studio, and more as a performer than a songwriter. He'd periodically wrestled with periods of little or no activity as a composer ever since *Self Portrait* in the late 1960s. The first half or so of the 1990s, however, would mark the most prolonged such bout he'd experienced. His course of action was not to withdraw from the creation of new recordings altogether but to turn toward the material that had inspired him to become a solo performer in the first place.

In his so-called Never Ending Tour, Dylan had been playing some traditional folk songs, usually in the acoustic portion of his shows. For his second studio album of the 1990s, he decided to concentrate on that aspect of his repertoire. At first, he tried the approach out on at least an album's worth of tracks with other musicians, produced by David Bromberg (who also played on the sessions) at Chicago's Acme Recording Studio; those recordings were shelved. All of the songs on 1992's *Good As I Been to You* featured nothing but his voice, acoustic guitar, and harmonica.

Devoted entirely to folk songs from an extremely wide array of sources, the record was (excepting the 1973 outtakes collection *Dylan*) his first all-covers album, though his 1962 self-titled debut LP had come close. *Good As I Been to You*, however, was not exactly a thirty-years-later follow-up. Dylan's voice had aged and coarsened, now sounding much like the aged blues and folk musicians he'd been inspired by as a young man.

Without any original tunes, *Good As I Been to You* could not be called a comeback or rebirth. Yet it was well received by critics and fans who welcomed his stripped-down return to his roots, *Rolling Stone* finding that "the album's intimate, almost offhand approach suggests what it would be like to sit backstage with his Bobness while he runs through a set of some of his favorite old songs." And so much did Dylan himself enjoy the exercise that he more or less repeated it with his next record.

San Diego Times Union critic **George Varga**, introduced in Chapter 13, and **Ron Loftus**, professor of Asian studies at Willamette University in Salem, Oregon, who has taught seminars on Bob Dylan, look for the high notes in *Good As I Been to You*.

Dylan's acoustic sets in concert (seen at Madison Square Garden in October 1992) presaged his two acoustic albums. *Richard Corkery/NY Daily News Archive via Getty Images*

Bream: What was your reaction when *Good As I Been to You* came out?
Varga: I gave it a fairly favorable review with a few qualifications. It was done very well. It seemed to be a welcome respite from the very overproduced '80s albums that preceded it.
Loftus: I loved the variety. Although it had a sort of tossed-off quality to it, the guitar playing is pretty damn good. He's famous for one take, but listening closely he prepared well to put those songs down. The lyrics are well delivered. I was very impressed with the album.

Bream: It might have been a reaction to *Under the Red Sky* with all the guests and the fancy production. Did you think this was a reaction to it, or more a contractual fulfillment, or a safe retreat, or just Dylan doing whatever he wants to do?
Varga: It could seem like contractual obligation, but, given the benefit of hindsight, it was a pretty bold, audacious thing to do. No one was expecting what was, in fact, his first all-covers album ever.

I read an interview with the recording engineer for both *Good As I Been to You* and *World Gone Wrong*. He said while the songs on the album were first takes, there were multiple takes of every song where Dylan would change tempo, the inflections would be different—kind of what we've come to expect from him live, but it was just him alone. So he clearly had a specific goal in mind.

Both albums were recorded in his Malibu garage. From what I've read, there was literally a lawn mower in one corner, so you can't ask for more of a downhome setting, albeit a downhome setting in a multimillion-dollar Malibu estate.
Loftus: That homespun feel and the tunes he selected were really appropriate to what he was doing. The two cuts that stood out to me were not the American ones—I like them as well—but "Jim Jones" and "Arthur McBride." They were worth the price of admission. I don't think he was ever doing them when he was younger.

Bream: Didn't he learn "Arthur McBride" from Paul Brady?

Loftus: Definitely. If you listen to that version, it's got that Irish tenor sort of feel. I think Dylan's has a completely different feel. He makes that story his own. He doesn't try to fake some Irish accent. He tells it like it is.

Varga: That's the key to the whole album. None of these songs are by him, yet he makes them indelibly his own in every case. He found or re-found his own voice on this, not through his own words but through the words of others and in some cases, centuries-old words.

Bream: What do you think of his singing here?

Loftus: I was very impressed. When Dylan is on, every word sounds like it is in the right place and you know that he knows what he's saying. Even though I don't get much out of the Lonnie Johnson song "Tomorrow Night," he nailed the vocal on it.

Varga: It didn't sound to me like some archival dusting off of old relics. These sounded as fresh and as contemporary as you could imagine. They spoke to his connection to not only these songs but to the whole tradition of these stories being passed on from one generation to another, and they're as vital as the person performing them. I don't think these were randomly selected songs. They seem to be an integral part of his musical DNA.

I think we would be remiss not to mention some of the negative aspects of the album. I believe all the songs on the album are public domain, a number of them are miscredited, "all arrangements by Bob Dylan"—which resulted in litigation on several songs because the arrangements clearly were very much based on someone else who had them recorded.

Bream: Doesn't this almost feel like a demo tape looking back at it?

Varga: The beauty of it to me is that unvarnished quality.

Loftus: It's not like the bootlegs or *The Basement Tapes* or anything like that in terms of the quality of recording. The quality is there and you can hear everything. I thought the recording was very clear, and didn't feel like it was recorded in a living room—or a garage with a lawn mower.

Varga: The songs fit together well, and what they thematically address are such Dylan topics: betrayal, escape, and the fact that he's not just fascinated with musical [history], but history in general, whether it be the Civil War or different periods. So these were like a nice old-shoe glove that fit him perfectly.

Loftus: One of the highlights of the record for me was "The Hard Times," a Stephen Foster song. The vocal was just tremendous on that—so emotionally rich.

Bream: What did you think of "Froggie Went a Courtin'"?

Varga: Who but Dylan would take this thirteenth-century English ballad about French imperialism and think to record it in the 1990s? It was inspired. I think some people complained that they thought the song was too long, but I thought it was just the perfect length.

Bream: Who knew it was this long?

Loftus: Once again, he didn't sing it as though he was singing down to people or mocking it or making fun. He sang it really straight.

Varga: "Little Maggie," the Stanley Brothers popularized it, and somewhere in the '90s Dylan guested on a Ralph Stanley album. Dylan, prone to hyperbole, said it was one of the biggest if not greatest musical treats of his life to sing with Ralph Stanley. I know he's a big fan of the Stanley Brothers, but I wondered if someone heard Dylan's version of this song, which led to him recording with Ralph Stanley.

Opposite: Dylan performed for five consecutive nights in August 1992 at Minneapolis' Orpheum Theatre, an old vaudeville house he had owned as an investment from 1979 to 1988. *Jim Steinfeldt/Michael Ochs Archives/ Getty Images*

Loftus: That seemed like a song that everybody did, but they took it kind of lightly, and he took it very seriously. He didn't start, as most versions do, with the verse about Little Maggie with her dram glass in her hand but with one where she has a pistol and a rifle. He's giving her more agency, more power.

Bream: The song "Tomorrow Night" has kind of this country crooning.
Loftus: Initially the song is too sentimental for me to get really excited about, but the more I listened to it the more I appreciated how he is phrasing everything just perfectly. I'm guessing he started to get interested in listening to the Bing Crosbys of the world and seeing what he could do as a crooner.
Varga: I love the Bing Crosby croon. The sentimentality of it seems just diametrically the opposite of what we associate with Dylan. But it seemed to be so heartfelt and true that it appealed to me.
Loftus: It sounds like it's effortless, but I'm sure there was a lot of effort [that went] into that.

Bream: Let's talk in more detail about the guitar playing.
Varga: It's clear that he had listened to and absorbed not only blues and folk but ragtime, swing—not only up-tempo but in the slow ballad style of swing. He clearly knows his Celtic music. If you stripped away the vocal and the harmonica and just had the guitar playing it would be fun and rewarding to listen to just by itself.
Loftus: He did it all with the flat-picking style, and he's playing a lot of lead notes, too, and it's impressive. Perhaps the thing about "Frankie and Albert" that stands out, that's usually played finger-picking style, but it's fast. I imagine that's pretty hard to do with a flat pick, and he did a great job.
Varga: "Tomorrow Night," I don't think it's knock-you-off-your-feet guitar playing, but it's impressive for the opposite reason. It's nuanced and delicate; it uses dynamics and space really well.
Loftus: I like the way the songs have real strong guitar, like "Jim Jones" and "Arthur McBride," where he takes instrumental breaks and you're just pulled into that. You're following the melody and you've been listening to the story and you want to get back to the story, but you really appreciate the break.

Bream: Any conclusions?
Varga: At the time it was released, it was a refreshing and unexpected change of pace. But if you look at it now, it was such an important album in terms of his left turn from the overproduced kind of slick '80s production albums that preceded it. It really laid the foundation for the three acoustic albums in a row that then led to this mighty triumvirate of albums beginning in 1997 with *Time Out of Mind*. This is an absolutely pivotal album and a really enjoyable album as well.

Neil Young dubbed it 'Bobfest' when Dylan's 30th anniversary with Columbia Records was celebrated at Madison Square Garden on October 16, 1992. Dylan was joined by pals (from left) Ron Wood, George Harrison, Johnny Cash, and Roger McGuinn. *KMazur/WireImage/Getty Images*

CHAPTER 29

WORLD GONE WRONG

with Jim Fusilli and William McKeen

1. World Gone Wrong
   (traditional, arranged by Bob Dylan) 3:57

2. Love Henry (traditional, arranged by Bob Dylan) . 4:24

3. Ragged & Dirty
   (traditional, arranged by Bob Dylan) 4:09

4. Blood in My Eyes
   (traditional, arranged by Bob Dylan) 5:04

5. Broke Down Engine (Blind Willie McTell) 3:22

6. Delia (traditional, arranged by Bob Dylan) 5:41

7. Stack a Lee
   (traditional, arranged by Frank Hutchison) 3:50

8. Two Soldiers (traditional, arranged by Bob Dylan) 5:45

9. Jack-A-Roe (traditional, arranged by Bob Dylan) . 4:56

10. Lone Pilgrim
    (Benjamin Franklin White/Adger M. Pace) 2:43

Released October 26, 1993

Producer: Debbie Gold

Recorded at Bob Dylan's garage studio in Malibu, California

Almost a year after the release of *Good As I Been to You*, Dylan put out another album of traditional folk material, *World Gone Wrong*. Some saw it as a measure of the depth of his passion for rediscovering his deepest roots; others viewed it as an indication of his faltering inspiration, at least as far as writing original material was concerned. What's undeniable is that there's no other instance of two consecutive Dylan records that are so similar to each other, though some differences are revealed upon close inspection.

Like *Good As I Been to You*, *World Gone Wrong* featured only Dylan's voice, acoustic guitar, and harmonica. It too was recorded rapidly at his garage studio in Malibu, though even more quickly than its predecessor, Dylan did not even change his guitar strings during the sessions. As a more notable difference, this time around the song selection was more tilted toward early rural blues, including numbers written by or learned from Blind Willie McTell, Willie Brown, Frank Hutchinson, and the Mississippi Sheiks.

According to Arthur Rosato, who worked with Dylan as an assistant and engineer, the production process was just as no-frills as the instrumentation. "We would record, we'd put it on a cassette, and he'd go sit out in his car and listen to it and then say, 'Okay, that was a take,'" he remembered in Clinton Heylin's *Bob Dylan: Behind the Shades Revisited* (2003). "Or in the pool room, he'd put it on a tiny little boom box and listen to it there. We'd never listen to it on playback through the studio speakers."

The lo-fi aesthetic, though on the verge of getting fashionable in alternative rock at the time, was not to everyone's taste. Huffed David Sinclair in the *London Times*, "It is hard to excuse the willful incompetence of the performances. His flat, croaky singing is accompanied by some shockingly duff guitar playing, and while a Dylan album without the fluffed notes would hardly be authentic, it is astounding, given the sophistication of modern studio technology, that a single acoustic guitar can be so badly recorded that it *distorts*."

Generally, however, the complaints were outweighed by reviews ranging from favorable to ecstatic. Some critics seemed as impressed by the liner notes as they were by the music, as Dylan's annotation, in contrast to *Good As I Been to You*, rigorously if quirkily documented the tunes' sources. Like *World Gone Wrong*, it wasn't a big seller, but it did win a Grammy for Best Traditional Folk Album.

Shortly after its release, Dylan performed some of the songs at a few shows at the Supper Club in New York with the intention of taping a TV special, as well as an accompanying album. Results from that project never saw the light of day, Dylan opting to fill the next few years of his release schedule with an *MTV Unplugged* album of November 1994 performances and a couple greatest-hits collections. His next album of studio material would not appear until 1997.

While he was in an acoustic phase, *MTV Unplugged* made perfect sense for Dylan. But he wanted to do the traditional songs heard on his two most recent albums *Good As I Been to You* and *World Gone Wrong*. However, MTV officials convinced him to perform some of his better known songs over two days in November 1994 at Sony Music Studio in New York City. His *MTV Unplugged* album was released in 1995. *Frank Micelotta/Getty Images*

Boston University professor of journalism **William McKeen**, introduced in Chapter 22, and **Jim Fusilli**, a pop-music critic for the *Wall Street Journal*, find some things right about *World Gone Wrong*.

Bream: I'd like to hear about your thoughts at the time this came out.
Fusilli: I was worried that Dylan had begun to meander a little bit. With the two acoustic albums, he focused himself and rooted himself into the music that helped launch his career and his interest in becoming a singer-songwriter. So I appreciated both of them.

McKeen: I kind of look at *Good As I've Been to You* as the historical album, these tales of people at sea and people in prison in Australia and all of that, and *World Gone Wrong* as more country blues. This became rather quickly one of my favorite Dylan albums. It was one I played almost daily for a year.

Bream: What was special about it for you?
McKeen: I was just kind of wondering where I was going, sort of drifting along, not in terms of work but life and relationships. I had no idea that another marriage and a ton of children were waiting for me. So this was that period in between, and the deep sadness in *World Gone Wrong* just really spoke to me. I love the intimate sound of the album. It's as if he's singing right into your ear. You put this on headphones and it's like inviting him into your skull. I thought it was a better-recorded album than *Good As I've Been to You*, and of course the album notes made it kind of special too, to hear holy writ from his Bobness.
Fusilli: There's an appealing intimacy. Dylan holds his guitar pick in a certain way, he chokes it very tightly. He attacks the strings, it's very funny. He doesn't have a light touch on acoustic guitar, and on this album you can hear the pick just as it touches the strings. You really are aware that it's Bob Dylan playing guitar on this album. I really appreciate that, because I like the way Dylan plays blues.

Bream: What did you think his sense of purpose was?
Fusilli: He made a really interesting folk-blues album, paid tribute to people who came before him, and maybe he felt his audience needed to know that. Dylan has a lot of young fans, and maybe he felt like he needed to put them in touch with the kind of people that influenced him at some point.
McKeen: I remember an interview in 1992 that Dylan did with Robert Hilburn [of the *Los Angeles Times*] and

he talked pretty openly about suffering from writer's block. I saw these albums as him recharging. He didn't have anything new and original that he wanted to share, so he went back to the sources that inspired him.

Fusilli: I think these two albums, particularly juxtaposed to *Under the Red Sky*, made it clear to Dylan that he needed a different kind of band and different kind of production going forward. *MTV Unplugged* is essentially expanding the harmonic platform that Dylan uses in the acoustic albums. These are players who are essentially articulating what Dylan was doing by himself on these two records.

Bream: "Jack-A-Roe" is some of the most artful and most musical guitar playing we've heard from Dylan in a long time.

Fusilli: Dylan has a tendency to muddy things up where he plays too much. This is Dylan's best kind of guitar work. This is what he was raised on.

McKeen: "Jack-A-Roe" is one of the songs that really appealed to me because it kind of has a great echo effect. It has the feeling of being a folk epic. By contrast, I thought *Good As I Been to You* was a little muddy, it wasn't quite as crisp.

Bream: He finally got around to recording a Blind Willie McTell song, "Broke Down Engine."

McKeen: I think "Blind Willie McTell" [recorded in 1983 but not released until 1991] is one of his greatest songs, so I was interested to hear him do that. But to me the highlights of the album were "Jack-A-Roe," "Two Soldiers," "Lone Pilgrim," and maybe the saddest song I've ever heard in my life, "Delia." I particularly like the way he did the Mississippi Sheik songs, because he brought something so different to the part. I think I had heard the Mississippi Sheik songs, but I went out and bought whatever the anthology is that he cites in there. I played them and thought, "Good god, he found something really different in those songs." "Broke Down Engine" was good, but it wasn't exactly the highlight of the album. As Jim said, maybe he's trying to educate us, too. He wants people to go find out more about this music. There is a little bit of Professor Dylan in these two albums in particular.

Bream: In the liner notes, he said this is a second-generation interpretation; go find the originals.

McKeen: I always liked an album that would inspire you to do more. That's what I thought about this album. I felt like this wasn't just a treading-water album, and neither was *Good As I Been to You*. He was trying to find that thing again. He was trying to change the whole musical context of his life.

Fusilli: One of the things I appreciate about Dylan, in contrast to people like Jagger and Richards, or like Lennon and McCartney—Dylan is constantly reminding us of the infinite well that is music. He doesn't tell us that music began with the electric blues coming out of the Delta. He is more of the long history of popular music. He reminds us we need to always look at popular music as this vast thing that comes from many streams. He could take a hokey pop song from the '30s and make it sound fresh again. He would never be concerned with the idea of hipness. If he liked the song, he played the song. He didn't care if you liked it or not. With this album he helps us along to find where he comes from.

McKeen: To hear the original "The World Is Going Wrong" and the original "Blood on My Eyes" by the Mississippi Sheiks, they're really great songs, really unusual and artistic. They have the fiddle going on them and all this other stuff. But when Dylan Dylanizes them, they seem completely different, and it's hard to imagine them beforehand.

Opposite: Dylan opted to perform an oldie, "Chimes of Freedom," at the inauguration of President Bill Clinton in front of the Lincoln Memorial on January 17, 1993. *Cynthia Johnson/ Liaison/Getty Images*

I think of Dylan as the Velcro singer. He attracts everything, all kinds of music. Here is one average-height, curly-haired dude, who is the embodiment of the American folk tradition of sharing.

Bream: Let's talk a little about Dylan's singing on this album.
Fusilli: It's not great, but appropriate for the music. He gets the most out of his voice at this point.
McKeen: I remember a review described his voice as sounding like it came out of a broken speaker. It was a great description. But I rather liked the singing here, because I always listened to it in these very intimate settings at three-thirty, four o'clock in the morning. The voice was just as important as the guitar playing. The guitar playing was so crisp, and the voice was so ragged and intimate.

Bream: What do you think of "Stack a Lee"?
Fusilli: It's a terrific rendition. The fact that he returns "Staggerlee" to close to its original form and takes it out of the pop world is a great gift to us.
McKeen: It makes a great companion to "Frankie & Albert" on *Good As I Been to You*. For a lot of people this might be the first time they ever hear this song. They haven't heard the four hundred thousand other versions, and he's the gateway drug.

Bream: One of the things that struck me in the liner notes is how much he credited other people, like Jerry Garcia introduced him to this song, or Tom Paley, and usually you don't see that kind of acknowledgment or generosity. He tends to be more mysterious.
McKeen: It's very nice, but I looked at the liner notes of *World Gone Wrong* as being kind of a statement of atonement for *Good As I Been to You* and its complete lack of any information about the songs.
Fusilli: Maybe we are unfair to Dylan, maybe we expect more from him than we might other people. Nobody ever said that Chuck Berry should have said that he got the guitar part for "Johnny B. Goode" from Carl Hogan.

Bream: Let's try to put in perspective *World Gone Wrong* in the Dylan catalog.
Fusilli: It depends on what you think of what followed it. I think it served as a refreshment for him and for us. It reconnected to his roots and reconnected us to his roots. I think what followed, for the most part, flows out of those two albums.
McKeen: I think of it is as rediscovery, reenergizing, the thing that links the previous great Dylan albums like *Infidels* or *Blood on the Tracks* or *Oh Mercy* with his later albums *Time Out of Mind* and *"Love and Theft"*, which I think is one of his finest. I don't think those later albums would have happened without this voyage of rediscovery of these two acoustic albums of the '90s.

Opposite: William McKeen: "I've always loved Dylan's liner notes. It's some of his best writing." *Ebet Roberts/Redferns/Getty Images*

CHAPTER 30

TIME OUT OF MIND

with Garland Jeffreys and David Yaffe

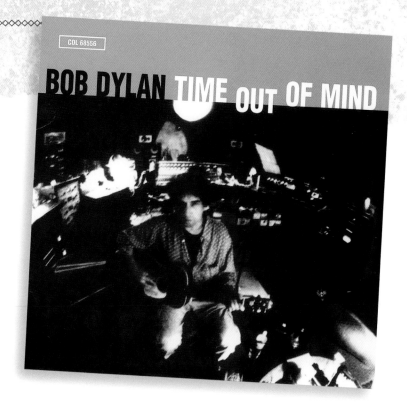

COL 68556

BOB DYLAN TIME OUT OF MIND

Released September 30, 1997

Producer: Daniel Lanois

Recorded at Criteria Recording Studios in Miami

All songs written by Bob Dylan.

Session musicians: Bucky Baxter (acoustic guitar/pedal steel), Brian Blade (drums), Robert Britt (guitar), Cindy Cashdollar (slide guitar), Jim Dickinson (keyboards), Tony Garnier (bass), Jim Keltner (drums), David Kemper (drums), Daniel Lanois (guitar), Tony Mangurian (percussion), Augie Meyers (organ/accordion), Duke Robillard (guitar), Winston Watson (drums).

By the autumn of 1997, Dylan hadn't released a new studio album for nearly four years and hadn't issued a record of original material for seven years. Both of those gaps were unprecedented, and though his Never Ending Tour continued to put him in front of audiences throughout the year, to some that seemed like a showcase for a living museum piece. In May 1997, he even seemed in danger of losing the "living" from that label, as he was diagnosed with a critical inflammation of the sac around his heart.

Yet just a couple of months later, he was back on the road. And just a couple months after that, a new record would put him back in the Top Ten and be acclaimed by many as among his finest. His critical and commercial standing had come off life support several times in the past, but as Nigel Williamson wrote in *The Rough Guide to Bob Dylan 1*(2004), "Even by Dylan's standards . . . *Time Out of Mind* was a spectacular comeback."

Producer Daniel Lanois was a chief agent of Dylan's resurrection, as he'd been for a previous comeback on 1989's *Oh Mercy*. Like *Oh Mercy*, *Time Out of Mind* was cut in a city in which Dylan hadn't previously recorded, the sessions taking place in Miami's famed

Criteria Recording Studios. While members of his road band played on the album, the tracks also benefited from contributions by veteran Dylan session drummer Jim Keltner, Asleep at the Wheel steel guitarist Cindy Cashdollar, and keyboardist Jim Dickinson. The haunting organ of Augie Meyers (most noted for his work as part of Tex-Mex rockers the Sir Douglas Quintet) was the album's most distinguishing trademark, other than of course the songs and Dylan's singing.

As for those songs, said Lanois at the 1998 Grammy Awards, "The words were hard, were deep, were desperate, were strong, and they came from having lived a number of lives, which I believe Bob has. So that's the record I wanted to make." Usually soaked in a swamp-rock aura, the record also drew from Sun Records–styled rockabilly ("Dirt Road Blues") and melodic balladry ("Tryin' to Get to Heaven," "Standing in the Doorway"), concluding with a sixteen-minute epic, "Highlands," that surpassed even "Sad Eyed Lady of the Lowlands" in length.

Actually finished before Dylan's spring 1997 health scare, the album was greeted as something of a Second Coming; Lanois was speaking at the Grammys, after all, since it won the award for Album of the Year. It even helped land Dylan on the cover of *Newsweek*, which called it "maybe [his] best since 1975's *Blood on the Tracks*. . . . It's far more accessible than such thorny later masterworks as *Infidels*—though it may also be his darkest record ever." Dylan acknowledged in the same article, "It is a spooky record, because I feel spooky. I don't feel in tune with anything. . . . It might be shocking in its bluntness. There isn't any waste."

Delving into the spooky record are **Garland Jeffreys**, a singer-songwriter in New York with a dozen albums to his credit, and Syracuse University professor of humanities and critic **David Yaffe**, who was introduced in Chapter 15.

Bream: When *Time Out of Mind* came out, it was seven years since Dylan had done an album of original music. Did you think it was a great comeback album?
Jeffreys: I think it's a tremendous record. I love the album. I don't think about it as a comeback album as such.
Yaffe: It's hard for me not to think of it as a comeback. When you hear the songwriting that he eventually did do, after the seven-year break of no original songs, him having gone deep into that well of great blues and great folk songwriting, it makes all the sense in the world. He had to really immerse himself in the songs that he loved.

I remember liking the sound on *Oh Mercy* and thinking of it as kind of an underrated record. Some people were calling that a comeback, the way that they called *Infidels* a comeback. But both of those albums are albums that Dylan fans really love, but they don't bring over everybody. They bring over the faithful; they don't bring the flock. *Time Out of Mind* brought everybody over.

It was just an amazing thing for people to hear how hard it was to be Bob Dylan. Who knew how miserable he was? That's not the only emotion on the album, because he does make a lot of jokes on it, but it's pretty bleak territory. And he had to be fifty-six and near death to get it across.

Bream: In some sense, is it a delayed sequel to *Blood on the Tracks* in terms of some of the content of the songs?
Yaffe: The emotional territory might be similar, but *Blood on the Tracks* is a relationship album and a breakup album. *Time Out of Mind* doesn't necessarily seem to be about a particular heartbreak. Maybe it's an accumulation of them. Maybe he's just disappointed by life. Maybe he's just got this ennui.

Bream: Some people say this is his album that discusses death.
Yaffe: That's true. I always thought that "Shooting Star" must have been for Richard Manuel [of The Band]. It would've fit. 'Cause it's about a suicide, I think. And "Long

Dylan played for 350,000 people, including Pope John Paul II, at Bologna on September 27, 1997. The pope cited one of Dylan's—"Blowin' in the Wind"—when he told the crowd that Jesus held the answers to their queries about life. *GERARD JULIEN/AFP/Getty Images*

Black Coat" is a morbid song. "Highlands" is a hilarious song, but it's also very sad, because it shows this guy drifting in and out of situations.

Jeffreys: I think there's a lot of this that just echoes everybody's life, period. This kind of broken love, broken-down love, meeting back together, coming back together—the sadness of it all, if that's in fact what it's all about. I think "Dirt Road Blues" is a fantastic song. I think "Love Sick" is fantastic. He goes all the way with that song in terms of expressing himself. "Cold Irons Bound," "Not Dark Yet"—fantastic songs. I'm not crazy about the very last song, "Highlands." I don't think it's fully realized.

Yaffe: There was the story that somebody walked in from the record label and heard Dylan recording. They said, "Can you make a shorter version of it?" And he said, "That is the shorter version of it." He had a version that was twenty-one minutes. He said, "Well, I've cut it down to sixteen," which was the longest song he ever recorded.

Bream: Another song that goes on pretty long is "Standing in the Doorway."

Yaffe: That is a really slow, sad song. Some of these tracks, where you have both Brian Blade and Jim Keltner credited drummers, it's hard to tell what's going on with the two drums. But on certain tracks, like this one, you can hear it more, because you have brushes and detuned drums, detuned hi-hat.

Jeffreys: The musicianship is remarkable. All these players playing together, or however they're playing, is just brilliant.

Yaffe: Maybe the best musicianship on any Dylan album. Because you had this combination of people who had been on the road for Dylan for years, like Augie Meyers and Jim Dickinson, and then you had these people that were Lanois people, like Brian Blade and others. Not everybody approved of what he did, but he was clearly a genius at fusing these two different bands.

Jeffreys: Lanois did a great job sonically on this record. He wasn't trying to duplicate Dylan's sound; he was trying to give him a sound, in my mind.

Yaffe: Dylan had never really allowed himself to be produced before the way he was produced on this album. When you think of the great '60s or '70s records, the producer really didn't do anything. All these people, they were just knob twirlers.

Bream: Dylan hasn't used a producer since *Time Out of Mind*.

Yaffe: I think that he was uncomfortable with the idea that he needed Lanois to have a comeback. *Time Out of Mind* was a great work of art. Anybody who's suffering, or has suffered, or has been fucked over by life in one way or another, can identify with this record.

In the middle of all this bleakness, you do have some jokes. And he sort of makes bad jokes. Like he makes bad jokes onstage sometimes, or he used to. But they're so bad that they're funny.

Bream: Let's talk about "Make You Feel My Love," one of his most straightforward love songs.

Jeffreys: I like the whole feeling of it . . . I like the lines "To make you feel my love. Nothing I would not do for you. I could make you happy, make your dreams come true." Even though those could be seen as simple lines or cliché in a certain way, I like 'em. "I'd go hungry, I'd go black and blue." It's a sincere song. I feel it.

Yaffe: I'm not saying it's without merit. I'm just saying that to me, it completely breaks the spell of the album. Like the album has a particular feeling that it's going for the whole time, and "Make You Feel My Love" is a speed bump, a sentimentality, and belongs elsewhere. If you got rid of it, then you'd have an extra few minutes maybe to have rounded out "Highlands."

"Make You Feel My Love" doesn't belong on the album. The fact that it was immediately covered by Billy Joel and Garth Brooks confirms my feeling.

Bream: You said it breaks up the flow of the album, and you're saying that as negative, but some people see that as a good thing?

Yaffe: Yeah, because it's so relentless in its misery, that it's this one rare light and one positive thing for like three minutes or something; it's a pretty short song. But I just always skip it.

Jeffreys: What do you think of "Love Sick?"

Yaffe: When it was used in a Victoria's Secret ad, I found that a little bit distracting. The more I think about the song, the more I think, in a way, that ad got it right. Because that ad shows Dylan as a stalker, right? You see these beautiful Victoria's Secret models, and then you see Dylan sort of ominously appearing, very airbrushed face.

Jeffreys: I think this is a tremendous song.

Yaffe: "I see lovers in the meadow, I see silhouettes in the window, I watch them 'til they're gone, they leave me hangin' on to a shadow." Now that's a stalker verse. That's as creepy as a Victoria's Secret ad.

[But] I love the groove on it; it's almost a reggae groove. It's a great song. People like to complain about Dylan that they can't understand the words. On this, you can hear every word. The pace of it, and the use of space, there's no mistaking every single word.

Jeffreys: That's probably also Lanois pushing the envelope and making sure that everything is being heard.

I like to have an up-tempo song open the record. I would have started with "Dirt Road Blues." That's a fantastic song. To have a sad song like "Love Sick" open the record, it's like you might as well throw the record in the garbage. I often want to have something that kicks off the album and then leads to the second track. But Dylan made an impression on me with "Love Sick."

Bream: The one song we haven't talked about yet, which a lot of people think is sort of the centerpiece of the album, is "Not Dark Yet."

Jeffreys: I love it.

Yaffe: I love it, too. And I didn't need Christopher Ricks to tell me that he was reading Keats.

Jeffreys: Maybe that's the best song on the record.

Yaffe: "I was born here and I'll die here against my will." It's like, yeah, I didn't ask to be brought into this earth in Hibbing, Minnesota, in 1941. Life is arbitrary. And then "It looks like I'm movin' but I'm standin' still." Like he's exhausted but he looks like he's still going forward, 'cause he's still on stage all the time.

Jeffreys: And he's still going.

Yaffe: He's spending his whole life on the road, right? In the Scorsese documentary [*No Direction Home* (2005)], he said, I was born a long way from where I was supposed to be, and now I guess I'm on my way home. Meaning that he's on the road. "I can't even remember what it was I came here to get away from." That's such a great line of ennui.

CHAPTER 31

"LOVE AND THEFT"

with John Schaefer and Wesley Stace

1. Tweedle Dee & Tweedle Dum 4:46
2. Mississippi 5:21
3. Summer Days 4:52
4. Bye and Bye 3:16
5. Lonesome Day Blues 6:05
6. Floater (Too Much to Ask) 4:59
7. High Water (For Charley Patton) 4:04
8. Moonlight 3:23
9. Honest with Me 5:49
10. Po' Boy 3:05
11. Cry a While 5:05
12. Sugar Baby 6:40

Released September 11, 2001

Producer: Bob Dylan (as "Jack Frost")

Recorded at Sony Music Studios, New York

All songs written by Bob Dylan.

Session musicians: Larry Campbell (guitar/banjo/mandolin/violin), Tony Garnier (bass), David Kemper (drums), Clay Meyers (bongos), Augie Meyers (organ/accordion), Charlie Sexton (guitar).

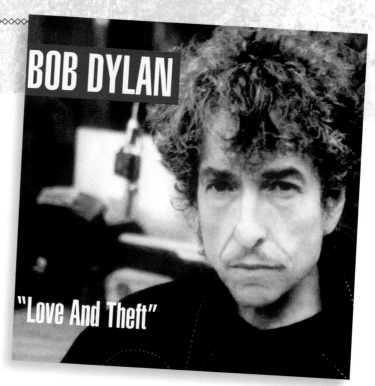

As the twenty-first century beckoned, there was no slackening of Dylan's Never Ending Tour schedule. In 1998 alone, his 110 shows included tours with Joni Mitchell, Van Morrison, Lucinda Williams, and (as opening act in South America) the Rolling Stones, giving him a chance to sing "Like a Rolling Stone" with the actual Stones every night. Nor was he just regurgitating the hits—in 2001, he'd play 121 different songs over the course of his 106 concerts.

As a recording artist and songwriter, however, Dylan wasn't nearly as prolific. The music industry had changed since he began his career, and stars were no longer expected to crank out an album a year, or even every other year. Having confirmed his stature as one of the twentieth century's most influential singer-songwriters many times over, he may no longer have felt the need to prove himself again and again after the novelty of another new Dylan record wore off. Whether these or other reasons were involved, it would be four years between 1997's *Time Out of Mind* and its follow-up, 2001's *"Love and Theft"*. Less patient Dylan fanatics were placated by the 1998 release of his oft-bootlegged 1966 Manchester, England, concert with the Hawks.

Producer Daniel Lanois had been key to the success of Dylan's two most recent albums that had been widely hailed as comebacks (*Time Out of Mind* and 1989's *Oh Mercy*). On *"Love and Theft"*, however, Dylan himself (under the pseudonym Jack Frost) returned to the producer's chair—a position he's occupied on his albums ever since. Recorded in New York in May 2001, the album features principally his touring band, with organist Augie Meyers (who'd been so crucial to *Time Out of Mind*'s spookiness) also playing a key role. More eclectic than its predecessor, *"Love and Theft"* drew from some vaudeville and Tin Pan Alley influences as well as the familiar folk, blues, and rockabilly ones. One of the songs, "Mississippi," had already appeared on Sheryl Crow's 1998 album *The Globe Sessions* before Dylan put it to his own use.

"Dylan's voice is almost completely shot here, yet what he does with it is most subtly nuanced and shrewdly judged," observed Michael Gray in *The Bob Dylan Encyclopedia* (2006). "And he is in such a good mood! This is the warmest, most outgoing, most good-humored Bob Dylan album since *Nashville Skyline*, if not *The Basement Tapes*."

Although the timing of its release—on September 11, 2001, the day of the tragic terrorist attacks on New York's World Trade Center and on the Pentagon in Washington, DC—was unfortunate, *"Love and Theft"* was Dylan's biggest hit in quite a while, peaking at #5. It was just as big a critical smash, topping the year-end lists of both *Rolling Stone* and *The Village Voice*, whose Robert Christgau gave it an A-plus grade in his *Consumer Guide*. Time hasn't dimmed much of its glow, the record getting named as the second best of the decade by *Newsweek*, and earning a #385 spot on *Rolling Stone*'s list of the 500 greatest albums of all time.

"Love and Theft" is the purview of **John Schaefer**, a longtime DJ on New York City's public radio station WNYC, and veteran singer-songwriter **Wesley Stace** (aka John Wesley Harding), who was introduced in Chapter 20.

Wesley Stace: "Suddenly John Waters is going to have a rival for the best pencil mustache in America." *Bernd Muller/ Redferns/Getty Images*

Bream: What expectations did you have for this album after *Time Out of Mind*?
Schaefer: My expectation was this is really going to be a kind of make-or-break record for him, at least in terms of my continued interest in following his career.
Stace: I liked *Time Out of Mind*, but it had kind of an overall gloominess to it that I found a bit wearing, ultimately. I wouldn't say I had any particular expectations with *"Love and Theft"*, but when it came out it totally blew me away. I consider it one of his four or five great[est] records.

I remember turning on [New York radio station WFUV] the Sunday that it was about to come out. FUV played "Summer Days." There were so many words. Words I hadn't heard him spit out in years. Those crazy jokes, like he was onstage saying these goofy things between the songs. His vocal delivery seemed more confident and wilder as the song went on. I thought, "Oh my god, this album is going to be absolutely phenomenal."

Schaefer: The ones that hit me most would have been "Cry Awhile," "Sugar Baby," and songs like that, where there's kind of a mournful streak. Even at the same time that he's clearly having a lot of fun as he was making this. In the first listen [after the 9/11 attack], getting to that sense of fun could be a dicey, difficult thing.

This is clearly a guy who was having the time of his life making this record with what was a really terrific edition of his band. I can't say enough about the interplay on this record between [guitarists] Larry Campbell and Charlie Sexton.

Stace: He knew the players very well, and so the album is really much more like what it might be when you saw him live. That really suits him, because none of them are trying to play over him. It's a very riff-heavy album.

Every song apart from one has a killer riff in it. That little figure in "Floater," I don't know where that came from, but that's brilliant.

Schaefer: Part of the fun of listening to the record, is like, "Oh where did that riff come from?! I've heard that before!"

Stace: That's an integral part. Presumably that's one of the reasons it's called *"Love and Theft"*.

You can't talk about *"Love and Theft"* without talking about plagiarism. It feels to me that you have some ridiculous apologists who are giving Dylan way too big a break in saying he's creating some kind of literary post-modern collage effect. Then you have the people who are saying he stole everything and it's worthless. Both positions are completely ludicrous. What he has always done as a musician is take the previous; he's standing on the shoulders of giants. He's always been happy to call a song the "Blind Willie McTell" this or this "For Charley Patton" or "Song to Woody"; he's particularly good at paying debt. When it gets sticky is when you know he seems to be pulling things that he won't in fact cop to and then says "different standards are applied to me because people pick over my work too much and don't get what I'm doing."

"Sugar Baby," the song by Dylan, is Dock Boggs' "Sugar Babe" plus "Lonesome Road" by Gene Austin. If I, as a musician, recorded a version of "Lonesome Road" now with that tune at that melody, I bet Dylan would sue me. He's got a copyright on it. All of his lip service to the folk process is in the end a little bit weird, because he'd sue you if you did to him what he does to other people. "Sugar Baby" is now Bob Dylan's song in the same way that "Scarborough Fair" became a Simon and Garfunkel song that they stole off of Martin Carthy; Paul Simon copyrighted it first.

Schaefer: That's a tradition started by W. C. Handy, isn't it?

Stace: We could talk about plagiarism all day and get nowhere, because to me nothing is getting in the way that *"Love and Theft"* [shows] a great artist at the absolute top of his game. Whether he stole or did not steal or whether it's all in his own head, I do not care. I would prefer that he be straightforward about it every now and then.

Schaefer: There are ways to do borrowing where you're not being a dick about it, but there are also ways to do borrowing that are so artistically creative and valid that you tip your hat to the person and say, "Well done." That is what makes *"Love and Theft"* so great.

Bream: Some people suggested that "Tweedle Dee & Tweedle Dum" was about the presidential election with George W. Bush and Al Gore.

Stace: Why do people say things like that? It's so obvious from listening to Dylan for the last fifty or however many years he has been going, that that is not what he is writing about.

Schaefer: That would never have even occurred to me. It's just kind of this window into this world of miscreants and outcasts and outright criminals and loners and losers that Dylan likes to see himself as a part of, as a chronicler of.

Stace: One of the charms of the album is that almost all Dylans are identifiable in it. Religious Dylan is in there. Folkie Dylan is in there. *Good As I've Been to You* Dylan is definitely in there. Sixties surrealist, poet, brain-cracked Dylan is in there. Somehow it's a melting pot for everyone Dylan has ever been.

I have a theory that the subject matter with Dylan in a sense never really changes. It's the society trying to get on and not be corrupted. But what's interesting is that when Dylan makes a really good album, what he does is he forms a completely new language to talk in. In *"Love and Theft"* he hit this language that suits him perfectly and which he had never quite done before. It's a jokey language that allowed for weightiness. It can include jokes, and there are some terrible lines on the record.

Schaefer: The music does cover several decades; it's basically like a walk through Bob Dylan's record collection, in a sense. Everything from '20s blues, '30s swing, '50s pop, Elvis style rock 'n' roll.

Stace: I think that's how it worked as well. He would come into the studio with like a Muddy Waters song and kind of go, "I want this to sound like this."

Schaefer: This is a Dylan record, but you're hearing the sounds of a genuine band at work here.

Stace: That's one of the reasons it's such a great record, because Dylan has always been bored in the studio. He likes to do a song a day. I think *"Love and Theft"* was recorded in twelve days, twelve songs. His production technique—willing to change the song at the drop of a hat because he was bored of the way you had just done it—I would contend very much that's what makes *"Love and Theft"* a terrific record. What you're hearing is a very natural thing. The clarity of all the instruments is terrific.

Bream: Are there any weak links on this album?

Stace: "High Water" I find to be the least satisfactory song on the album; I don't like it terribly much. The lyric doesn't in the end add up in a way that the order of verses takes it forward; it seems fragmented to me. I want it to be very compelling.

Schaefer: I had the same reaction with "Mississippi," which is a lovely song, some really neat mandolin playing, but it feels like the character has stayed in Mississippi one day too long. This song may have gone on one or two verses too long.

Stace: The reason you may be feeling that is because essentially it's another album outtake. It was wise to put it second because it doesn't really feel like the rest of the album, at all. It was a leftover from *Time Out of Mind,* and it had already been released by Sheryl Crow. I really like it. The B section of that verse, I find it musically triumphant, because I've never heard that in a song before. That bass keeps going either up or down; whatever it's doing, it's marvelous. But it doesn't quite fit with the other songs because it doesn't feel like something from 1962 or before, do you know what I mean? It feels like something up to date.

Schaefer: To come back to the idea that you don't always know what he's writing about, with these songs on *"Love and Theft"* we're getting these character studies but not the full story. We're getting part of the picture but not all of it.

Stace: It's what Dylan has always done, though. I don't necessarily think that the narrator of "Desolation Row" verse one is the same as verse two or the same as verse three. They're randomly cut-up and edited songs and often re-edited in post-production. Not only that, but I think the songs are not consistent within themselves. I'm not saying it matters, I'm not criticizing it, I just think that's a fact. That's why I think "Bye and Bye," that last verse is so shocking because it doesn't seem like anything else in the song at all. These songs are like that, cut-up within an inch of their life. It's only Dylan's voice and strength of delivery that are holding them together at all.

Schaefer: Since you are getting a very strong character study, but he's almost taking like a Cubist approach, a verse might be in third person and then suddenly it's in the first person. If you take a song like "Floater," what's the story there? I don't know what's going on here. But you have this vaguely sketched character, and Dylan clearly likes these characters. No matter how creepy he makes them, no matter how puzzling or strange or disturbing the imagery might be, he clearly is invested in and loves these characters. They can be pretty gothic, be very ambiguous, but that just leaves more room to me as the listener to figure out what's going on.

Bream: The humor on the album, do you think that's part of Dylan doing the vaudevillian thing?

Stace: To me it's all part of the kind of vista he's trying to give us of expression. I mean, there's a knock-knock joke on the album. That's pretty crazy. The sense of humor is great, and I really think it's a very important part of the album. That to me does talk to why *"Love and Theft"* is in inverted commas, because there's a little debt to minstrelsy, little debt to vaudeville, and a little debt to white appropriating black culture.

Schaefer: I think "Throw your panties overboard," or hunting naked in the moonlight, whatever that line is, they're funny images. They're kind of tossed off in a way that is not prurient. You listen to it and you think, *That is Dylan as the vaudevillian that he's in his heart of hearts wanted to be.*

And it's not just humor, it's not just the little funny asides. There's a sense of high spirits, which might be anachronistic these days. Our favorite artists are supposed to be too cool for school.

John Schaefer: "Look, Dylan borrows, he steals, but Woody Guthrie did that." *Fin Costello/Redferns/Getty Images*

CHAPTER 32

MODERN TIMES

with Peter Jesperson and Bill Shapiro

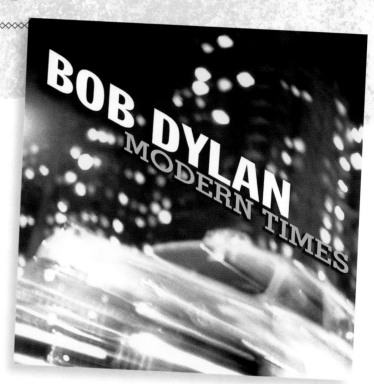

Released August 29, 2006

Producer: Bob Dylan (as "Jack Frost")

Recorded at Clinton Studios, New York

All songs written by Bob Dylan.

Session musicians: Denny Freeman (guitar), Tony Garnier (bass/cello), Donnie Herron (steel guitar/violin/viola/mandolin), Stu Kimball (guitar), George G. Receli (drums/percussion).

In the five years between the release of *"Love and Theft"* and *Modern Times* Dylan was about as busy as possible, without issuing a studio album. Besides keeping up his hectic tour schedule, he participated in a string of projects that almost seemed to cast him as a fulltime archivist of his own legacy. There were three more volumes of his *Bootleg Collection* series, including historic live tapes from a 1964 New York Philharmonic Hall concert and the 1975–76 Rolling Thunder Revue tour. There were discs of previously unissued material from shows in 1962 and 1963. There was also the Martin Scorsese PBS documentary *No Direction Home* (2005), though this covered Dylan's life and career only until 1966.

While Dylan's involvement in these endeavors might have been on the indirect side (though he allowed himself to be interviewed for *No Direction Home*), there were other activities in which he wielded a much stronger hand. To mixed reviews, he starred in and cowrote the 2003 film *Masked and Anonymous*, much of which seemed to lampoon his own legend. To much better reviews, he issued the nonlinear autobiographical book *Chronicles* (2004), which spent nearly five months on the *New York Times* bestseller list. In 2006 he began hosting his own radio series, *Theme Time Radio Hour*, on XM Satellite Radio on which he provided commentary on a wide range of music.

With all this on his plate, it might have seemed that Dylan, like many another superstar veterans of his age, could be content to indefinitely coast on his royalties and fame (including a special Pulitzer Prize in 2008). Yet his new material had not stopped, only slowed. In early 2006, Dylan recorded *Modern Times* in New York, using (as he had on *"Love and Theft"*) his touring band, and working with typical speed, the sessions lasting about three weeks. Like *"Love and Theft"* and its predecessor *Time Out of Mind*, *Modern Times* was a musical buffet of Americana. Unlike those two records, it was a #1 album, his first since 1976's *Desire*—and his first ever to debut at #1 on Billboard's album chart.

Surveying summaries of the record's reviews is rather like looking at a straight-A student's report card. The album was honored with almost across-the-board five-star huzzahs, as well as winning Grammys for Best Contemporary Folk/Americana Album and (for the track "Someday Baby") for Best Solo Rock Performance. It was selected as album of the year by both the *Village Voice* and *Rolling Stone*, the latter publication also ranking it as the eighth best album of the 2000s.

If there were any sour notes to be heard, they were contentions that Dylan had lifted material from other songs and literary sources without credit. The *New York Times* even ran an article about the resemblance of some lyrics to work by Civil War poet Henry Timrod. This hasn't stopped *Modern Times* from often being hailed as the crowning jewel in a roots trilogy of sorts that started with *Time Out of Mind*, though Dylan has said he didn't view the albums as such.

Singing the praises of *Modern Times* are **Peter Jesperson**, former Replacements manager and a record label talent executive for some forty years who currently works with New West Records, and **Bill Shapiro**, the host of the radio show *Cypress Avenue* in Kansas City since 1978 and the author of *The CD Rock and Roll Library* (1988) and *The Rock and Roll Review* (1991).

Dylan began playing keyboards more often than guitar in concert, including at The Fleadh 2004 in Finsbury Park in London. *Dave Hogan/Getty Images*

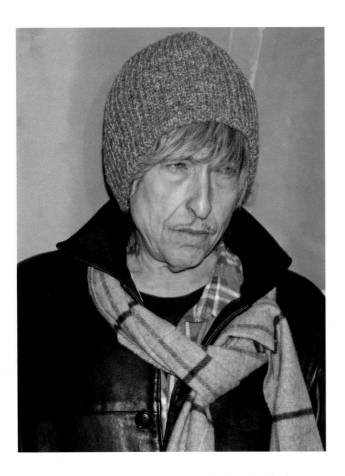

Dylan donned a bit of a disguise for the premiere of his film *Masked and Anonymous* at the Sundance Film Festival in 2003. *George Pimentel/WireImage/ Getty Images*

Bream: When *Modern Times* was released, it was hailed by some as the final piece in the trilogy of his artistic renaissance along with *Time Out of Mind* and *"Love and Theft"*.

Jesperson: Those three were A-plus records. But Dylan himself said he thought the trilogy actually began with *"Love and Theft"*.

Shapiro: I think *Modern Times* is probably Dylan's last great album.

Jesperson: I would agree, although I wouldn't put it past him to paint another masterpiece. The one thing I do feel has changed drastically since *Modern Times* is the singing has become craggier than ever, and much as I still like it, I can see it's harder for others to stomach or tolerate.

Shapiro: For a guy who has had to deal with issues about how well he sings for a long, long time, this recording is as good an example of the breadth of what he can do. He works everywhere from covering Bing Crosby and crooning and some of these blues sounds that were so much of an element of what he did in the first place.

Bream: This seems like a tribute to American music, the sounds he grew up on, the pre–rock 'n' roll music.

Shapiro: I agree with that. There are some strong blues influences here. I hear Muddy Waters, Memphis Minnie, and Bing Crosby. It's very much the Americana sound before anybody was dubbing it that.

Jesperson: There are some rockers to me, though they are blues based: "Thunder on the Mountain," "Rollin' and Tumblin'," "Levee Gonna Break."

Bream: These may be old forms of music, but in "Thunder on the Mountain," he has a line about current star Alicia Keys. What was your reaction to that?

Shapiro: I thought he had immaculate taste.

Jesperson: It made me laugh out loud. I just get a kick that it comes so early on the first song on the record.

Bream: Much of the discussion about this record has been about how much borrowing he does or paying homage to other songs, whether it's Memphis Minnie, Slim Harpo, Muddy Waters, or Bing Crosby. For almost every song, you can cite the precursor. Are these homages? He's not giving credit in the songwriting.

Jesperson: I'm conflicted about it to some degree. I do understand what they say about folk music being handed down, passed around and shared, adapted and changed and updated over the years. But when you take "Rollin' and Tumblin'" and you take the title and you put your name on it as a writer, I'm conflicted on that. I don't know if I'd be the one to call him out and say this is wrong. For someone like Dylan for whom this music was so important, it would seem like he'd want to pay respect to the people that created it. On "Workingman's Blues," he uses the refrain "bring me my boots and shoes," which I thought was a curious line when I first heard it, and I did some digging around and found out that line comes from a lot of old songs. Willie Dixon used it, and Big Joe Williams, and a jazz singer I wasn't familiar with by the name of June Christy. That sort of borrowing is cool in the grand tradition.

Shapiro: I think the borrowing is just inherent. To me, the classic example [in which] he's drawing on historic sources is "Nettie Moore," which may be my favorite track on the whole recording. That's a nineteenth-century English ballad. I guess he's claiming it, but he's also identifying it.

Jesperson: "Nettie Moore" and "Workingman's Blues" are the two heavy songs for me on this record, the ones that would stand on any list of great Dylan songs. Another interesting factoid I came across was that the cowriter of the original "Nettie Moore" was James Lord Pierpont, who was also the composer of "Jingle Bells." "Nettie Moore," the vocal on it sends chills up and down my spine. Not to be clichéd here, but he sings it like he means it. It's such a committed vocal.

Bream: Some writers have pointed out that snippets of lyrics on *Modern Times* can be traced to Ovid, Henry Timrod, and other poets.

Shapiro: We all borrow. C'mon. There's very little true originality. Yet Dylan, who was probably the most original artist of our time, is constantly the one that critics want to dig into and find the attribution to suggest that perhaps he's not as original as he really appears to be, which is a fool's errand, in my opinion.

Bream: That's what folklorists do. Is this a very folklorist record?

Shapiro: I think so. It's very much in the tradition of the troubadour and the tradition of the wandering minstrel that took him away from Minnesota in the first place and was very much the earmark of his early career until he scared everybody to death by plugging in. He's a guy who is very much aware of the folk tradition.

Jesperson: He tends to put an awful lot of things into most of his compositions, so that something that may be largely folklorist may have other elements altogether. There was one of the early tracks on the record where he's singing one thing that sounds like doom and gloom and the next verse is very romantic. Rarely does he do something that's all one thing, at this stage of his career. Something like "Blowin' in the Wind" or "The Times They are a-Changin'," he would stay on point for a whole song; I don't find that happening with this particular record. It's an amalgamation of things, almost a collage that juxtaposes ideas or concepts.

Bream: Almost all of these songs are longer than six minutes. Does it make it a challenge to listen to or is this what we've come to expect from Bob?

Jesperson: I didn't find it a problem. I've always loved the long songs from "Sad Eyed Lady of the Lowlands" to "Desolation Row" to a number of tracks on *Blood on the Tracks*. It struck me how many words there are on this record. "Spirit on the Water" has twenty verses. "Workingman's Blues" has eight verses and four choruses. "Ain't Talkin'" nine verses and nine sorta choruses. He's clearly got a lot to say. It does seem like there's an urgency to the writing, and he doesn't feel compelled to turn it off to make it a nice, concise three-minute song. He gives himself and the band a lot of elbow room to paint these sound pictures.

Shapiro: I couldn't agree with you more. The larger the canvas the more we have to garner from the artistic expression.

Bream: "Workingman's Blues" is one of his more political songs in recent years. What did you make of him becoming political again?

Shapiro: It didn't hit me as strongly as it obviously hit you. His political stance has always been exact, and at the same time it's been askew. He's such a chameleon.

Jesperson: I did feel that there is some contemporary social commentary going on there. But there's also times where I look at it and think the world goes in cycles so much that this could be a sly parallel he's drawing from an older time. Hard to know where he's getting at. The mystery is what keeps us listening.

Bream: Could "Workingman's Blues #2" be a tip of the hat to Merle Haggard? Merle had a song called "Working Man's Blues," which was a number-one country song in 1969.

Shapiro: Also a damn good song. I'm a big Haggard fan, and I think it's among his very best.

Jesperson: Maybe that's why Bob called it "Workingman's Blues #2." I also crack a smile when he sings "I sleep in the kitchen with my feet in the hall" [in "Workingman's Blues"]. Which obviously comes from a Fats Waller song. I love how he throws those things in randomly.

Bream: If this album didn't come out late in his career, would we have made such a fuss over this album?

Shapiro: I think so. This is a very, very special recording that in so many ways illustrates so many different facets of his career. Dylan is encyclopedic in so many ways. We get little samples of that lyrically, musically, and title wise. This is a marvelous pastiche of all kinds of elements being brought together and fed to us in a unique form. Dylan has been the only artist who has been consistently able to do that sort of thing.

Jesperson: I think it absolutely holds up. In some ways, it couldn't have been made at another point in time. The ingredients that we are hearing are clearly a combination of Dylan's past work and contemporary feels, sounds, and subject matters in some ways. I think this record, any year it came out, would have been recognized as a great work from start to finish.

Bream: His blues doesn't snarl as much here. It's a cleaner vocal sound than we usually get from Dylan.

Jesperson: He does put a little snarl into "Someday Baby." It's a little jaunty, a little sassy. It's got some wicked lines in there. Certainly the refrain "someday baby you ain't gonna worry poor me anymore." That's a fairly gritty delivery. Some of these songs that aren't bluesy, he does do the croon. He's talked about over the years that Johnny Ray was a favorite singer of his. He loved Dean Martin. A lot of the pre-rock people he was influenced by and didn't feel comfortable singing those kinds of songs until he was a little older.

Shapiro: I think that's one of the things that gives Dylan potency for me today. He does have roots in the pre-rock era. That era came into being into the '50s and came into full flower in the 1960s, but [the] pre-rock era has been overlooked except for some specialty bands. But Dylan is the one artist who has managed to incorporate those sounds, those artists, along with everything that has come since that time. And through his own vision has made them work together, and made one side more or less clarify the other.

Bream: If you had to rate this album: masterpiece category, damn good album, where?

Shapiro: I'd clearly rate it in the masterpiece category.

Jesperson: I agree. To me, *Modern Times* would be in my top twelve or fifteen Dylan records out of his thirty-five studio albums.

Shapiro: This is an amazing recording that I continue to go back to, probably even more so than some of the early classics. Every time I do, it can still manage to raise the hairs on the back of my neck.

Jesperson: "Someday Baby," I'm completely in awe that he can conjure a performance like that at this stage of his life. It's quite staggering to me that he's been this great for this long.

Opposite: The Never Ending Tour took Dylan and Willie Nelson to Yogi Berra Stadium in Montclair, New Jersey, on June 24, 2005. *Michael Loccisano/ FilmMagic/Getty Images*

CHAPTER 33

TOGETHER THROUGH LIFE

with Kevin Barents and Alex Lubet

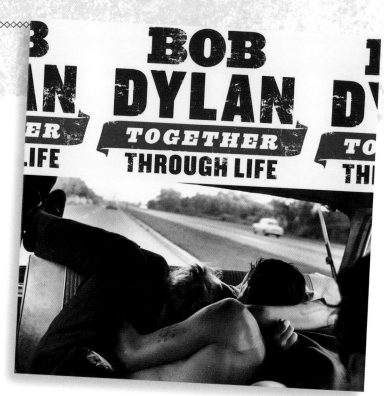

Released April 28, 2009

Producer: Bob Dylan (as "Jack Frost")

Recorded at Groove Masters Studio in Santa Monica, California

Session musicians: Mike Campbell (guitar/mandolin), Tony Garnier (bass), Donnie Herron (steel guitar/banjo/mandolin/trumpet), David Hidalgo (accordion/guitar), George G. Receli (drums).

Time Out of Mind, *"Love and Theft"*, and *Modern Times* are sometimes viewed as the most impressive trilogy of Dylan albums other than *Bringing It All Back Home*, *Highway 61 Revisited*, and *Blonde on Blonde* (though those three were recorded and released in a far shorter period of time). It might have been unfair to expect him to maintain the momentum, and while 2009's *Together Through Life* topped the charts and got its fair share of good reviews, ultimately it wasn't regarded as being in quite the same league. Like those previous albums, it stitched numerous styles together in a quilt often branded Americana, though this time with the help of Robert Hunter.

Hunter was long known to Grateful Dead fans as a frequent songwriter partner with that band's guitarist, Jerry Garcia. He'd also cowritten a couple songs with Dylan on 1988's *Down in the Groove*, around the time Dylan briefly toured and recorded a live album with the Dead. All but two of the songs on *Together Through Life* had Dylan-Hunter composer credits, exceptions being "Dream of You" (written by Dylan alone) and "My Wife's Home Town," on which Dylan, Hunter, and blues great Willie Dixon share credits owing to the melody's similarity to a Dixon tune recorded by Muddy Waters.

Asked about how the process worked when he collaborated with Hunter, Dylan gave a characteristically enigmatic explanation to Bill Flanagan in an interview published on the *Huffington Post* website: "There isn't any process to speak of. You just do it. You drive the car. Sometimes you get out from behind the wheel and let someone else step on the gas." Another inspiration for the material was French film director Olivier Dahan, who'd asked Dylan to write songs for *My Own Love Song*. Dylan came up with "Life Is Hard" as (according to his interview with Flanagan) "a ballad for the main character to sing towards the end of the movie," and while Dahan would have liked more tunes for the soundtrack, Dylan ended up using it in the batch of tracks that evolved into *Together Through Life*.

Like its predecessor *Modern Times*, *Together Through Life* was recorded with members of Dylan's road band, augmented by Tom Petty guitarist Mike Campbell and Los Lobos' David Hidalgo. If the music was rooted in the sounds of the twentieth century, the marketing was not; a three-disc deluxe version added a CD of the "Friends & Neighbors" episode from his radio series and a DVD of an interview with his first manager, Roy Silver.

In keeping with Dylan's contention to journalist Flanagan that "the new songs have more of a romantic edge" than those on *Modern Times*, *MOJO* magazine found that at the album's "heart there is a haunting refrain. Because above everything this is a record about love, its absence and its remembrance." If it seemed sentimental to some listeners, his next album would take a far more surprising and harder turn in that direction.

Kevin Barents has taught a course on Bob Dylan at Boston University since 2007, and **Alex Lubet**, introduced in Chapter 23, is a singer-songwriter and professor of music at the University of Minnesota in Minneapolis. Together, they will discuss *Together Through Life*.

Dylan participated in the 37th AFI Life Achievement Award: A Tribute to Michael Douglas at Sony Pictures on June 11, 2009 in Culver City, California. *Kevin Winter/Getty Images for AFI*

Bream: This album started out as a soundtrack assignment to a movie that most people have never seen, *My Own Love Song* by French director Olivier Dahan. How do you think the assignment of doing a soundtrack colored what this album became?
Lubet: It started with the song "Life Is Hard," and that seems to be a through-line for a lot of the songs. One of the things I like about the album so much as kind of an old guy—I'm sixty —is that it's so age-appropriate in so many ways. Although the theme of being associated with age wasn't in the film, it resonates deeply with the songs both in terms of words and music.
Barents: He clearly likes to get homework assignments like this, where this song is for a road-trip movie. The album has road-trip imagery, place names, and that sort of thing. Also the fact that he's collaborating on this album, I think he's looking for a way to enter into another stage without preplanning or being formulaic.

Bream: Dylan eventually said this was part of his trilogy with *Time Out of Mind* and *"Love and Theft"*. Did you see it that way, as sort of almost like a trilogy on mortality and regret?
Barents: I definitely see it being a continuation in terms of themes and music in a lot of ways, although I see this as being in some ways more of a bridge to something else. For me,

that it echoes his strategy immediately after some of his other masterpieces. In '66, when he finished what he called his Electric Trilogy, at the height of his popularity and critical acclaim, he famously sort of dropped off the planet, recorded the songs on *The Basement Tapes*, many of which are covers of traditional songs, cowritten with members of The Band or improvised. Then in 1975, after writing what for me is I think unquestionably his greatest album lyrically, *Blood on the Tracks*, what did he do? He teamed up with Jacques Levy, with *Desire*, one of his loosest, prosiest albums in some ways.

So we have a similar move here with *Together Through Life*, moving through sort of a different thing in some ways. Purposely I think less ambitious than what preceded it, not because he's lazy, but because he needs to shift gears and sort of change himself. He's purposely moving to something a little bit looser, a little more cliché-ridden, perhaps a little more standard musically and lyrically.

Lubet: In a lot of ways this album is the way that he would do *Highway 61* if he were fifty years older. It's surreal on the one hand, but it's very definitely a blues and '50s genre album. It's pretty strongly inspired by Chess Records, as [Dylan] said. And yet not. There are certain things that are really quirky about it that make it reference the older styles, but it can't possibly be them. One of the things that makes it that is that the driving instrument throughout so many of these songs is David Hidalgo on the accordion. As far as I know, the accordion was never permitted in Chess studios.

Barents: The accordion sort of replaces the harmonica on the Chess recordings. And yeah, a totally different tone and a different feel.

Lubet: Then it crosses a number of other genres that he wouldn't have thought of. There's Tejano music, there's Cajun music, there's songs that were sort of French popular songs; there's also something like Charles Aznavour that Dylan also loved.

Barents: Now he can jump genres effortlessly, in a way that he hasn't always been able to do in his career, and also keep things consistent lyrically.

But not everybody has felt that way about this album. Some people find it a bit monotonous in some ways. Some people would say that it's too consistent. But it shows a virtuosity and a deep knowledge of several different types of music.

Lubet: That's why I can't see it being tedious. Something that's got French popular songs and Tejano and Cajun music, along with the blues and the old rock 'n' roll numbers, but also the playing is amazing on this album. There are very major Dylan writers who say that the band—and this isn't quite his touring band—is not good. But I side with Dylan, and he says it's one of the best bands he's ever had.

Barents: I agree. It's great to hear Hidalgo on accordion; it's great to hear Mike Campbell on the guitar. From the first song, we get a very interesting sound. When I first heard it, it sounded kinda like [Tom Waits'] *Rain Dogs*. The guitar sounds a lot like Marc Ribot on that album. What would you say that "Beyond Here Lies Nothin'" is?

Lubet: It sounds a lot like the grooves of the person I think he channels more than anyone else on the album—Howlin' Wolf.

Bream: What do you think of "I Feel a Change Comin' On"?

Lubet: Lyrically it's really dense. The title refers to Sam Cooke's "A Change Is Gonna Come," and the chord changes also refer to Sam Cooke—[his] "You Send Me."

Barents: It's by far my favorite song on the album. The lyrics about aging are perfectly matched to that kind of light nostalgia-inducing music. To me, that sounded so much like "Easy" by The Commodores. And even a little bit of something like "Handbags and Glad Rags" by The Faces or something like that; it has that kind of '70s-ish feel to it.

Lubet: I love the line about listening to Billy Joe Shaver and reading James Joyce. It goes back to things like Ma Rainey and Beethoven, and those weird, surreal connections that he made during his first electric period. And then the thing about the blood with the

Opposite: Dylan toured minor-league baseball stadiums with Willie Nelson and John Mellencamp in the summer of 2009, including the Dell Diamond in Round Rock, Texas. *Gary Miller/FilmMagic/ Getty Images*

land. I listened to that line over and over and over again, and I was sure he was talking about the blood of the Lamb, who's Jesus, of course, but also—

Barents: That's what I thought he said the first time, too. It was only looking at the lyrics that I saw it was "land."

Lubet: The blood of the land. And to me, that often hails Woody Guthrie—"This Land is Your Land." There's a lot of sort of lyrical polyphony in this song. There're clearly complex references. The line "the fourth part of the day" actually comes from Jewish scripture from the Talmud.

Barents: That's such a beautiful recurring line, "The fourth part of the day is already gone." That could really be the last line of a sonnet. It could work as perfect iambic pentameter, such a really evocative line.

Bream: What role do you think Robert Hunter had?

Barents: He's often overlooked as one of the great American songwriters of the last forty years or so. He's written dozens of classic [Dead] songs, from "Dark Star" to "Ship of Fools." So I'm really glad that Robert Hunter got a little attention here with this collaboration. They're really well matched to work with each other. Hunter is kind of a master of the sort of geographic love songs that this album has a lot of. Hunter has name-checked half the towns in America. Especially place names that are in the American South and West, which Dylan has said that he consciously restricted his palette to for this album.

Lubet: Dylan is someone who likes to just change it up. He enjoys collaborating, actually, a lot of the time with instrumentalists or other singers. But it's not the first time he's collaborated with a lyricist, or even with Hunter. From what I understand, Hunter's very good at songs that have more of narrative through-line, and Dylan's often tend to be more a swath of images. You can hear the Hunterness, if you will, of the lyrics, in that they do tend to have that kind of storytelling element to them.

Bream: What did you think of Dylan, the great borrower, giving credit to Willie Dixon in "My Wife's Home Town"?

Lubet: I think there's also no way around it, because it's just so obvious, in that particular case. On the other hand, "If You Ever Go to Houston" is led by "Midnight Special," but I think that may not be a copyrighted song. It's got a huge chunk of "Midnight Special" in it.

Bream: Let's talk about "Life Is Hard," the French-flavored number.

Lubet: "Life Is Hard" is a French chanson type of song. Dylan actually loves that music. He's friends with Charles Aznavour and Hugues Aufray, who has conflated some of those songs. That song sounds kind of Tejano to me, actually. Old school. To me, that's the most Latin song on the album.

Barents: Yeah, an old-timey sound. A song about depression. But the thing I like the most about this album is Dylan's singing. It's emotive, it's expressive, it's delicate in a way that I've never heard it in concert. It's got great phrasing. It's something he's perfected also on [2012's] *Tempest*, which to my mind is a much superior album in a lot of ways, but it's something he was working toward with *Together Through Life*. Where he often has the cymbals perfectly matched to the musical rhythm, just lyrically have everything kind of click like a box or something. "Life Is Hard" does that a lot, too.

Lubet: For the longest time, people thought that Dylan only knew four chords. That's never been true. He has been able to, when he wanted to, pull out a much deeper harmonic palette. These songs have a harmonic sophistication about them that maybe people didn't know that Dylan had. That may also be reason that there's accordion instead of harmonica—maybe not feel[ing] like it fits in with that kind of harmonic sophistication. I think he's had this all along. He just never pulled it out because it didn't serve his purposes.

Opposite: Kevin Barents: "Dylan doesn't change to match his surroundings, but so that he doesn't match his surroundings." *Harry Scott/ Redferns/Getty Images*

CHAPTER 34

CHRISTMAS IN THE HEART

with Stephen Thomas Erlewine and David Hinckley

Released October 12, 2009

Producer: Bob Dylan (as "Jack Frost")

Recorded at Groove Masters Studio in Santa Monica, California

Session musicians: Tony Garnier (bass), Donnie Herron (steel guitar/mandolin/trumpet/violin), David Hidalgo (accordion/guitar/mandolin/violin), George G. Receli (drums/percussion), Phil Upchurch (guitar), Patrick Warren (piano/organ/celeste).

Christmas releases have been a tradition among major recording stars since the dawn of the record industry. Some of the heroes of Dylan's youth, like Elvis Presley and the Everly Brothers, put out Christmas albums; major rock stars and producers of the 1960s like the Beach Boys and Phil Spector put together Christmas LPs; and the Beatles made annual Christmas discs, even if those were distributed only to fan club members. When Dylan issued a Christmas album in 2009, however, it was as much of a shock as his actual conversion to Christianity thirty years earlier. Here was a singer who'd been raised as a Jew and had spent much of his career running in opposition to, or even disdaining, show business institutions. What changed his mind now?

In an interview with Bill Flanagan for Street News Service, Dylan said he'd first been asked to do a Christmas album quite a few years earlier by then–Columbia Records president Walter Yetnikoff. As to why he didn't do one back then, "There was always a glut of records out around that time of year, and I didn't see how one by me could make any difference." As to why he did it in 2009, he elaborated, with characteristic vagueness, "It just came my way now, at this time. Actually, I don't think I would have been experienced enough earlier anyway." As another motivation, all of his royalties from the album benefited the charities Feeding America (in the United States), Crisis (in the UK), and the United Nations' World Food Programme because, as he told Flanagan, "They get food straight to the people. No military organization, no bureaucracy, no governments to deal with."

For all its lack of similarity to any previous Dylan album, *Christmas in the Heart* was recorded in much the same way as he'd done his most recent record (*Together Through Life*, released earlier in 2009). Working in a Jackson Browne–owned Santa Monica studio, he again used members of his touring band, with David Hidalgo of Los Lobos again guesting on various instruments. Rather than twist holiday standards into idiosyncratic shape, Dylan played it straight, elaborating (again to Flanagan), "There wasn't any other way to play it. These songs part of my life, just like folk songs. You have to play them straight too."

That came as a disappointment to some reviewers hoping for a quirkier take on Yuletide tunes. "Filled largely with the most familiar carols, *Christmas in the Heart* is a full-on embrace of the old, not-so-weird America, a tribute to the kind of mass-market holiday records that his own Jewish family might have picked up in suburban Minnesota in the '50s, as a near freebie at the gas station," wrote Chris Willman in *New York* magazine. "In *Christmas in the Heart*, Dylan's being Bing again, not born-again." Enough listeners found it palatable, however, to top *Billboard*'s holiday albums chart, capping Dylan's quirkiest commercial success of all.

Unwrapping this Dylan holiday gift are **David Hinckley**, who reviews TV and music for the *New York Daily News*, and allmusic.com senior editor **Stephen Thomas (Tom) Erlewine**, who was introduced in Chapter 25.

Bream: When you heard about this Christmas album, did you view it as product, continuation of the Dylan tradition of covering all kinds of American music, or what?
Hinckley: I thought it was very much in his tradition. I was surprised at the specifics of it but not at all surprised that he did it—just because no pitch was not in his arsenal.
Erlewine: I didn't view it as pure product. I couldn't imagine who the audience would be a good piece of product for. I was surprised at its existence, and then once I actually listened to it, it very much seemed part of his lineage and made sense. It fell in with how he's fascinated with song and loves to get into the roots of that.

Bream: The songs are done straightforward and traditional. Did you expect him to go more adventurous?
Hinckley: I was probably a little bit surprised that he didn't go a little further from traditional arrangements and traditional vocal styles. But after the first song, "Here Comes Santa Claus," it seemed like it was not going to. What he wanted to do with this record was make it very straightforward. I think it's his most pop record, actually.
Erlewine: After *Time Out of Mind* and *"Love and Theft"*, you see him playing around more with pop and sort of old-fashioned vocal crooning. This is an outgrowth of that. I expected more of a blues or roadhouse feel to the record, like on "Must Be Santa."

Hinckley: "Must Be Santa" was the only one with a get-up-on-the-bar-and-perform kind of feel to it.

It struck me that he was treating these as folk songs, not as Christmas songs. These are songs everyone knows. While not everything on *Christmas in the Heart* is on the level of Gershwin or Irving Berlin or Cole Porter, nonetheless he has such respect for the carols in particular as songs that he wouldn't fool with any of them.

Erlewine: There's no other way to tackle these songs. These songs are like part of the air; you're just letting the song go through you, in a way. You have heard different interpretations of these songs, but that doesn't seem to fit where Dylan is coming from with this album. Because I agree with David; it's part of a tradition. It's not necessarily folk, but it's part of American song. The whole album seems to grow out of that love for American song form and Americana.

Bream: When was the last time he did such straightforward singing and such a strong sense of melody?
Hinckley: I've heard him do it in concert sometimes. On record, not so much. When you listen to this album, it's almost "follow the bouncing ball on 'First Noel.'" You put on this record and you can sing along with it.
Erlewine: There is a shift after *Time Out of Mind* to *"Love and Theft"* where the vocals are more prominent, and it's almost like a gateway to this kind of singing. Being more unadorned and being able to put the phrasing and delivery front and center.

Bream: Did you think his voice was musical enough to pull off this approach?
Hinckley: I absolutely did. I thought it was great. Obviously, we know his voice is gravelly. But it was great for Christmas songs because they're songs anybody can sing, even more so than the standards album he'll do.
Erlewine: I think that Dylan often gets a bum rap in terms of the musicality of his singing because there's always been this hang-up about the gravel in his voice or he's nasal. I think he's actually a really musical singer. Look at how he phrases things. He really knows how to modulate his delivery, so I was excited to hear what he was doing with these songs. He knows what makes a song work, not just in terms of writing but in terms of performance, and I think the record bears that out.
Hinckley: I'd put any of these Dylan songs up against any Christmas album where the singers are technically much better singers. But I would listen to this. It's more enjoyable to me.

Bream: What did you make of the first verse in Latin for "O' Come All Ye Faithful"?
Hinckley: There he played with his emphasis on syllables, emphasizing the syllable you don't think he's going to emphasize. In the Latin part, he did that a couple of times. That was the only time on the record I noticed it. It seems to me that's a very traditional thing to do; I hear that a lot in churches, doing the first verse in Latin if it's more reverent or if it's truer to the spirit.

Bream: "Must Be Santa" is pure polka—a sound that's big in Minnesota.
Hinckley: I thought it was great. This isn't a dance album, but I think he wanted to put something in that had more movement in it. Doing that as a polka was a brilliant stroke. It broke up the record in a way that didn't sound silly.
Erlewine: It's joyous. It's probably my favorite cut on the record because it does have movement and they had a great time playing it.

Opposite: Pedal steel guitarist Donny Herron has Dylan's back on the Never Ending Tour at the Hollywood Palladium in Los Angeles in 2009. *Jim Steinfeldt/ Michael Ochs Archives/Getty Images*

This Dylan-signed Fender Stratocaster was among other memorabilia from prominent musicians put up for auction at Christie's in 2006. *Stephen Chernin/ Getty Images*

Bream: "Christmas Island," is it cool or kitsch?

Hinckley: There's inherent kitsch in it. I think the Andrews Sisters did it, and Leon Redbone did it, and there's always a little tongue-in-cheek going on with him. But I don't think the kitsch was disrespectful, I don't think it was laughing at the song. We all get to have a little chuckle along with it. "Hang your stocking on a great big coconut tree." There's no way you're going to sing that that's not going to get a little bit of a rise.

It does hark back to records from a pop era in which we find a certain amount of goofiness. In that sense, you could say there's a kitsch element. But all through this record, the background vocals—the female dominated ones—are something that could have been off an Andrews Sisters record. Over the years, his background vocals have been so gospel-ish. These are just ripe—they just float over the record.

Bream: That high, pure, sustained note that Dylan hits at the end of "Winter Wonderland," did you ever think he could hit a note like that at this point of his career?

Hinckley: I was a little surprised. Pleasantly surprised.

Erlewine: It's another one of the delightful things about the record. There's a lot of small little presents tucked away.

Hinckley: He throws in "amen" at the end of "Little Town of Bethlehem" at the end of the record. Oh, what a nice little touch.

Erlewine: This record can be enjoyed or it can go in the background, too, as holidays records are intended to do—to set the mood. That doesn't really happen with other Dylan records.

Bream: On "I'll Be Home for Christmas," he's raspier than Louie Armstrong.

Hinckley: That goes to his point of not wanting to spend time in the studio. I think that works to his advantage. There's nothing homogenized about a record like this. I don't think he set out as producer saying, "Let's be raspy here" and "Let's be smoother here." It's just the way it comes out when he sings at this point.

Bream: The detractors and cynics have said the album is a hoax, his worst since *Self Portrait*. Is it?

Hinckley: He's never had any trouble polarizing people. But you can see why people didn't like this record or *Under the Red Sky* or *Self Portrait*. This is a much gentler record. If you're trashing it because it's so gentle and laid-back and doesn't seem to have any agenda beyond singing songs that he loves to sing, there's not much you can do about that.

Erlewine: I think people often attacked this record for the idea of the record without ever listening to it. It's a very warm-spirited album. They don't go beyond "Dylan can't sing so this will be a funny record" or "It's just not worth the time."

There's a comfortable feel here. It doesn't feel like he's trying to be alienating to fans. It's like this is where his head space is at. After the death scare [in 1997], he's funnier on record and he's trying these weird little projects.

Bream: When you pull out your Christmas records, where does this come in your order of priority?

Hinckley: There's probably ten or twelve I pull out at first. I don't play them in particular order. Phil Spector is in there, Elvis is in there, Sinatra is in there, Emmylou Harris is in there, and Dylan is in there.

Erlewine: I personally go into phases for holiday music. There will be a couple years where I'm into Sinatra or into a family mixtape we have. Some sort of things that aren't that great but you have emotional attachment to. But this is one that continues to have some resonance for me.

CHAPTER 35

TEMPEST

with Frances Downing Hunter and Kevin Odegard

Released September 10, 2012

Producer: Bob Dylan (as "Jack Frost")

Recorded at Groove Masters Studio in Santa Monica, California

All songs written by Bob Dylan, except where indicated.

Session musicians: Donnie Herron (steel guitar/banjo/mandolin/violin), David Hidalgo (accordion/guitar/violin), Stu Kimball (guitar), George G. Receli (drums), Charlie Sexton (guitar).

Opposite: A Dylan caricature created by Chris Ware. *MCT via Getty Images*

As Dylan neared and passed his seventieth birthday, the honors just kept a-comin'. On February 9, 2010, he performed "The Times They Are a-Changin'" at a White House celebration of music from the Civil Rights movement. And on May 29, 2012, President Barack Obama presented him with the Presidential Medal of Freedom. "There is not a bigger giant in the history of American music," proclaimed President Obama at the ceremony, adding that Dylan redefined "not just what music sounded like but the message it carried and how it made people feel."

The concerts and recordings kept coming too, though for a few years after 2009's *Together Through Life* and *Christmas in the Heart*, records were restricted to compilations and archive anthologies of previously unreleased material. There was a collection of early 1960s publishing demos; a boxed set of mono editions of his early albums; and a 1963 concert at Brandeis University in Massachusetts. But he hadn't stopped writing, and he recorded a new album in early 2012 in Santa Monica. *Tempest* was released in September of that year.

Dylan's twenty-first-century albums are not as different from each other as his earlier ones, and *Tempest* again tapped into the mix of roots influences often dubbed Americana by the media and music industry. Again Dylan recorded with his road band, the personnel differing only slightly from the players he'd used on his past few records. And again the album contained a song of epic length, the title track lasting nearly fourteen minutes.

By this point, Dylan albums could be guaranteed to generate a shelf-load of laudatory reviews. "Sometimes in oracular free associations, sometimes in terse narrative, Mr. Dylan has a lot on his mind: women, class, journeys, power, the inscrutable will of God and the omnipresence of death," wrote Jon Pareles in the *New York Times*. "He sings forcefully, in a raspy, phlegmy bark that's not exactly melodic and by no means welcoming. Battered and unforgiving, he's still Bob Dylan, answerable to no one but himself." *Tempest* was also a hit, reaching #3 on the US charts and getting listed by *Rolling Stone* as the fourth-best album of the year.

Frances Downing Hunter, editor of *Professing Dylan* (2015) and an associate professor of English at Arkansas State University who teaches a class on the poetry of Bob Dylan, discusses *Tempest* with singer-songwriter **Kevin Odegard**, who played on *Blood on the Tracks* and was introduced in Chapter 15.

Bream: When *Tempest* came out, it received quite positive press. Was it overhyped?
Hunter: He's not in voice in the same way that he was on *Blood on the Tracks*. The images perhaps are looser than they were, but he's moved to a universal stage, away from personal pain. The maturity shows through. [There're] some songs I like more than others, but I do think it's going to be remembered as one of his best, partly because of what he says about America.
Odegard: There's a lot to love about this record. Dylan's a voracious reader. He absorbed everything he read, and now we had a more mature storyteller who inhabits his characters only occasionally autobiographically on this record. It is as much a reader's record and a story record for me, the obstacle being that croak. I have a hard time getting over that deathly croak. As you have to suspend your belief system sometimes to follow a movie plot, you really have to not

pretend this is gonna be a healing experience, because it's very off-putting. This record has not sold. It has not lived up to the critics' hype.

Hunter: It's not a feel-good album. I think there's so much truth in it that we shoot the messenger. I like the way it begins with "Duquesne Whistle." You've got that outsider, that outlaw, that journey motif, warriors, mythological hero. I even see Shakespeare's *The Tempest* in it as well. The themes and the overall scope are grand, and that doesn't necessarily translate into popular taste. It is an apocryphal vision. It's sung in riddles.

Odegard: It's not a record from the '60s. It's not groundbreaking musically. It's more of the '30s and '40s. I don't really think he cares at all to be groundbreaking or to blaze new trails. He's a historian. And he really paints pictures that are fantastic. They sometimes reference sources. He reinhabits history with these fantastic, wonderful characters.

Hunter: It's cinematic, almost. We're in flashback, we're in future, we're in past.

"Tin Angel" is the one I like the least, because it's cynical, it's kind of hardened, jaded. I don't know whether Dylan has become embittered, or is still carrying that bitterness in "Tin Angel." Because the woman, she's older, she's jaded, she's reprehensible.

Odegard: She's fickle in "Tin Angel." She is the criminal—it's a sexist tale. He's brave enough to be sexist. You're not brave if you don't really put those things out there in the story. This is a dark tale.

Hunter: I see a pattern throughout *Tempest*—and of course in earlier works as well—there are always the two women. The ideal, the Mary figure, the earth mother, the mother of Jesus—the Madonna whore, to some extent. And then the other woman, that present woman who will do. I think he's spent his life trying to understand them, and he's written some of the most beautiful love songs in the canon of American music.

He sets it up in "Duquesne Whistle," even from the very beginning. He talks about the mother of our Lord, the heavenly intercessor for the sinner, and then he talks about the woman in the bed, the other woman, the erotic versus platonic love. Takes the good one to save his soul, but the other one puts out warmth and solace, for the moment. But you know, there are not that many women in *Tempest*. There's none in "Roll On John" and it's not female concerns he deals with at all in the title song, "Tempest," and of course certainly not in "Pay in Blood" or "Early Roman Kings."

Odegard: I think those [last] two songs [you mentioned] are related.

Hunter: Oh, I do, too. Because "Pay in Blood," it's not a traditional way of looking at the situation. I think he's thinking that he'd like to kill somebody. And he'd like to kill them for what they've done to this country. He's harsh when he says in "Pay in Blood," "I could stone you to death for the wrongs that you done."

Odegard: He's inside a Quentin Tarantino character, a bad guy. He's cinematic as well, and he's inhabiting a movie character with some great lines. Earlier in "Early Roman Kings" with the sharkskin suit, that's Wall Street, to me.

His voice—the croak—it makes you not hear it the first time. But the maddening thing about Bob Dylan, and especially this album, is that if you get involved, you're pulled into this world. And you love it. You get pulled into all these characters and the story lines, and it's an album that I have fallen in love with in spite of the fact that I hate listening to that croak.

Hunter: I try to see the croak as a device, as a voice that he has decided to use to emphasize the ravages, not only of time but of what has been done to our country—the corporate greed. I think Dylan is doing kind of an apocryphal wake-up call for the country. He sees where the ship of state is headed. There's a bleak and tragic undertow there. But even in "Tempest," in forty-five verses, it never sinks; there's still hope for what may come.

Opposite: Mostly a piano man these days, Dylan picked up his guitar for a tune at Bluesfest near Byron Bay in Australia on April 25, 2011. *TORSTEN BLACKWOOD/AFP/Getty Images*

Bream: Let's talk about "Roll On John." Is it totally about John Lennon or does it have a broader meaning for all of us to roll on?

Hunter: It's a tribute to John, certainly. It's also Dylan paralleling himself, his own situation, along with that of John's, but he's still here. He's not shot down in the Wild West scene of America with no gun control. And he says it's too late now to sail back home. Cover him up and let him sleep. He's ending with the two Englishmen, Lennon and Blake, with "Tiger, Tiger," and I like the soft repetitive dirge of it.

Odegard: When Bob Dylan talks about John Lennon, he's got respect. He lives in that superstar world; he made friends with John. He trusted John, and I think he really felt a great loss when John Lennon was shot. And he's angry about that, too. It's also about Bob Dylan.

He liberally quotes Beatles songs and John Lennon songs in here, but you can see the parallels to his own career all the way throughout the song, right on through "Tiger, Tiger burning bright, I pray the Lord my soul to keep, In the forest of the night." He's talking as much about himself as he is about John Lennon there.

Hunter: It's like he's saying, "Roll on, John, but save a seat in the boat for me."

Bream: I think that gets to maybe what the central theme of this album is. It seems pretty obsessed or fixated with mortality.

Odegard: Every step of this album, every song. How many songs did you quote that people died in? I think it was three or four.

Hunter: You think about Shakespeare, and Hamlet had ten dead, and we thought that was carnage. But my goodness, we got sixteen hundred in "Tempest" alone, and then there's blood and guts in just about half the others.

Odegard: The biggest body count of any Dylan record.

Hunter: He's talking for forty-five verses, in this song, of course.

Bream: And no choruses.

Odegard: The band carries this one. "Tin Angel" has an incredible hooky bass figure that just sucks you in from the first stanza. Great musicianship throughout.

Bream: The album borrows pretty blatantly from other things, such as Muddy Waters on "Early Roman Kings."

Odegard: I think that he is reimagining history and introducing an audience to things they may have never heard before. How many people who listened to *Tempest* ever heard of Muddy Waters? Bob had a license to do that. He's not afraid to recycle great themes.

Hunter: I like "Duquesne Whistle." It sets the themes for the whole album. Its fury announces the danger as the freight train clangs through small-town America.

Odegard: That's my favorite song on the record. "Long and Wasted Years" is a very wistful approach, and, for me, it's a great letter to [early girlfriend] Suze Rotolo.

Hunter: It's a lyric poem, almost, filled with regret. It's a man who's tired of blame, he's empty of his anger, he's empty of his idiot wind, he's filled with guilt. He wishes, I think, that he could go back, whether it's to the relationship with Suze, which was pure and young and new, before she sent those boots of Spanish leather back, or whether it's with Sara and a marriage that he thought was worth saving but couldn't save at the time.

Odegard: I like to play a casting game with "Long and Wasted Years," and I see Phil Ochs in this song; I definitely see a lot of Suze Rotolo. He's talking to her when he says, "Come back, baby, if I ever hurt your feelings, I apologize." And he references *Freewheelin'*, the cover: "We cried on that cold and frosty morn, So much for tears, so much for these long and wasted years."

Dylan receives the Presidential Medal of Freedom from President Barack Obama on May 29, 2012. *MANDEL NGAN/AFP/ Getty Images*

Bream: Do you think with *Tempest*, he's taking stock of his own life?

Hunter: It's natural for a person who's approaching death to look back at that perfect youth, and the memory of his youth. But I think it could be Suze, and it could be Sara as well.

Odegard: Dylan's most successful relationship was—is—with us, with his audience.

Hunter: They never failed him.

Odegard: It's the great success of his life, that he's connecting with his audience. He is seeking closure, he's confessing, he's telling as much truth about himself as he possibly can, because we are his greatest relationship.

Hunter: He also judges himself from time to time, in the album, rather harshly—as hard, really, as he judges anyone else. When he says "Two-timing Slim," I think he's talking about that other side of self, who I was then, and I rebuke that person now; I'm not that person anymore. But we all make mistakes in youth that haunt us.

CHAPTER 36

SHADOWS IN THE NIGHT

with Tom Moon and John Schaefer

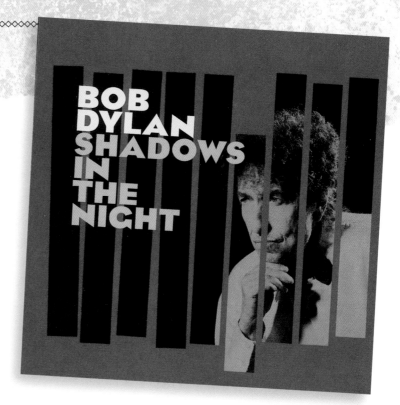

Released February 3, 2015

Producer: Bob Dylan (as "Jack Frost")

Recorded in Studio B at Capitol Studios, Hollywood, California

Session musicians: Tony Garnier (bass), Donny Herron (pedal steel guitar), Charlie Sexton (guitar), Stu Kimball (guitar), George G. Receli (percussion)

Additional musicians: Andrew Martin (trombone), Dylan Hart (French horn) on "I'm a Fool to Want You," Alan Kaplan (trombone), Francisco Torres (trombone), Joseph Meyer (French horn) on "The Night We Called It a Day," Daniel Fornero (trumpet), Larry G. Hall (trumpet), and Andrew Martin (trombone) on "That Lucky Old Sun"

On May 13, 2014, Dylan cryptically streamed a new song—"Full Moon and Empty Arms," made famous by Frank Sinatra in 1945—on his website, www.bobdylan.com, with no explanation. Seven months later, Columbia Records announced that Dylan's next album, *Shadows in the Night*, would feature ten standards that Sinatra had recorded. In a statement released by the label, Dylan explained:

> It was a real privilege to make this album. We knew these songs extremely well. It was all done live. Maybe one or two takes. No overdubbing. No vocal booths. No headphones. No separate tracking, and, for the most part, mixed as it was recorded.
>
> I don't see myself as covering these songs in any way. They've been covered enough. Buried, as a matter a fact. What me and my band are basically doing is uncovering them. Lifting them out of the grave and bringing them into the light of day.

Dylan and his band recorded the project at Capitol Studios in Hollywood, where Sinatra cut many of his recordings. Dylan produced the sessions with veteran engineer Al Schmitt, a twenty-one-time Grammy winner known for his work with George Benson, Steely Dan, and Sinatra, among others. "Frank [Sinatra] had this ability to get inside of the song in a sort of a conversational way. Frank sang to you—not at you. I never wanted to be a singer that sings at somebody. I've always wanted to sing to somebody," Dylan told Robert Love, editor of *AARP The Magazine*.

Shadows in the Night debuted at #7 on Billboard's album chart and received many glowing reviews. Calling it "strikingly unadorned and as emotionally raw as anything in the artist's canon," *Los Angeles Times* critic Randall Roberts wrote that the album reflected "a soaring lifetime's worth of emotion conveyed with the fearlessness of a cliff diver spinning flips and risking belly flops in the open air." Greg Kot of the *Chicago Tribune* concluded, "There are countless standards albums that bring forth more technically proficient singing. Dylan doesn't pretend otherwise. But few are as emotionally transparent."

However, the recording wasn't for everybody, including a "Panel of Dads" assembled by *Newsweek* magazine to comment on the album. Opined one dad, age sixty, "He never was a singer, but he's trying to be a singer."

Dylan addressed critics of *Shadows in the Night* in a rare speech on February 6, 2015, when MusiCares, the Grammys musicians' assistance foundation, honored him at a gala. During the event, Bruce Springsteen, Willie Nelson, Norah Jones, Beck, Bonnie Raitt, and others performed Dylan's songs. After pointing out that these standards are usually recorded nowadays by Michael Bublé, Linda Ronstadt, Rod Stewart, and even Paul McCartney, Dylan claimed, "The reviews of their records aren't like mine. In their reviews, no one says anything. In my reviews, they've got to look under every stone and report about it."

Dylan, alongside former president Jimmy Carter and National Academy of Recording Arts and Sciences president Neil Portnow, is honored at the MusiCares 2015 Person of the Year Gala.
Lester Cohen/WireImage/Getty Images

Looking under every stone of *Shadows in the Night* are NPR critic **Tom Moon**, introduced in Chapter 26, and WNYC DJ **John Schaefer**, who was introduced in Chapter 31.

Bream: What was your reaction when you heard that Dylan was doing an album of standards?

Schaefer: Here's a guy whose prodigious reputation is based on his songwriting. And here he's going to give us an album where the focus is going to be on perhaps the least momentous part of his arsenal of musicianship, namely his voice. So the idea that he would have a whole album that would kind of deflect attention away from the songwriting and aim it directly on his voice seemed to me bizarre, but also totally Bob Dylan.

Moon: My first reaction was "great," because if this last stretch of his career has told us nothing else, it's that he is rethinking every bit of his art, and it was only probably a matter of time before he decided to dive in and be an interpreter.

Schaefer: Not just his Never Ending Tour, but from listening to his radio show, you get the strong impression of just how important what we can call pre-rock music has been to him. Whether that's the Great American Songbook or country blues or early R&B or jump blues.

Bream: Why do you think he did this record?

Moon: In much the same way Louis Armstrong was sort of tolerated as a singer until he was huge, Dylan's always been tolerated as a singer simply because the material was so genius. Well, he turns his focus to material that's genius from a whole different realm, and I feel like he had something to prove about himself just as a pure vocal interpreter.

Schaefer: I have two answers. One is I think he did this as a band album, to show off just how talented and versatile his band is. The other is: *You think you know me; watch this.*

The album that this reminds me of is *Thelonious Monk Plays Duke Ellington*. Because here was a guy who built his career on his own unique approach that was kind of fractured and kind of scraping along the keyboard in a way that seemed not to be conventional or conventionally pretty, and people thought, *Well, that's because that's the only way he can play the piano.* And here he was taking on the songs of Duke Ellington, as if to

Frank Sinatra cut many of his recordings in the same Hollywood studio where Dylan and his band would later record *Shadows in the Night. Votava/Imagno/Getty Images*

say, "Hey, I can do this too." And here's Dylan taking on these great old songs, many of them closely associated with Frank Sinatra. There's a similar aesthetic, or a similar kind of look-what-I-can-do at work here.

Moon: A lot of these songs were also done before Sinatra, by Bing Crosby—I hear Crosby in here too.

Schaefer: I hear Sinatra as a reference, but it's not like he's trying to sound like Sinatra.

Moon: And the instrumentation, especially the pedal steel, the slide guitar, it's like that says the wonderful orchestration with thirty strings and really colorful brass can be distilled down. That is very much part of the genius of this, this band sitting all together. This is live music. And it has that breadth, and it has that spaciousness. And they figured out how to take a lot of the big orchestral cues that were Sinatra's hallmark and bring them into something very small and interior.

Schaefer: Can I just shout out to Donny Herron, the pedal steel player—I think he just makes this record. The steel guitar on "Autumn Leaves"—you don't need to hear the thirty strings at that point. He is the secret weapon that makes this album flow the way it does, to have the gentle, almost languorous swing that it has at times.

Bream: Let's talk about the concept of the arrangements.
Schaefer: Dylan was on record as saying if these were not covers, they were uncovers. He was trying to scrape away decades of accumulated sounds that had been layered on these lovely songs, and he wanted to get back to the original. And I think that has proven to be the case more often than not on this record. Yes, "The Night We Called It a Day" has an almost orchestral sound, but it's more Nelson Riddle than Gordon Jenkins.
Moon: Also, "Lucky Old Sun," there are horns on there. But it's very much like the spare, austere, we're-gonna-present-the-melody approach. And for someone who's not really known for having a great range as a singer, and to cover a lot of melodic ground, he really gets it.
Schaefer: The way that voice fits the music is kind of surprising. There are a couple of tracks where the fit is less than comfortable. I thought "I'm a Fool to Want You" was a challenging way to open the record, because as he gets into the upper registers, the voice is obviously strained, and he's not trying to hide it. In "Stay with Me," the strain of the voice leads to a certain kind of step-wise motion in spots, where you want to hear more of a legato kind of flowing sound. But you hear "Why Try to Change Me Now?" where the line between croak and croon is really blurry.

And then "What'll I Do," the kind of lived-in quality of the voice suits those lyrics so beautifully that it would be a crime to try and pretty up, to try and fix the patchy or pitchy moments. Because they just suit the song. "That Lucky Old Sun" is an absolute moment of musical genius—it is just so timeless. It seems to be the summation of everything Dylan was going for on this record.
Moon: And it's so relaxed. It's almost like the complete opposite of that sort of shouting approach to standards that we've heard so much. It really sneaks up on you. And the notion of that—music like this having lots of shadow in it—is really wonderful. I'm not sure about "I'm a Fool to Want You"; it's such a standard-y standard. I think there he's hamstrung more by the way the tempo is and by the intervals.
Schaefer: I did feel that was an uncomfortable fit for his voice. But that raises the question of the consistency of tone and of pace throughout the record, which some people might find ultimately kind of monochrome but which is reminiscent of some of the classic late-night Sinatra albums of the mid fifties.
Moon: *Only the Lonely.*
Schaefer: This does have the feel of what in later years we would call a concept album, which is exactly what *Only the Lonely* was.

Bream: All of these songs are pretty much about romantic regret.
Moon: That's right. And in that sense, you could start with any of them. I'd put "Autumn Leaves" as Track One because I think it bookends with "Lucky Old Sun" really well. But also, it has that sense of Dylan, as a singer, really trying to grapple with exactly how much to sing. And in a sense, he over-sings "I'm a Fool to Want You," and he under-sings, in a really entrancing, beautiful way, "Autumn Leaves."

Bream: Were you surprised at his vocal abilities here?
Moon: I didn't expect it to be anywhere near as good as it was. But as someone who knows how to deliver a lyric and create a phrase that hangs in the air—and because there's not a million baubles, bangles, and beads around it, it really hangs in the air—I

think that's genius. It's not genius in the conventional pretty-voice sense, but we're in an era where all these voices are so glossed up, hearing something that's just this verité is wonderful.

Schaefer: Despite what I said at the beginning about his voice, Dylan has been incredibly sophisticated in the way he has dealt with his instrument throughout his career. And a lot of the raspy, almost tuneless quality that you get from some nights of the Never Ending Tour, he knows what he's doing, and you can feel the intent as he applies a layer of sandpaper and a bit of rasp to something that maybe didn't have it to begin with. There are people whose ear for timbre and texture, and their sort of intuition for how to get a musical idea across, gives them the opportunity to take an instrument you think you know and say something new with it. And that is what makes this record so endlessly interesting.

Bream: Do you think, because it's Bob Dylan and he's age seventy-three, that we cut him some slack on this project?

Moon: No. And in fact, I think that a lot of what was coming in the media, when the early tracks were put out well before the record, was that usual sort of knee-jerk, *Uhh, you're kidding me, Bob.* Outside of the world of Dylan fanatics, this is a tough sell, period. Even people who are curious about Dylan approach this with skepticism. I don't think anybody in the critical press cut him slack. I think the Dylan die-hards probably cut him all kinds of slack for fifty years.

Schaefer: I agree to a point. When the reviews began, I did get the sense that the people who were not convinced were somewhat muted in their criticism because it was Bob Dylan. I do feel that this album is not an unalloyed triumph. There are parts of it that don't really work.

Moon: It's really interesting the way the media treats people who are that iconic. Sinatra, at the end of his career, those duet records were not great records. And they didn't get called out.

Schaefer: This is Dylan with the same band that you have seen out onstage with him for years and years, and look what they're doing. This is a complete musical detour. To the general musical audience, this must have been like a bolt out of the blue.

Bream: Just as the *AARP* interview was a bolt out of the blue.

Moon: Or the Victoria's Secret commercial. But he figured if he was going to do an interview at all, it makes sense, right? That demographic does still buy CDs.

Bream: Where does this fit on the spectrum of rock-era singers doing standards?

Moon: This is completely fresh and deserves a place in that small shelf with the ones that really worked well—I'd put [it with] the Willie Nelson [*Stardust*] and the first Linda Ronstadt one [*What's New*].

Schaefer: I rank it really high, just as I would Bryan Ferry's first go-round [*As Time Goes By*].

Bream: What is this to the Bob Dylan canon?

Moon: It's a curiosity in his discography, for sure.

Schaefer: But it is also a statement of affection, and perhaps unexpected affection. And a throwing down of the gauntlet to say, "I've reached a point in my career where I can follow the things that I like, and if it takes me to some place that people don't want to go, that's fine, but that's where I'm going."

IN SHOW & CONCERT!

BOB DYLAN
AND HIS BAND

OCTOBER 28, 29 & 30TH
PARAMOUNT THEATRE
IN OAKLAND

TICKETS AVAILABLE AT APECONCERTS.COM AND TICKETMASTER.COM

ANOTHER PLANET ENTERTAINMENT

Appendix 1

NOTABLE BOB DYLAN RELEASES IN ADDITION TO HIS STUDIO ALBUMS

The Bootleg Series

The Bootleg Series Vol. 1–3: (Rare & Unreleased) 1961–1991.
  Released March 26, 1991
The Bootleg Series Vol. 4: Bob Dylan Live 1966: The "Royal Albert Hall" Concert.
  Released October 13, 1998
The Bootleg Series Vol. 5: Bob Dylan Live 1975: The Rolling Thunder Revue.
  Released November 26, 2002
The Bootleg Series Vol. 6: Bob Dylan Live 1964: Concert at Philharmonic Hall.
  Released March 30, 2004
The Bootleg Series Vol. 7: No Direction Home: *The Soundtrack.*
  Released August 30, 2005
The Bootleg Series Vol. 8: Tell Tale Signs: Rare and Unreleased 1989–2006.
  Released October 6, 2008
The Bootleg Series Vol. 9: The Witmark Demos: 1962–1964.
  Released October 19, 2010
The Bootleg Series Vol. 10: Another Self Portrait (1969–1971).
  Released August 27, 2013
The Bootleg Series Vol. 11: The Basement Tapes Complete.
  Released November 4, 2014

Live Albums

Before the Flood. Released June 20, 1974
Hard Rain. Released September 13, 1976
Bob Dylan at Budokan. Released April 23, 1979
Real Live. Released November 29, 1984
Dylan & the Dead. Released February 6, 1989
MTV Unplugged. Released May 2, 1995
Live at the Gaslight 1962. Released August 30, 2005
Live at Carnegie Hall 1963 [EP]. Released November 15, 2005
In Concert: Brandeis University 1963. Released April 11, 2011

Notable Various-Artists Concert Albums Including Bob Dylan Performances

The Concert for Bangladesh. Released December 20, 1971

Tribute to Woody Guthrie Part 1. Released January 12, 1972

The Last Waltz. Released April 7, 1978

The 30th Anniversary Concert Celebration. Released August 24, 1993

Greatest Hits/Best-of Compilations

Bob Dylan's Greatest Hits. Released March 27, 1967

Bob Dylan's Greatest Hits Vol. II. Released November 17, 1971

Bob Dylan's Greatest Hits Volume 3. Released November 15, 1994

The Best of Bob Dylan [non-US version]. Released June 2, 1997

The Best of Bob Dylan Vol. 2. Released November 28, 2000

The Best of Bob Dylan [US version]. Released November 15, 2005

Dylan [different album than the 1973 LP titled Dylan]. Released October 2, 2007

Beyond Here Lies Nothin': The Collection. Released October 24, 2011

Other Compilations

Biograph. Released June 10, 1985

Bob Dylan: The Collection [issued through iTunes]. Released August 29, 2006

The Original Mono Recordings. Released October 19, 2010

The 50th Anniversary Collection: The Copyright Extension Collection Vol. 1.
   Released December 27, 2012

The Complete Album Collection Vol. 1. Released November 4, 2013

50th Anniversary Collection 1963. Released December 2, 2013

Thematic Compilations of Note

Live 1961–2000: Thirty-Nine Years of Great Concert Performances.
   Released February 28, 2001

Blues. Released June 27, 2006

Appendix 2

ABOUT THE COMMENTATORS

Eric Andersen has recorded twenty-five albums of original material including the critically acclaimed *Blue River* (1972), *Ghosts Upon the Road* (1989), and *Beat Avenue* (2003). Bob Dylan released a version of Andersen's song "Thirsty Boots" on his album *Another Self Portrait (1969–1971): The Bootleg Series Vol. 10* (2013).

Nicole Atkins is a singer, songwriter, and visual artist from Asbury Park, New Jersey. She's released several albums and EPs. She has toured the world with her band as well as with such artists as Nick Cave & the Bad Seeds, the Black Keys, Eels, and the Avett Brothers. www.nicoleatkins.com

Kevin Barents has taught a writing class on Bob Dylan at Boston University since 2007. He has discussed Dylan and his classes in interviews on NPR's *Weekend Edition* and in *Bostonia*, *BU Today*, and the *Boston Globe*. His poetry has been published on *Slate* and *AGNI online*, among other places.

Jim Beviglia is the author of *Counting Down Bob Dylan: His 100 Finest Songs* (2013) and *Counting Down Bruce Springsteen: His 100 Finest Songs* (2014). He is also a featured writer for *American Songwriter* magazine and maintains a blog at countdownkid. wordpress.com, which contains his thoughts on new and classic songs.

Lin Brehmer has been a radio program director, music director, or DJ since 1977. Since 1991, he has hosted the morning show at the legendary WXRT, Chicago. As program director at KTCZ in Minneapolis from 1990–91, he headed up a celebration of Bob Dylan's fiftieth birthday with a ten-hour "Bob-a-thon."

Jonatha Brooke, originally part of the duo the Story, has released nine solo albums, *Plumb* (1995) and *Ten Cent Wings* (1997). She writes songs for film and TV, and for artists such as Katy Perry and the Courtyard Hounds. Her one-woman musical, *My Mother Has 4 Noses*, opened Off Broadway in 2014. www.jonathabrooke.com

David Browne is a contributing editor at *Rolling Stone* and the author of *Fire and Rain: The Beatles, Simon & Garfunkel, James Taylor, CSNY, and the Lost Story of 1970* (2012), as well as biographies of Sonic Youth and Jeff and Tim Buckley. He formerly served as the pop music critic for *Entertainment Weekly* and the *New York Daily News*.

Marshall Chapman has recorded more than a dozen albums, the latest being *Blaze of Glory* (2013). Her songs have been recorded by Emmylou Harris, Joe Cocker, Irma Thomas, Jimmy Buffett, and many others. Chapman has co-composed the off-Broadway musical *Good Ol' Girls* and written the books *Goodbye, Little Rock and Roller* (2004) and *They Came to Nashville* (2010). www.tallgirl.com

Longtime *Village Voice* dude **Robert Christgau** isn't dead and can still get work. He has written five books based on his journalism and also published his memoir *Going into the City* (2015). He writes for *Medium's Cuepoint*, *Billboard*, *The Barnes & Noble Review*, and NPR's *All Things Considered*. He is a Visiting Arts Professor in NYU's Clive Davis Institute of Recorded Music.

Charles R. Cross is the Seattle-based author of nine books including best-selling biographies of Jimi Hendrix and Heart. His *Heavier Than Heaven: A Biography of Kurt Cobain* (2002) won the 2002 ASCAP Award for Outstanding Biography. Cross was editor of *The Rocket* from 1986 through 2000, chronicling the rise of the Pacific Northwest music scene. www.charlesrcross.com.

Rodney Crowell is a songwriter, singer, producer, and author. He is a two-time Grammy winner and a member of the Nashville Songwriters Hall of Fame. Crowell's most recent offerings were *Old Yellow Moon* (2013), a duets disc recorded with Emmylou Harris, and a solo effort called *Tarpaper Sky* (2014).

Anthony DeCurtis is a contributing editor for *Rolling Stone* and a distinguished lecturer in creative writing at the University of Pennsylvania. He coauthored Clive Davis' autobiography, *The Soundtrack of My Life* (2013). He is also the author of *Rocking My Life Away: Writing about Music and Other Matters* (1999) and *In Other Words: Artists Talk about Life and Work* (2006).

Kevin J. H. Dettmar is W. M. Keck professor and chair of the Department of English at Pomona College. A scholar of literary modernism by vocation, Dettmar has become a popular music critic by avocation. He coedited *Reading Rock & Roll: Authenticity, Appropriation, Aesthetics* (1999), wrote *Is Rock Dead?* (2006), and edited the *Cambridge Companion to Bob Dylan* (2009).

Daniel Durchholz, a St. Louis–based music critic, is coauthor of *Rock 'n' Roll Myths: The True Stories Behind the Most Infamous Legends* (2012), *Neil Young: Long May You Run—The Illustrated History* (2012), and *MusicHound Rock: The Essential Album Guide* (1998). www.danieldurchholz.com

Stephen Thomas Erlewine is a senior editor of pop music at Rovi, whose database of music information and reviews can be seen on Allmusic.com. He has written countless reviews and biographies for this database, including for several Bob Dylan albums. Erlewine has also written liner notes for Sony/Legacy and Raven Records.

Jim Fusilli is the rock and pop critic of the *Wall Street Journal*. He is also founder and editor of ReNewMusic.net and the author of eight novels. www.jimfusilli.com

Holly George-Warren is the author of more than a dozen books, including *A Man Called Destruction: The Life and Music of Alex Chilton* (2014) and *Public Cowboy No. 1: The Life and Times of Gene Autry* (2009). She has contributed to the *New York Times*, *Rolling Stone*, the *Oxford American*, *Mojo*, and *Entertainment Weekly*.

Janet Gezari is Lucretia L. Allyn Professor of English at Connecticut College, where for a few years she taught a course on Bob Dylan. In 2010, she was a Berlin Prize Fellow at the American Academy. Her most recent book is *The Annotated Wuthering Heights* (2014).

Tony Glover was a member of the folk-blues group Koerner Ray & Glover in the early 1960s. He has accompanied Jesse Fuller, Big Joe Williams, Bob Dylan, Patti Smith, the Doors, Bonnie Raitt, the Allman Brothers Band, Lucinda Williams, the Jayhawks, and the Replacements. He wrote three harmonica instruction manuals and cowrote *Blues with a Feeling: The Little Walter Story* (2002).

Gary Graff is an award-winning music journalist based in Detroit and writes regularly for *Billboard*, the *New York Times* Syndicate, Digital First Media nationwide, United Stations Radio Networks, Greater Media Interactive, *Revolver*, *Classic Rock*, and *For Bass Players Only*. He has authored, coauthored, and edited books about Bob Seger, Neil Young, Bruce Springsteen, and rock 'n' roll myths.

Geoffrey Green, professor of English at San Francisco State University, has taught a course on Bob Dylan and American culture since 2007. Author of several books, he wrote an essay on Dylan, "Hellhound on My Trail," that appeared in *Interdisciplinary Humanities* (Fall 2006). A musician, Green supported his education playing guitar. He played with Muddy Waters, Chuck Berry, Chubby Checker, and Danny Kalb, among others.

Joe Henry is a singer, songwriter, recording artist, and three-time Grammy-winning producer, who has collaborated with Mose Allison, Harry Belafonte, Solomon Burke, Ornette Coleman, Elvis Costello, Ramblin' Jack Elliot, Salif Keita, Madonna, Brad Mehldau, Meshell Ndegeocello, Bonnie Raitt, and Allen Toussaint. He cowrote *Furious Cool: Richard Pryor and the World That Made Him* (2013).

Geoffrey Himes has written about music for the *Washington Post* since 1977. During that time, he has also contributed to the *New York Times*, *Oxford American*, *Rolling Stone*, the *Los Angeles Times*, *Downbeat*, and *Smithsonian Magazine*. A songwriter, poet, playwright, and an author, Himes wrote *Born in the USA* (2005) about Bruce Springsteen.

David Hinckley is the television critic and former music critic for the *New York Daily News*. He saw his first Bob Dylan concert in 1965 and came away feeling mildly ambivalent. Proving there can be redemption for the appreciation deficit of youth, he saw the 1974 Dylan/Band tour twice and wishes at least once a week he could see it again.

Frances Downing Hunter, associate professor of English at Arkansas State University, teaches the poetry of Bob Dylan. She studied at Oxford University with Dylan scholar Sir Christopher Ricks, author of *Dylan's Visions of Sin* (2005). A poet and novelist with several books to her credit, she is also the editor of and contributor to *Professing Dylan* (2015).

Jason Isbell, the 2014 Americana Music Association's artist of the year, is an acclaimed Americana singer-songwriter who has released four solo studio albums, appeared on three studio albums with the Drive-By Truckers, and tattooed a lyric from Bob Dylan's "Boots of Spanish Leather" on his arm.

Garland Jeffreys is a New York–based singer-songwriter whose songs have been covered by artists as diverse as punk pioneers the Circle Jerks and the neo-folk band Vetiver. He has played with Dr. John, Sonny Rollins, James Taylor, Linton Kwesi Johnson, Phoebe Snow, Sly & Robbie, and many others. His most recent albums are *The King of In Between* (2011) and *Truth Serum* (2013).

Peter Jesperson cofounded Twin/Tone Records in Minneapolis, Minnesota. In 1980, Jesperson discovered and signed the Replacements. He joined New West Records in L.A. in 1999. He now serves as VP of production and catalog for the label, working with John Hiatt, Buddy Miller, and Steve Earle, along with recent signings Nikki Lane, Floating Action, and Rodney Crowell.

Joe Levy is editor at large for *Billboard*. The former executive editor of *Rolling Stone*, he has worked at *The Village Voice*, *Spin*, *Details*, and *Maxim*. Levy is an adjunct professor at NYU's Clive Davis School of Recorded Music and is frequently seen on *The Today Show*, *CBS This Morning*, and VH1.

Alan Light is the author of *Let's Go Crazy: Prince and the Making of Purple Rain* (2014). The former editor-in-chief of *Vibe* and *Spin* magazines, he is a frequent contributor to the *New York Times* and *Rolling Stone*. Light is also the author of *The Holy or the Broken: Leonard Cohen, Jeff Buckley, and the Unlikely Ascent of "Hallelujah"* (2013).

Ron Loftus was among those 4,200 people who purchased Bob Dylan's first album and has been listening ever since. After completing a PhD in modern Japanese history, Loftus became a teacher at a small liberal arts college. He has taught "Changing Times: The Music and Lyrics of Bob Dylan."

Alex Lubet is a professor of music at the University of Minnesota in Minneapolis. He teaches courses on the early history of rock music, including a class entitled "Bob Dylan." His essays on Dylan appear in *Highway 61 Revisited: Bob Dylan's Road from Minnesota to the World* (2009), *Professing Dylan* (2015), *Cognitive Critique*, and *Fordham Urban Law Journal*.

Evelyn McDonnell has written or coedited six books, from *Rock She Wrote: Women Write about Rock, Pop, and Rap* (2014) to *Queens of Noise: The Real Story of the Runaways* (2013). A longtime journalist and now professor at Loyola Marymount University, she has been a pop culture writer at *The Miami Herald* and a senior editor at *The Village Voice*.

William McKeen is the author of seven books and the editor of four more, including *Highway 61* (2003), *Rock and Roll Is Here to Stay* (2000), and *Bob Dylan: A Bio-Bibliography* (1993). He teaches at Boston University, where he chairs the Department of Journalism.

Don McLeese has written about (and interviewed) Bob Dylan as pop music critic for the *Chicago Sun-Times* and *Austin American-Statesman* and senior editor for *No Depression*. Now a professor at the University of Iowa, he was a frequent contributor to *Rolling Stone* and has written for many publications, including the *New York Times Book Review*, *Entertainment Weekly*, and the *Oxford American*.

Dennis McNally is the author of *Desolate Angel: Jack Kerouac, the Beat Generation, and America* (1979); *A Long Strange Trip: The Inside History of the Grateful Dead* (2002); and

On Highway 61: Music, Race, and the Evolution of Cultural Freedom (2014). He became the Grateful Dead's authorized biographer in 1980 and the band's publicist in 1984. www.dennismcnally.com

Minneapolis-based singer-songwriter **Paul Metsa**, who like Bob Dylan grew up on Minnesota's Iron Range, has released twelve albums on his own label (www.MaximumFolk.com). He is the author of *Blue Guitar Highway* (2011) and a radio host. *The Huffington Post* called Metsa "the other great folksinger from Minnesota's Mesabi Iron Range." www.paulmetsa.com

Tom Moon is the author of *1000 Recordings to Hear Before You Die* (2008) and a regular contributor to NPR's *All Things Considered*. A saxophonist and lifelong student of music, Moon spent twenty years as a staff critic for the *Philadelphia Inquirer*. His work has appeared in *Rolling Stone*, *GQ*, *Esquire*, *Musician*, Medium.com, NPR Music, and many other publications.

Ric Ocasek is a singer, songwriter, guitarist, and producer. He has made seven albums with the hitmaking band the Cars, including the 2011 reunion disc *Move Like This*, and has released seven solo albums, the most recent being *Nexterday* (2005). Ocasek has produced albums for Bad Brains, Guided by Voices, Hole, No Doubt, Bad Religion, Jonathan Richman, and Weezer. www.ricocasek.com

Kevin Odegard was a brakeman on the Chicago and Northwestern Railroad when he was asked to play guitar on Bob Dylan's *Blood on the Tracks*. He coauthored *A Simple Twist of Fate: Bob Dylan and the Making of* Blood on the Tracks. He is currently working on a fictional story about a '70s band reunion gone criminally awry. www.kevinodegard.com

Ike Reilly is the frontman of the indie-rock band Ike Reilly Assassination. He was a doorman at the Park Hyatt Chicago for more than a dozen years before devoting himself fulltime to his music career. He has released five albums, the latest of which is 2009's *Hard Luck Stories*.

Kim Ruehl settled in Seattle in 2003 and was the Roots Music Correspondent for *Sound* and *CityArts* magazines, and the About.com folk music expert from 2005–2014. Her work has appeared in *Billboard*, *Shuffle*, and *Yes* magazines and online at NPR, Folk Alley, and the Bluegrass Situation. Ruehl is the editor of *No Depression*, the online incarnation of the alt-country/roots/Americana music magazine.

Robert Santelli is the executive director of the Grammy Museum in Los Angeles and the author of a dozen books on American music, including *Greetings from E Street: The Story of Bruce Springsteen and the E Street Band* (2006) and *The Bob Dylan Scrapbook* (2005). His most recent book is *This Land Is Your Land: Woody Guthrie and the Journey of an American Folk Song* (2012).

John Schaefer is the host of New York public radio WNYC's innovative music/talk show *Soundcheck*. He has also hosted and produced WNYC's radio series *New Sounds* and the *New Sounds Live* concert series. Schaefer has written extensively about music, including the books *New Sounds: A Listener's Guide to New Music* (1987) and *The Cambridge Companion to Singing: World Music* (2000).

San Francisco Chronicle pop music critic **Joel Selvin** started covering rock shows for the paper shortly after the end of the Civil War. His writing has appeared in a surprising number of other publications that you would think should have known better. People all over the world are still pissed off about things he has written in books and magazines. His books include *Smartass: The Music Journalism of Joel Selvin* (2010). www.joelselvin.com

Bill Shapiro is a Kansas City–based lawyer who has hosted a weekly show, *Cypress Avenue*, devoted to "an intelligent look at rock music," on KCUR-FM, Kansas City's Public Radio station since 1978. He has published two books, *The CD Rock & Roll Library* (1988) and *The CD Rock & Roll Review* (1991).

Colleen Sheehy is the director and CEO of the Plains Art Museum in Fargo, North Dakota. She served for fifteen years as director of education at Weisman Art Museum in Minneapolis, where she was a curator of "Bob Dylan's American Journey." She coedited *Highway 61 Revisited: Bob Dylan's Road from Minnesota to the World* (2009).

Wesley Stace, born in Hastings, Sussex, United Kingdom, has released seventeen albums under the name John Wesley Harding. His most-recent album is *Self-Titled* (2013). He has published five novels: *Misfortune* (2006), *By George* (2008), *Charles Jessold, Considered as a Murderer* (2011) and, most recently, *Wonderkid* (2014). He is the host of *Cabinet of Wonders*, a variety show based in New York City.

Ahmir "Questlove" Thompson is drummer for the Roots, leader of the *The Tonight Show Starring Jimmy Fallon* band, club DJ, actor, instructor at NYU, author of the memoir *Mo Meta Blues: The World According to Questlove* (2013), and a producer who has worked with Elvis Costello, D'Angelo, Jill Scott, Erykah Badu, Common, Jay Z, Al Green, Amy Winehouse, and John Legend, among others.

Richie Unterberger is the author of numerous rock history books, including books on the Velvet Underground, the Who, and a two-part history of 1960s folk-rock, *Turn! Turn! Turn!* (2002) and *Eight Miles High* (2003). His book *The Unreleased Beatles: Music and Film* (2006) won a 2007 Association for Recorded Sound Collections Award for Excellence in Historical Recorded Sound Research.

George Varga has earned three Pulitzer Prize nominations for his work as pop-music critic for *U-T San Diego* (formerly the *San Diego Union-Tribune*) and Copley News Service. Varga is also a contributing writer for *Jazz Times* magazine and hosts the UT-TV music show *Live from the Fourth Floor*.

Since the release of her self-titled, critically acclaimed 1985 debut album, **Suzanne Vega** has sold more than 7 million records, performed in sold-out concert halls around the world, and been nominated for seven Grammys. Her latest album is *Tales from the Realm of the Queen of Pentacles* (2014).

Dan Wilson is a Grammy Award–winning singer, songwriter, producer, multi-instrumentalist, and occasional cartoonist. He is best known as the lead singer of the Minneapolis band Semisonic. Wilson has released three solo albums: *Live at the Pantages* (2011), *Free Life* (2012), and *Love Without Fear* (2014). www.danwilsonmusic.com

David Yaffe is a professor of humanities at Syracuse University. He is the author of *Fascinating Rhythm: Reading Jazz in American Writing* (2005) and *Bob Dylan: Like a Complete Unknown* (2011). His writings have appeared in many publications, including *The Nation*, *Harper's*, the *New York Times*, *The Village Voice*, *New York Magazine*, *Slate*, *Bookforum*, *The Chronicle of Higher Education*, *The Oxford American*, *Tablet*, and *The Daily Beast*.

Paul Zollo is a singer-songwriter, recording artist, author, photographer, and music journalist. He is currently the senior editor of *American Songwriter* magazine. His book *Songwriters on Songwriting* (2003) includes his 1991 interview with Bob Dylan. His other books include *Hollywood Remembered* (2011) and *Conversations with Tom Petty* (2012).

Appendix 3

COMMENTATORS RANK THE ALBUMS

With so many opinionated Dylan experts involved in *Dylan: Disc by Disc*, we couldn't resist subjectively ranking Dylan's albums. We asked the commentators to rank the studio albums, from best to worst. *Note:* Our survey took place before 2015's *Shadows in the Night* was released.

1. *Blonde on Blonde*
2. *Blood on the Tracks*
3. *Highway 61 Revisited*
4. *Bringing It All Back Home*
5. *The Freewheelin' Bob Dylan*
6. *John Wesley Harding*
7. *The Times They Are a-Changin'*
8. *The Basement Tapes*
9. *Desire*
10. *Another Side of Bob Dylan*
11. *Time Out of Mind*
12. *"Love and Theft"*
13. *New Morning*
14. *Nashville Skyline*
15. *Modern Times*
16. *Oh Mercy*
17. *Bob Dylan*
18. *Infidels*
19. *Planet Waves*
20. *Slow Train Coming*
21. *Street-Legal*
22. *Tempest*
23. *World Gone Wrong*
24. *Good As I Been to You*
25. *Shot of Love*
26. *Pat Garrett & Billy the Kid*
27. *Empire Burlesque*
28. *Together Through Life*
29. *Self Portrait*
30. *Under the Red Sky*
31. *Saved*
32. *Knocked Out Loaded*
33. *Christmas in the Heart*
34. *Dylan*
35. *Down in the Groove*

INDEX

ABOUT THE AUTHOR

Jon Bream is an award-winning music critic who has worked for the Minneapolis *Star Tribune* since 1974, giving him the second longest tenure of any current pop-music critic at a US daily newspaper. He is the author of the biographies *Prince: Inside the Purple Reign* (1984), *Whole Lotta Led Zeppelin* (2008 and 2015) and *Neil Diamond Is Forever* (2009). Bream's reviews and features have been published in countless newspapers from the *Boston Globe* to the *Los Angeles Times* and in various magazines from *Billboard* to *Vibe*. Bream has interviewed the King of Pop, the Queen of Soul, Prince, U2, three Beatles, four Rolling Stones, and all of Maroon 5. Bream has seen Bob Dylan in concert in five different decades and has interviewed him and hung out with him several times.